The Theatre of
GROTOWSKI

The
THEATRE
of
GROTOWSKI

JENNIFER KUMIEGA

Methuen . London and New York

for my mother
for my father
and for Dave
but most of all for myself

First published in this paperback edition in 1987,
in Great Britain by Methuen London Ltd,
11 New Fetter Lane, London EC4P 4EE
and in the United States of America
by Methuen Inc,
29 West 35th Street, New York, NY 10001
Originally published in hardback in 1985
by Methuen London and Methuen Inc
Copyright © 1985, 1987 by Jennifer Kumiega

Printed in Great Britain
by Redwood Burn Ltd, Trowbridge
Filmset in Monophoto Ehrhardt by
Northumberland Press Ltd, Gateshead, Tyne and Wear

British Library Cataloguing in Publication Data

Kumiega, Jennifer
The theatre of Grotowski.
   1. Grotowski, Jerzy   2. Theater——Poland——
   Production and direction
   I. Title
   792'.0233'0924   PN2859.P66G7

   ISBN 0–413–46640–X
   ISBN 0–413–58040–7 Pbk

Some of the photographs in this book come from private collections
and it has not always been possible to trace the copyright owners.
The publishers and the author apologise for any failure
to acknowledge ownership and will make amends
in the next edition if further information is forthcoming.

The photograph of Jerzy Grotowski on the front cover
is by Andrzej Paluchiewicz.

Contents

Acknowledgements

The research for this book (both academic and active) has spread over many years and has involved much travelling and time spent living and working in other countries. In this, I have been helped generously by many individuals and organizations, all of whom I thank. In particular I would like to mention: The Polish Cultural Institute in London, the Ministry of Art and Culture in Warsaw, the British Council and Bristol University – for assistance with grants and travel; Zbigniew Osiński and Interpress Publishers in Warsaw for the loan of photographs; the administrative staff at the Laboratory Theatre – especially Stefa Gardecka – for continual support; Jan Fiolek, Wojciech Bernecki and Dave West for photographs taken for the book; all the photographers who gave generous permission to publish their work.

And my love and thanks to: My uncle, Zbych Kumiega, for introducing me to the theatre of Jerzy Grotowski; My sister Lesley Kelly, for bibliographical advice and research, and for indexing the book; my former tutor at Bristol University, Ted Braun, for his guidance; Nick Hern of Methuen for time; Nick Sales, Nicholas Janni for discussion and shared work; Jerzy Grotowski and the members of the Laboratory Theatre for giving me so much; Małgosia Spurring for sharing most of it; and Sandra Reeve for her love and skill.

Finally, my book would not have been started or finished without the following people:
My parents – Nora and Tadeusz Kumiega – who have given many years of moral, financial and practical help; My Teacher – John Garrie–Rōshi; and Dave West.

List of Illustrations

Introduction

More than twenty years have passed since the Western world first became aware of the existence of Jerzy Grotowski and his Polish Laboratory Theatre: in that time their work has undergone considerable change. From the austere practitioners of a 'holy' art, working with very limited resources in a small, provincial Polish town, they became, by the end of the sixties, a group renowned internationally for the technical skill and power of their acting. The reception in their own country was disappointing, but to some, at least, in the West, Grotowski's appearance was barely less than messianic. It seemed to many that theatre was faltering under the weight of technical refinements. Facing the straightforward commercial competition of cinema and television, directors had begun to make a necessity of what was once luxury. To the conventional aids of lighting and sound were added the accumulated resources of technological invention, and only the most acute were able to keep the art of the actor alive amidst the fairground spectacle. Grotowski called this trend 'artistic kleptomania ... conglomerates without backbone or integrity', and recognizing the inevitability of the decline of the domain of theatre, he sought through his work and research to give renewed vitality to an age-old truth: that the core of theatre is the communion between actor and spectator. By eliminating a dependence on what is superfluous to this core, he arrived at the concept of the 'poor theatre'.

But by the time that the rest of the world was becoming familiar with this proposition, Jerzy Grotowski was already changing direction. And by the turn of the new decade, in 1970, he had announced his abandonment of a strictly theatrical context for his work, and the beginning of experiments into 'paratheatrical' forms. Since that time the work of the Laboratory Theatre, as a group and as individuals, has not ceased to evolve and change. The voluntary closing of the Laboratory Theatre Institute in Wrocław in August 1984 was another step in that evolution.

It seems, however, an unavoidable aspect of renown that an individual becomes frozen into one particular public image or another. This applies particularly, of course, where their work is seen as 'inaccessible', or there has apparently not been a readiness to talk freely and to publicize activities and theories. For many people, even those interested in international developments in theatre, Jerzy Grotowski is still the austere director of those early years, proposing an 'elite' theatre for a dedicated few. This is not in the least surprising. I know only too well, after twelve years of research on the subject, how difficult it is to acquire reliable information about the activities of the Laboratory Theatre Institute.

One of the major aims of this book, therefore, has been to present a perspective on the *development* of the work of Grotowski and the Laboratory Theatre. However, since this is one of the first major published works on the subject, it also has to fulfil other needs. I felt it would be valuable to present some kind of factual history of the Laboratory Theatre company, and a description and analysis of their theatrical productions. I have also offered an external perspective on, and assessment of, the theories developed at the Laboratory Theatre, which have been so influential in the past two decades. I have tried, as simply and factually as possible, to describe some of the 'post-theatrical' work undertaken at the Laboratory Theatre, in which I have been personally involved. And finally, I have made available, through reference and quotation, some of the original written material I have acquired and translated in my research.

The need for such a wide and general scope has obviously entailed some compromise. Inevitably, there were aspects of the research – important for me – which didn't reach these pages. In particular, when I first began studying the work of Jerzy Grotowski for my degrees at Manchester, and later Bristol, University Drama Departments, I had wanted to place my subject within the political, social and cultural context of Poland. Now, after many visits to Poland and the events of the past few years, that is an intellectual task I would rather avoid. I am more regretful, however, about the limited space I have been able to give to a real investigation of Grotowski's theories of actor training and the creative process, and the Laboratory Theatre experiments on the 'borderline of art'. That aspect, more than any other, is one that deserves a volume to itself.

From his earliest work as a young director of 26, Grotowski has subjected theatre to an extreme and intensive process of research. Perhaps the greatest value of that research – at least for those who came into contact with the Laboratory Theatre work – was that it forced theatre to redefine itself. There were surely few people who were able, in the face of Grotowski's insistent questioning, to remain complacent and self-satisfied with their own work and motives in theatre (which is what made him such an uncomfortable colleague). And this is an aspect of the Laboratory Theatre work that should not be allowed to pass away. Theatre *should* have its own watchdog – ideally one within each country, each culture – capable, as Charles Marowitz wrote more than a quarter of a century ago, of 'peering intently into its own nature to discover something about its own chemistry'.

Another vital aspect of the Laboratory Theatre work with continuing relevance for other countries and other systems is that of 'active culture' and the emphasis on 'process' rather than 'product'. The establishment and organization by Grotowski of creative work to be directly experienced by members of the public – rather than the creation of 'works of art' for their passive consumption – is at odds with his popular image as an advocate of an 'elite' theatrical experience. But the fact is that he has now been committed to 'active culture', in different forms, for many more years than he ever dedicated to theatre as an artistic discipline. These two aspects of the Laboratory Theatre work – the self-questioning of its research and the experiments to extend the accessibility of the creative process – constitute its major heritage. They should be an inspiration to all those – from performers and members of their audiences to teachers and officials on administrative and funding bodies – who are concerned to maintain theatre as an arena for living and creative contact.

There are a few practical points about this book that I wish to explain at this stage:

1. I have made the assumption that readers will be familiar with Grotowski's book *Towards a Poor Theatre* and the theses contained within it – poor theatre, the holy actor, the 'total act' etc. This is not only for ease of reference but because I believe anyone interested in the work of Grotowski (and indeed in theatre in general) should read *Towards a Poor Theatre*. It contains some fundamental statements about theatre that had never been said before, and that needed saying. Some people (including Eric Bentley) have objected to the way the book was written, finding it alien and obscure. I have never failed to find inspiration in it, no matter how many times I read it.

2. Despite the lack of reference material concerning Grotowski and the Laboratory Theatre, there are one or two more recent publications to which I am indebted. The first is a very detailed and scrupulously researched work by Zbigniew Osiński, published in Warsaw in 1980 and called *Grotowski i Jego Laboratorium*. This book, together with the chapter on Grotowski in Kazimierz Braun's *Nowy Teatr na Świecie 1960–1970* (Warsaw 1975) and the chapter on the Laboratory Theatre in Czesława Mykita-Glensk's *Życie Teatralne Opola* (Opole 1976) have been particularly useful for little known facts about Grotowski's early years. In addition I should mention the research carried out by Leszek Kolankiewicz into the paratheatrical work, which was compiled in 1979 in the pamphlet *On the Road to Active Culture* (translated Bolesław Taborski). And finally Małgorzata Dzieduszycka's own account of *Apocalypsis Cum Figuris* has been helpful with some of the more obscure textual references in the production.

3. One unavoidable problem with researching material about, and by Grotowski is translation. The problems arise partly because Grotowski is describing processes and concepts that are difficult to express verbally. In addition he has a very individual, often grammatically peculiar way of expressing them. Where possible I, together with my father, have made my own translation of Polish material. However, there are instances in the book where I use other translations – e.g. where a translation has become standard and accepted (as in the case of *Towards a Poor Theatre* and the *Holiday* texts), or where I have been unable to acquire the original Polish. These will be obvious by reference to the bibliography.

4. I have made use of a system of annotation whereby all references and quotations are followed by a series of numbers which refer directly to a general bibliography at the end of the book. The numbers follow the sequence: bibliography reference number/page number of cited work.

5. Throughout the book I have used where possible a convention of non-sexist language that may require explanation for some readers. I have simply refrained from using the terms 'he', 'his', 'himself', 'man', 'mankind' etc. when the sex of an individual is not specified (although I obviously have not altered any such usage in quotations). Equally, since I do not like the use of such terms as 'actress' (or 'authoress') I have made the assumption that the following terms refer to both sexes: actor, director, spectator, participant, author, critic, writer etc. This convention, which very occasionally calls for slightly unorthodox grammar, may initially seem awkward: but it is only a question of usage and habit.

Stefa Gardecka – Administrator of Laboratory Theatre. (Phot: Wojciech Bernecki)

SECTION I
History

This first section of the book, comprising Chapters One to Five, presents Grotowski's early years, the establishment of his theatre company in Poland, and their work up until 1970. As such its deals strictly with the *theatrical* phase of their work, and this is one of the reasons why the section is called 'History'. It is also called 'History' because, having had no direct experience of this phase of the Laboratory Theatre work, my research for this section was mainly academic (i.e. a gleaning of historical facts) rather than experiential. Even so, I have made no effort to present an exhaustive biography and history, but have selected what seems to

1 Entrance to
Laboratory Theatre Offices.

me relevant information to show the development of the theatre's work and Grotowski's theories.

The story is, on the whole, told chronologically, with Chapters One and Three presenting historical periods of activity, while Chapters Two and Four deal with the theatrical productions from those periods. Chapter Five deals with the final phase of their theatrical work before the transition to post-theatrical work (1970 being the year of change) and their final production, *Apocalypsis Cum Figuris*.

During the full course of their activity, Grotowski's theatre company changed the name of their institute six times in all, and on each occasion the change of name was indicative of an evolution in their attitude to their work: The Theatre of Thirteen Rows (1.9.59); The Laboratory Theatre of Thirteen Rows (1.3.62); The Laboratory Theatre of Thirteen Rows – Institute of Research into Acting Method (1.1.66); Institute of Research into Acting Method – Laboratory Theatre (1.9.66); Actor's Institute – Laboratory Theatre (1.1.70); Institute-Laboratory (1.1.75). For the sake of simplicity I will use the title Theatre of Thirteen Rows for the period covered by Chapter One (to the end of 1961) and Laboratory Theatre, or Institute, from thereon.

CHAPTER ONE
Theatre of Thirteen Rows

In 1963, in the magazine *Encore*, there was published one of the first reports acquainting the British public and theatre world with the activities of the young Polish theatre director, Jerzy Grotowski, and his Laboratory Theatre. It was written by Michael Kustow who had just returned from a visit to Poland for an ITI Congress where he and several other delegates had, almost by chance, come across Grotowski's work. The article preceding Kustow's in the same edition of *Encore* was written by Charles Marowitz, and concluded significantly with the words:

> The great irony in England today is the fervour that can be roused for a moribund art-form.... I react badly to indiscriminate enthusiasm, and find it appalling for *theatre* to be madly approved of in the abstract and abominably practised in the particular. *More* theatre is not *better* theatre and better theatre does not necessarily mean highly subsidised main stream work. But without demeaning any of the activity that already exists, I would point out that the one sort of theatre which is practically non-existent in England is laboratory-theatre, studio-theatre, theatre peering intently into its own nature to discover something about its own chemistry. Until such theatre is (a) understood, (b) encouraged, (c) financed, the cause of theatre may be widely championed but the state of theatre will progressively disintegrate. [341/245]

Ironically, these words are just an echo of a similar cri de coeur published by Peter Brook four years earlier in the same magazine. Brook questioned the lack of energy and drive in our 'lazy and passionless' British actors, so few of who 'think theatre, dream theatre, fight for theatre'. But their inertia, he claimed, was due to a structural fault in the system – dependence on the box office. Brook's plea (and that of Marowitz above) remains as vital today as when the words were first written:

> I would like to see a start made – and the principle established – with one tiny theatre with a hundred seats, even fifty seats, but subsidised to the hilt.... It will be run by a director and a new sort of committee.... Its appeal must be that it can *dare completely*. [178/73]

In the very year that Peter Brook was making his plea, 1959, this dream was being realized unrecognized by the theatrical world. In Opole, a small provincial town of 50,000 inhabitants sixty miles from Auschwitz in Poland, Jerzy Grotowski established what was at that time called the Theatre of Thirteen Rows (Teatr 13 Rzędów). At its inception it was merely another small, new theatre, perhaps remarkable only for the youth and inexperience of its inaugurators. But in the following years Grotowski was to try to its limits both the socialist principle of total state subsidy, and the seemingly utopian vision formulated by Stanislavsky and others of a 'spiritual order of actors'. At the age of only 26, Grotowski had attained his position as director of the Theatre of Thirteen Rows via a conventional, established route in terms of training and experience, but nevertheless one from which he had drawn the fullest benefit and advantage.

Grotowski was born in Rzeszów, near the Eastern border of Poland, on 11 August 1933. His father worked in forestry and his mother was a schoolteacher. His only brother, three years his senior, was to become a professor of theoretical physics at the Jagielloński University at Cracow. At the outbreak of the Second World War, at the age of six, Grotowski settled with his mother and brother in the small village of Nienadówka, about twenty kilometres north of Rzeszów (his father having left Poland to settle in Paraguay, where he lived until his death in 1968). The small Grotowski family spent the entire occupation in these rural surroundings, with Grotowski travelling to Rzeszów to attend the school where his mother was a teacher. In 1950 the family moved again, to Cracow, where Grotowski completed his secondary education (although he had earlier missed a year due to a serious illness). In July 1951 he applied for admission to the Acting Department of the State Theatre School in Cracow, and two months later took the two-part entrance examination, comprising both practical and theoretical subjects. The verdict on his practical work was on average only 'satisfactory', and his admission to the school was decided by a very good written paper (from a choice of three topics Grotowski had decided to write on: 'In what way may theatre contribute to the building of Socialism in Poland?').

On 1 October 1951 Grotowski became a student in the theatre school. By the time he had completed his studies and received his actor's diploma in 1955, he had already made his first journalistic pronouncements, with four articles published that year. At the beginning of October Grotowski was to have taken up work at the Old Theatre (Stary Teatr) in Cracow, immediate employment being the normal procedure in Poland's highly systematized education process. This commitment was officially deferred, however, to permit him to attend a directing course at the State Institute of Theatre Art (GITIS) in Moscow from August 1955. During this time he worked on productions under the tutelage of Zavadsky, and was able to make a more detailed study of the work of such great Russian innovators as Stanislavsky, Meyerhold and Vakhtangov.

According to the Polish writer Kazimierz Braun, ill-health again interrupted Grotowski's studies, and it was in order to recuperate that he made his first journey to Central Asia, spending two months travelling there in summer 1956. This was his first direct contact with the East, but it was evidence of a fascination that had been engendered during his childhood. He had at that time become acquainted with esoteric literature, and during his higher education in Cracow he made contact with those working in the area of Eastern philosophy, and participated in organized meetings and discussion groups. It was an interest that he also brought to bear in later years, in ways both manifest and implicit. Subsequent visits to the East were to culminate in 1970 in a six-week solitary odyssey through India and Kurdistan which had a profound and transformative effect upon him and his work.

But when Grotowski returned to Poland in 1956, it was at one of the most significant moments in his country's recent, troubled past. The purpose of his return was to take up, in October, both studies in directing and a junior teaching post at the Cracow Theatre School. But the events from this period (which later came to be called the 'Polish October') involved him equally, and it is worth recounting them briefly because of the social and cultural changes they brought about in Poland.

Since the death of Stalin in 1953 a gradual 'de-stalinization' had been spreading outward from the Soviet Union. The resulting relaxation naturally reached the satellite countries more slowly, but when it did arrive the reaction tended to be more forceful. Russia had a sturdier tradition of Communism on which to rely, but in Poland the political reversal released a flood of frustrated liberalism, which threatened to overwhelm the none too secure structure of the Party. Movements of doubt and protest, led by artists and Party intellectuals such as Jan Kott and Leszek Kołakowski gathered momentum. The party leaders uneasily became aware that appeasement might not suffice: paramount was the need to halt the demo-cratization, but in a way that did not damage the flimsy fabric of the people's cooperation. Already there was unrest, with serious riots in Poznań. The two conflicting forces operative in Poland at that time were the Poles' obsession with independence, and the need to placate the Soviet Union.

Luckily for Poland on this occasion, there was a potential leader amongst the politicians recently released from prison and re-instated, and moreover one capable of balancing the conflicting political needs of the moment – Władysław Gomułka with his professed creed of a 'Polish Road to Socialism'. At the 8th Plenum of the Central Committee of the Polish United Workers Party held on 19–21 October 1956, Władysław Gomułka was elected First Secretary, and, during concurrent meetings with the Soviet authorities, his election was accepted and a certain degree of internal freedom agreed upon. The over-optimistic liberals within Poland were eventually to be disillusioned during the fluctuating periods of liberalism and optimism that followed (leading to the events of 1968 and Gomułka's deposal in 1970). But his achievements on regaining power in 1956 were immediate and a matter of record: including the abolition of compulsory agricultural collectivization, the revitalization of the private enterprise sector, and a more energetic flow of cultural communication between Poland and the Western world.

In his meticulously detailed study of Grotowski's work, published in Poland in 1980, Zbigniew Osiński documents Grotowski's political activities during this period. The facts of these activities may come as a surprise to Western readers, who will be more familiar with Grotowski's later 'apolitical' stance. But as Osiński points out, Grotowski is by temperament an activist, and hence it is not surprising that he did not remain in the background during these events. In the months following the 'Polish October', Grotowski enjoyed what Osiński describes as a 'short, but tempestuous adventure', [361/26] actively and vociferously participating in meetings of the political youth organizations, becoming (in January 1957) a Secretary of the Central Committee of the Socialist Youth movement, and publishing politically orientated articles with such titles as 'The Academic Left' [6] and 'Civilization and Freedom – This is the Only Socialism'. [7] This is neither a period of his life, nor a part of himself that Grotowski would wish to deny. Eighteen years later he referred to it in an interview, contrasting it with the apolitical attitude of his maturer years:

> In another period of my life, let's call them the October and post-October years, I wanted to be a political saint, one of the foremost. And I was so fascinated by Gandhi that I wanted to be him. I came to the conclusion that not only was this improbable for objective reasons, but incompatible with my nature – although equal to fair play I am incapable of a total and generalized assumption of everyone's good intentions. . . .
>
> If I were ever to build the self-portrait of my dreams – at the very centre would be a liberated life, the original state, freedom. . . . For me, freedom is connected with the supreme temptation. It exists for the individual, even if unaware of it. . . . Freedom is associated neither with freedom of choice, nor with sheer voluntarism – but with a wave, with giving oneself up to this huge wave, in accordance with one's desire. And when I speak of desire, it is like water in the desert or a gasp of air to someone drowning. [169/22–23]

In the years between the events of 1956 and the beginning of his professional directorial career in Opole in 1959, Grotowski remained for the most part in Cracow, completing his directing studies at the Theatre School and working on his first productions in the professional Old Theatre. Amongst these was a production of Ionesco's *The Chairs* (premiere 29.6.57), significant at that time in terms of the contemporary influx of Western authors and material (a translation of the work had appeared two months prior to the premiere in the monthly magazine *Dialog*). The following month Grotowski visited France for the first time for the annual International Youth Meeting in Avignon (during which time he learned of the work of Jean Vilar and his teacher, Dullin) and before returning to Poland spent some time in Paris. Between December 1957 and June 1958 Grotowski organized and led a series of regular, weekly talks on Oriental philosophy in the Student Club in Cracow. The subjects covered included Buddhism, Yoga, the Upanishads, Confucius, Taoism and Zen-Buddhism. During this period he also directed several plays for the Polish Radio, including a work based on Kalidasa's poem *Shakuntala* in his own radio adaptation, for which he received an award.

Amongst other significant creative work in this period there was a production called *Gods of Rain* (premiere 4.7.58) based on a play by the contemporary author,

Jerzy Krzyszton. It evinced what one critic described as a 'violent collision between director and author, theatre and literature' [361/42] as well as aspects of Meyerholdian constructivism. It was presented on a triple stage, the actors were in masks, and Grotowski had grafted onto the original extracts from other poets and writers (a total of six in all), as well as using a film montage for the prologue. Four months later Grotowski directed another version of this same work, under a different title, as a guest director at the Opole Theatre of Thirteen Rows, which he was to take over himself in less than a year.

At the beginning of 1959 Grotowski once again visited Paris, where he met Marcel Marceau and was much impressed by the mime artist's work. And in March of that year Grotowski directed his final production at the Old Theatre in Cracow, before moving to Opole: Chekhov's *Uncle Vanya*. The press reaction to the performance was for the most part fairly cool, including one review by Ludwik Flaszen, shortly to become Grotowski's colleague. He described Grotowski's Chekhov as conventional, disciplined and intellectual, lacking only distance and humour: 'After this contemporary surgery Chekhov is no longer an archaeologist of the soul but a young, rural schoolmaster from the age of positivism'. [361/56]

Ludwik Flaszen, three years Grotowski's senior, was at that time an acknowledged literary and theatre critic. He had been Literary Director of the Słowacki Theatre in Cracow for three years, as well as being the author of a book, *The Head and the Wall*. In the early spring of 1959 he was approached by the Opole authorities with the proposition that he take over directorship of the small Theatre of Thirteen Rows with the aim of revitalizing it. This theatre had originally been set up in early 1958 by two actors, who had defected from the conventional Teatr Ziemi Opolskiej in Opole to establish a contemporary alternative in the town. They had been given a long, low room in the market-place of the town, where they had constructed a small proscenium stage and set out thirteen rows of seats. But after only two performances (the second directed by Grotowski) the theatre closed down: the financial authorities had categorized the enterprise as a 'private business' and the actors were unable to pay their taxes. [173/157]

On being approached, however, Flaszen felt that the practical role of directorship was not within his capabilities. In May 1959 he contacted Grotowski with whose work he was familiar, although there had been no personal acquaintance. Their meeting has been picturesquely described in a 1966 interview with Flaszen:

> At a Cracow crossing two people met: Jerzy Grotowski and Ludwik Flaszen. The first had come to the conclusion that he was thoroughly fed up with the Old Theatre and with old theatre. Flaszen was also fed up with old theatre – theatre was an art located at the tail end of other artistic disciplines.... [31]

At subsequent meetings with the Opole authorities Grotowski put forward proposals for the following season's repertoire, and a tour of the major Polish cities. Most importantly, he laid down conditions for the establishment of the theatre, including a free hand in the selection of the repertoire and group, the establishment of the post of literary director, a permanent subsidy, and a budget level permitting work without continual upsets. These conditions, which were accepted, together with the subsidy granted by the Opole People's Council, permitted the establishment of what was called 'the only professional experimental theatre in Poland'.

The company with which Grotowski started work in Opole for the 1959/1960 season was small, and from the beginning the emphasis in practical work was towards the ensemble principle. Grotowski:

> It seems that we have the smallest group in Poland. Nine people, two of them women. . . . the actors are working very seriously and with great self-sacrifice. . . . It is sufficient to say that one of the actors is also the stage manager, another a stage hand. [361/66]

This group was quite fluid during the first few years, but of the original nine actors, three remained with Grotowski to form part of his permanent company: Rena Mirecka, fresh from actor training at Cracow Theatre School; Zygmunt Molik, who also trained at Cracow but had since worked at the Teatr Ziemi Opolskiej in Opole; and Antoni Jahołkowski, who had transferred to Grotowski's group from another theatre. In 1961 they were joined by Zbigniew Cynkutis (also a defector from the Teatr Ziemi Opolskiej) and Ryszard Cieślak. With the addition of Stanisław Scierski in 1964, the Laboratory Theatre acting company was complete (apart from the only non-Pole, the South American Elizabeth Albahaca, who joined in the late sixties). The basic stability of this central group of actors has been one of the significant factors in their development and the quality of their work. Flaszen:

> Theatre history proves that the greatest theatres were created when, in the course of practice, a sense of 'group' was emerging. Stanislavsky and his actors, Meyerhold, Brecht etc. Could those individuals have led effectively for just one production? [143/325]

Ludwik Flaszen himself, Grotowski's co-founder, naturally took the post of Literary Director – although the role he actually played went beyond a responsibility for literature and was crucial in the development of the theoretical concepts that motivated the theatrical experiments. Grotowski saw Flaszen's role, which he likened to that of a Devil's Advocate, as absolutely essential in a research-orientated theatrical establishment. Flaszen described the relationship thus:

> While I was sometimes a spokesman, my essential work all these years has been talking with Grotowski – a kind of dialogue covering many years. . . . we agreed to be absolutely sincere with each other. I told him what I really thought about what was happening – its possibilities. I pointed out to him what was himself and what was the inherited tradition and the mistakes of the past. For example, when I analyzed Grotowski's work for him, I tried to find all that had become merely a shell, the reasoned or the artificial. I analyzed what could be rejected. When I felt my analysis was helpless, I knew I was dealing with something alive. [143/303, 304]

2 Ludwik Flaszen.

Whilst the theatre received a grant from the municipality, it must be borne in mind that in the beginning this was a very small subsidy indeed. Jan Kott has pointed out that Poland was probably the only country at that time to allow itself the luxury of a 'theatre-laboratory' and yet was so poor that its actors had to starve: 'Poverty was at first a practice of this theatre; only later was it raised to the dignity of aesthetics'. [322/199]

There was a great deal of critical comment on the choice of Grotowski as the new director of this provincial theatre, the majority by no means favourable. Grotowski was already familiar to the critical fraternity from his theatrical activities in Cracow and from his published writings (over twenty articles by this time, mostly in local Cracow newspapers or youth magazines). An academic analysis of these theoretical manifestos would reveal clear indications of his later stringent and committed approach to theatrical technique. But at that time the tone of youthful dogma, dedicated to transforming theatre, antagonized the theatrical establishment, who similarly found his theatrical practice too flamboyant and intellectual. Kazimierz Braun has written in summary of Grotowski's writings that they contained 'the formulation of an excessively broad and eclectic baggage of experience and knowledge, such as a youthful artist might amass, in which Stanislavsky went hand in hand with Brecht and Oriental theatre with Vilar'. [173/158]

It will be useful at this point to consider the theatrical climate within which Grotowski established his new theatre. The period from 1939–1956 had been one of almost total stagnation in the theatrical world in Poland. Not only were all theatres closed down during the war, and many theatre artists killed or imprisoned, but even after liberation there was an enforced programme of Socialist Realism (proclaimed in 1949 at the Congress of the Polish Writers Union). This, combined with a policy of centralized administration, succeeded in destroying all the creative independence that makes theatre so valuable. But with the general relaxation of restrictions in the mid-fifties, the Polish theatre began to flourish again. On the administrative side a reversal of the centralization process of the Stalinist period gave greater independence to local councils and theatre directors to develop individual style. (Flaszen has pointed to the significance of this, which encouraged 'regional ambitions' and, reinforced by an atmosphere of greater artistic liberty and a general 'diversification of life' made possible the kind of personalized research that Grotowski foresaw for his institute).

The political changes also brought behind them an influx of avant-garde influences from the West – these merely served to stimulate the revival of the Polish theatre's sturdy and unique traditions. The absurdist movement in particular, so emphatic in its effects in the West, had little to add to the Poles' own artistic consciousness of a grotesque absurdism that dates back to Stanisław Witkiewicz (Witkacy 1885–1939) and Witold Gombrowicz (1905–1969). But the Poles relished the freedom that this period brought, and by the end of the fifth decade the conditions were favourable for the success of such politically conscious dramatists as Mrożek and Rożewicz.

In terms of staging, an emphasis was placed on design and technical media, as well as on cerebral interpretation of text at a time of relative liberalism in the literary arts. Roman Szydłowski notes with pride in the opening chapter of his multi-lingual government handbook, *The Theatre in Poland*, that 'there are not many countries ... where the sets are applauded as the curtain goes up'. [408/9] And Jan Kłossowicz, in an article in the bi-lingual magazine *The Theatre in Poland* in 1971, gives a general picture: 'A peculiar style of new baroque emerged, a style of staging replete with political content, and at the same time bewildering in the wealth and excess of concept, colour and form'. [309/4] To visitors from the West, the Polish theatre of the early sixties seemed particularly exciting, and was considered to be of a very high quality when compared, say, with the average British equivalent. Alan Seymour reported, after a visit in 1963:

> Polish Theatre has a verve and brilliance intoxicating to anyone tired of the 'buttoned-up emotions' (I quote a much-travelled Pole) of London's theatre world. At the very least, performances have an all-round excellence, of acting, direction and design. When the excellence catches fire as it so often seems to, the theatre again becomes a place of magic rather than ritual tedium. [387/33]

But there were those within Polish theatrical circles who were less enthusiastic, particularly about the effect of these developments on the craft of acting. Jan Kreczmar – an established post-war Polish actor – charted the development of the ethics and practice of the actor's art in Poland in an article in 1968. He contended that the application of the approved but fossilized Stanislavsky system within the State theatre schools had resulted in mediocrity and a reliance on 'psychological and intuitive acting', which led in turn to undisciplined self-indulgence on stage. In a reaction against this, and influenced by the 1949 call for Socialist Realism, there was a concerted attempt to formulate and impose a theory known as 'intellectual · theatre' with which Kreczmar identified himself. At this point the naturalistic actor, who had previously dominated the Polish theatrical scene, became demoted, and in retrospect Kreczmar recognized the damage done to the actor's art as the actor became the transmitter of the author's and director's creations: 'We are so terribly afraid of offending against good taste, culture and moderation in sentiment, that our stage quite often represents a picture of greyness. . . .' [324/8]

This picture of a cerebrally influenced process of stage creation has parallels in the recent history of British theatre. The sixties saw the emergence of non-actor directors of great power and skill: in their methods, it has been argued, the aspect of 'interpretation' was emphasized to the detriment of 'experience'. In 1969 J. C. Trewin wrote in a manner reminiscent of Kreczmar:

> It is as if an actor or actress were in the anteroom, refusing to go further, refusing to fling the door wide. . . . it is curious, for there are many current actors of high spirit and intelligence. Can it be that they and their directors – who so often have the final word – are intent on interpreting a play to us rather than letting us experience it? [421]

And it was partially this aspect of reticence in the face of experience that contributed to Peter Brook's condemnation of the British stage:

> The English version of half-truth is so skilful that it's much harder to recognise. . . . When you have a beautiful approximation of the truth and the style with which it's executed is admired more than anything else, then it's always harder to look for the real thing when what's offered in its place is almost it. [182/19]

But in Poland in 1959, when Grotowski founded his small experimental theatre company in Opole, there were additional forces at play affecting the balance of disciplines in the theatre: the avant-garde influences from the West and the Poles' reaction to them; the emphasis on the textual and technical aspects of scenic production; the prominence of either an un-disciplined or an over-intellectual approach to acting. The result of all this was to reduce the actor to the status of puppet, or as the critic Jan Kłossowicz expressed it in his 1971 article – 'an executor of the will of the all-powerful director'. [309/4] Within this context Grotowski was proposing an artistic programme *in opposition* to the main stream, as was evident from his theatrical statements and practice. It could be said of his earliest work, in fact, that its strongest characteristic was precisely that of contradiction and defiance of existing practice – a polemical attitude which, twenty years later, Grotowski claimed to have been a conscious principle throughout his work:

> I would like to remind you that the work of our institution has invariably followed a path complementary to – and so in a way at variance with – current trends in culture. Such is our calling. [95/40]

It became apparent in time that what Grotowski was proposing was a total revaluation of the actor's art. He wanted the actor to be elevated from merely one of several factors in a theatrical event to the essence of theatre itself: simultaneously there should be a reduction of the artistic means of expression extraneous to the actor. This basic premise became known as 'poor theatre'. In 'After the Avant-Garde', a retrospective talk delivered in Paris in 1967, Flaszen considered the new theatre's programme as a heritage of the avant-garde writers of the fifties, such as Beckett, Ionesco and Genet:

> Indeed, these writers did not leave behind them a form of theatre, but literary works written for the stage. Theatrical scripts, but not a craft of acting. And they left us not a new function for theatre, only a rebellion against the old function, onto which the rebellion itself was grafted. [135/110]

He goes on to describe the eliminatory process to which Grotowski proposed to subject theatrical art, with a particular emphasis on the decayed relationship between theatre and text:

> To create theatre we must go beyond literature; theatre starts where the word ceases. The fact that a theatrical language cannot be a language of words, but its own language, constructed from its own substance – it's a radical step for theatre, but Artaud had already realized this in his dreams....
>
> The same line of thought that sees a possibility for theatre today through a state of isolation, tells us not only to go beyond the discursive word, but also to reject everything not strictly essential for the theatrical phenomenon.... The proper subject-matter of theatre, its own particular score belonging to no other form of art is – in Grotowski's words – the score of human impulses and reactions. The psychic process, revealed through the bodily and vocal reactions of a living, human organism. That is the essence of theatre. [135/112]

It is therefore not surprising that when Grotowski's Theatre of Thirteen Rows was first established, there was some resistance, even antagonism, to the ideas set forth by Grotowski and Flaszen, which were in direct and conscious opposition to the prevalent styles of staging in their own country. In particular, as Jan Kłossowicz pointed out: 'Grotowski referred to Stanislavsky's theory in 1959 when the entire Polish theatre was set to react against the ossified, deformed "system", the observance of which has for so long been recommended'. [309/5] Many seemed to find the partnership of Grotowski and Flaszen – and the resulting conceptual clarity – particularly threatening. As one critic said: 'It is difficult to decide what is more frightening, the theatrical ideas of the men of letters or the literary desires of the men of theatre'. [256] There were critics, for the most part theatrical theoreticians and historians, who were eventually able to recognize in the theories a revaluation and deeper exploration of Stanislavskian precepts. But many practitioners, actors in particular, were repelled by Grotowski's dogmatically purist and dedicated approach.

But to return to the very beginnings of the Theatre of Thirteen Rows, it must be said that this was not immediately apparent in Grotowski's first production. Quite soon after the new theatre company had set themselves up in Opole, and under the pressure of the impending opening to the 1959/1960 season, *Orpheus* (text by Cocteau) had its premiere on 8 October 1959. One of the actors has reported that Grotowski had every aspect of this production worked out in advance of the rehearsal period, which lasted less than three weeks. And Kazimierz Braun has described *Orpheus* as 'acted in a bizarre and awkward manner, on an ordinary end-stage. The stage design was basically realistic, although clearly slapdash and thrown together, and the costumes were conspicuously shoddy.' [173/161] *Cain* (text by Byron), which critics familiar with Grotowski's work have called the first really important premiere of the Theatre of Thirteen Rows, followed on 30 January 1960. Osiński:

> This performance, like the earlier *Orpheus*, was based on richly augmented visual and theatrical elements and technical tricks, and not on the art of the actor. It was – as Grotowski described it later – 'more in the nature of an exorcism of conventional theatre than a proposition of a counter-programme' and in consequence 'formulated the negative programme of this company'. [360/16]

In the months following the premiere of *Cain*, the Theatre of Thirteen Rows took their two productions on tour in Poland, giving performances in Katowice, Cracow and Warsaw. Concurrently, Grotowski was working on a production of *Faust* (after Goethe) at the Polish Theatre (Teatr Polski) in Poznań – the only theatrical piece of work he was to do outside his group – which had its premiere in April 1960. This period also marks the nadir of the Theatre of Thirteen Rows' fortunes in terms of audience attendance. Flaszen has ascribed this at least in part to the indifference of the provincial audiences in Opole, which, he says, also affected the larger, more conventional theatres. However, the fact remains that on occasions it was necessary to cancel performances for lack of spectators, although on principle a production would be presented with only two or three people present. It was this fact that first drew the attention and admiration of Zbigniew Cynkutis, at that time a newly-graduated actor working at the conventional Teatr Ziemi Opolskiej in Opole, but soon to transfer to the Theatre of Thirteen Rows to work and remain with Grotowski until the present. In an interview I conducted in April 1981, he recalled:

> Although these people had been called dilettantes by those wiser than I, what I found there gave me hope. There was something I hadn't met in the conventional theatre or even during study – I mean the discipline of those on stage.

3 Goethe's *Faust* directed by Grotowski at Polski Theatre, Poznań.

There was construction, structure, consciousness, and there was risk. It was something they did with belief, trust and with hope. And furthermore, they gave their performance with only five people sitting and watching.... So I felt that this group had respect for those coming to see them, even when it was such a small number. There was something between them and each visitor.

But throughout its history, Grotowski's group has shown itself to be never at a loss for a strategic response at moments of apparent adversity, and such was the case at that time. In May 1960 there was set up an organization called the Circle of Friends of the Theatre of Thirteen Rows, whose members numbered about eighty, and whose honorary president was Józef Szajna. Concurrently, and directly connected with this group, there were established regular fortnightly discussion groups, led by Grotowski and Flaszen, in which practical aspects of the new theatre's artistic policies could be considered in relation to contemporary theatre practices. Osiński calls both the Circle and the discussion groups ('Conversatoria') 'a factor in the development of an atmosphere favourable to the work of the Group'. And also, with unintentionally sinister overtones – 'a fight for the public through their systematic education'. [361/75]

The Theatre of Thirteen Rows ended their first season with a production of Mayakovsky's *Mystery-Bouffe* (31.7.60) and opened the new season with a theatrical

4 Cast of *Mystery-Bouffe* (Grotowski top left).

treatment of Kalidasa's poem *Shakuntala* (which Grotowski had already directed
as a radio play). It was for this production that Grotowski began his collaboration
with the architect Jerzy Gurawski – in experimentation into the scenic relationship
between actors and spectators – that was to last until the production of *The Constant
Prince* in 1965.

In the meantime, in October 1960, Grotowski finally received his diploma from
the Cracow Theatre School, and the professional title of a qualified director. And
in June of 1961 came the last production of that season, and by far the most
significant to date, of *Dziady* (Forefathers' Eve – words by Adam Mickiewicz). This
was the first of a series of the great national classics that Grotowski was to stage
during the following few years. In historical terms the production was also significant for another reason. Eugenio Barba, a student from Norway visiting Poland
with a UNESCO grant, came to see one of the performances. He was to stay for
two years, working as an assistant to Jerzy Grotowski, and the role he has played
(and still plays) in familiarizing the Western world with Grotowski's work and
facilitating contact between the two has been highly significant.

The conclusion to the 1960/61 season at the Theatre of Thirteen Rows can also
be seen as the end of the first period of work for Grotowski and his young theatre

group. They had already completed two full seasons of productions and tours, and despite opposition were still firmly in residence in their provincial 'laboratory'. Up to this point, they could be said to resemble any other young theatre group, who had managed to secure for themselves the minimum resources for their experiments. Because of the nature of those experiments they had earned some degree of renown, and even notoriety, in their own country, although they remained almost unheard of outside Poland. But Grotowski's theories were now no longer merely the dogmatic formulations of an inexperienced and youthful artist, as Kazimierz Braun once described them. They had been tested and refined to some extent by practice, and what was beginning to evolve was a set of propositions, profoundly simple, which were soon to become internationally known and to revolutionize the craft of acting.

CHAPTER TWO

Orpheus to Dziady

Viewed as a whole, the work of the Laboratory Theatre has constituted an un-compromising and painstaking investigation of almost every area of study involving the actor, and the actor's body and craft. Within Grotowski's earliest theoretical writings there is contained the central proposition that theatre, in order to survive, must concentrate itself and focus upon the actor and what can be achieved scenically, through the acting processes, and in relation to the spectator who is the other half of the dynamic, theatrical equation. Once he was established as Director of the Theatre of Thirteen Rows in Opole, Grotowski was in a position to test his theories freely, but had to carry out his investigations within the inevitable limita-tions imposed by the necessity of constructing public performances. In the process he discovered for himself (or had pointed out for him by critics) those aspects of his theories which did not co-exist comfortably (or at all) with the realities of theatrical and artistic convention.

This chapter will consist, in the main, of a chronological investigation of the actual productions constructed and directed by Jerzy Grotowski at the Theatre of Thirteen Rows between its opening in September 1959 and the end of 1961 (i.e. the historical period covered in the preceding chapter). None of the productions was in repertory for long and therefore the accounts are based almost exclusively on documentary evidence, comprising for the most part either statements of intent on the part of the creators, or critical reviews. Neither source could be said to be completely reliable, so an academic reconstruction is neither possible, nor being attempted. But I hope that what emerges will nevertheless serve to present the principal themes of Grotowski's work during this period, and also constitute a concrete framework and point of reference for the subsequent evolution of his theories.

Apart, therefore, from a certain amount of descriptive reconstruction (where possible) to do with scenography, costume, properties, sound, etc., I will trace the development, through the successive productions, of the following central themes of Grotowski's work: (i) the emergence of the principle of 'poor theatre'; (ii) the attitude to, and treatment of, literature and text; (iii) spatial construction and relationships (environmental theatre); and (iv) the actor-spectator relationship. I will be placing particular emphasis on the experimentation into the dynamic three-way relationship of actor/spectator/space. The initial explorations seen in the early productions demonstrate a preoccupation with viable methods of audience 'participation', which was to overshadow much of Grotowski's work, and was never finally to be resolved in a theatrical context.

But it must be stressed that Grotowski never aimed in his experiments at a search for a definitive theatrical form, whether spatially or in the actor/audience relationship. He tried instead to be open in each production to the form organic to that play or performance. This exploration of spatial concepts and relationships was one of the most exciting elements of the early work, and in the process Grotowski tried and discarded many (by now) well-used formulae. He inaugurated a procedure of staging in which each production became an experiment *per se* in some aspect of the actor/audience spatial relationship, an approach which the American critic, J. Schevill, found revolutionary, as he recalled in 1973:

> I have a new vision now of what space can mean in a theatre. . . . If every play has its own unique space, it is not enough to begin with the idea of a flexible theatre. What is more important is the vision of a company, uniting director, playwright, designers, and actors, creating their vision of space in each work. . . . Even if a company plays only in its own theatre, it must find ways to abolish the idea of aesthetic, theatrical space and explore the transformations of dramatic space. This may mean not only the abolition of fixed seating and barriers of any kind between audience and actors, but also an architectural and psychological ability to transform the basic theatre into the ideal space for a particular production. [386/300, 301]

This, in essence, was the basic premise of 'environmental theatre', although the theory did not become conceptualized as such until the late sixties. In an article in 1975 Brooks McNamara cites as the first American 'environmental theatre' production a presentation of Ionesco's *Victims of Duty* by Richard Schechner and his Performing Group in New Orleans in 1967. On this occasion Schechner moved the seating and theatrical appliances out of the studio theatre and converted it into a living room, which was inhabited by both actors and audience. (Grotowski, as will be seen in this and later chapters, inaugurated similar experiments in *Dziady* 1961, *Kordian* 1962 and *Akropolis* 1962, with the actors in *Akropolis* even constructing the architectural space during the course of the action.) Schechner later formulated the ideas explored in his production of *Victims of Duty* in an article in *The Drama Review* entitled 'Six Axioms for an Environmental Theater', and established the Performing Garage in New York as a neutral space for designing theatrical environments. Brooks McNamara traces the development of this spatial form from its earliest roots in folk tradition and ritual. As a discipline it became distinct from the performance forms which moved into 'formal theatre structures', in which there is a physical separation of the actor from the audience:

> In the environmental tradition, this separation has never been seen as necessary, and performance space has been viewed as a single, all-encompassing unit. The result has been that the boundaries between actor and spectator have been informal or indefinitely drawn, and there has been not only close contact but often an intermingling of the two groups. [344/4]

In an article in 1976 analyzing 'The Disintegration of Theatrical Space', Javier Navarro de Zuvillaga further distinguished two basic methods of delineating theatrical space which have evolved from the environmental tradition. The first, having developed from folk performances, parades and processions, he calls 'theatre of the found environment': this has been explored in various forms of street theatre; the guerilla theatre and Happenings of the sixties; and in more sophisticated interpretations by the Bread and Puppet Theatre and the Living Theatre. The second category he refers to as 'theatre of the prepared environment':

> It unfolds within a closed space which is conveniently prepared for each production, but always based on the assumption that this space is common to actors and spectators.... This idea of living together and the vital common experience within the same space is its clearest characteristic.... Why should only the actor and not the public as well feel a relationship with dramatic space and time in a direct manner? [228/27–28]

This is a question, de Zuvillaga says, that has concerned amongst others Appia, Meyerhold, Okhlopkov, Artaud and Brecht. And their questioning has influenced the work of Grotowski, whom de Zuvillaga describes as 'one of those who did most to rediscover theatre by replanning theatrical space ... a space which lives during the performance and which should be a protagonist as much as the actors and audience'. [228/25]

De Zuvillaga has also, accurately, singled out Artaud as the most significant influence, not specifically for his spatial propositions as such (which were largely theoretical and unrealized), but because these were 'the spatial translation of his idea of addressing oneself directly to the public through their feelings and not their understanding of the spoken word'. [228/25] Environmental theatre has to a great extent been developed and explored in the context of theatre forms employing with ever less compromise and ever more confidence non-verbal means of expression and communication: and Grotowski could be said to be in the forefront of this development. In this respect the concept of environmental theatre, the exploration of the actor-spectator relationship in physical and psychological terms, and the attitude towards and employment of literature and text in Grotowski's theatre are all essential and interdependent aspects of a central line of enquiry: one serving a vision of theatre as revolutionary and a dynamic force for change in humankind.

ORPHEUS (ORFEUSZ) text by Jean Cocteau
Premiere: 8 October 1959

As has already been noted in the preceding chapter, *Orpheus* was prepared in less than three weeks, in a form pre-determined by Grotowski. It opened the 1959/1960 season by the new company occupying the Theatre of Thirteen Rows in Opole. The establishment of the company had provoked an energetic debate in the local and national press as to the rights and qualifications of the Cracovian team to set up an experimental 'laboratory' theatre in the small provincial town. The production was therefore seen as a 'statement of intent' on the part of the new Theatre of Thirteen Rows, underlined by the appearance with the production of a lengthy 'programme' booklet which was more in the way of a manifesto (and was jokingly referred to by one critic as 'a short philosophy course'. [353/201]) The booklet was the first of many to appear subsequently in conjunction with productions. They were used as a platform for the publishing of theoretical statements by Grotowski and Flaszen, information relating to the production including photographs and textual excerpts, extracts of press response, and publicity relating to future activities. This first issue was provocative: it reprinted some of the more sceptical press debate, together with a written response. It also published a statement by one of the company's supporters, Józef Szajna, and a poem written for the occasion by the Wrocław poet Tymoteusz Karpowicz entitled 'Elephants (For the Seekers of the New in Theatre – against spectators without imagination)'. [97]

From this very earliest production Grotowski showed his readiness to enter into a polemical relationship with the written text (and by implication with spectators and critics, particularly those who take for granted the theatre's subsidiary role in a faithful presentation of text). As with later, more traditional (and thus respected) texts, the philosophy of the writer was inverted and the production used as a vehicle to deny its own implicit faith or doctrine – in this case what Grotowski saw as the negative aspects of existentialism.

This is how one contemporary review by a Polish critic assessed the aim:

> The director wished to transmit the philosophical contents through purely theatrical means. Therefore the literary aspect becomes a scaffolding, on which theatre can build its own construction. Each sentence, almost each word has its own internal rhythm. The action is formulated like in a musical score. Not only the movement, but the pace of the action are subject to a precise discipline, while the scenic space matches to some degree the rhythm of the composition.... Moments of reflection, of seriousness, follow grotesque interludes, and then we see the characters again as if through a distorting mirror. [321]

Grotowski was not content, however, to use *only* theatrical means to press home his point, and the production ended with his own re-written version of Cocteau's concluding prayer, in which he clarified his message:

> We thank you ... world, that you dance your order, the order of your laws and the order of our intellect, which is capable of absorbing your laws.... We thank you, world, that we possess consciousness which permits us to overcome death: to understand our eternity contained in your eternity. And that love is the tutor.... We thank you, world, that you exist. [14]

This conscious pantheism can be seen as deliberate intellectual provocation during a period when the Polish literary and theatrical worlds were responding with enthusiasm to the post-1956 influx of Western and European writers, in particular the absurdists. In an interview published shortly after the premiere of *Orpheus*, Grotowski said:

> We have no wish to perpetuate absurdism, we see and want to find some kind of hope. Translated into the terms of theatre this hope can be found between the two extremes of reality: the tragic and the grotesque. We undertake this search in our own name, and not that of the author, which by no means implies a disrespect of playwrights. [13]

Kazimierz Braun, who saw Grotowski's first production with his Theatre of Thirteen Rows company, recalled in particular one scene from *Orpheus* which he found both humorous and significant. The scene is that in which Heurtebise the Glazier is revealed as an angel to Eurydice, who sees him floating in the air by the window. The original script of Cocteau's play offers suggestions for how this can be achieved mechanically, and Braun prefaces his account with examples of complex solutions that were devised in other Polish theatres presenting the play:

> But in the Theatre of Thirteen Rows that scene was done very crudely – undoubtedly because of lack of funds and through haste. Quite simply Heurtebise (Zygmunt Molik) grasped the window-frame with his hand and hung there. I was sitting nearby and could see the veins standing out on his forehead with the strain. . . .
>
> I don't know for certain, but I feel that that scene with the flying angel might have been decisive. Maybe it inspired them with the energy for further work and pointed out the direction of further research? In any case I find something highly instructive and symbolic in the scene. An actor must rise in the air. But how? It's not possible. He hangs onto the window-frame. He experiences all of his weight and his lack of skill, and most likely the humour of the situation, both physical and psychological. And thus he must learn to fly. In reality. Both physically and psychically. He must free himself from the weight of his body. And he must free himself from the illusory demands – and the aesthetics – of old theatre. [173/162]

CAIN (KAIN) text by George Gordon Byron
Premiere: 30 January 1960 (Polish premiere)

Bolesław Taborski, the Polish writer and translator who has written a major academic work on 'Byron and the Theatre', asked Jerzy Grotowski (by letter in 1972) his motives in choosing *Cain* for production: 'Why did I do *Cain* in 1960? I came across the text rather by chance, and it interested me because it contained, as it were, the "whole world" and the "whole life" of man. Just as *Dziady* or *Faust*, for example'. [409/352] This difficult drama had also been selected for production at one time by Stanislavsky (1919). And although Grotowski has denied any conscious significance in his choice, the references to the production in Stanislavsky's *My Life in Art* are striking in the image they convey of the magical and communicative power of theatre, overcoming all barriers and evoking an almost religious awareness and respect in the audience:

> They listened to what was going on on the stage in the deepest of silences. The serious, thoughtful mood of the dramatic poem prevented them from staging an ordinary theatrical ovation. After the end of the performance the spectators sat for a long time without any movement and departed without any noise, as if they were leaving a temple of worship after prayer. [400/556]

The same degree of respect was, however, by no means evident in Grotowski's staging of the 'thoughtful ... dramatic poem'. He responded to the text with the polemical attitude characteristic of this period of his creative work. In the usual extensive programme notes Ludwik Flaszen explained how they interpreted Byron's attitude. At the conclusion of Byron's original text, he writes

> There remains only a revolt, the desperate 'no', full of pathos and dead seriousness, absolute pessimism ... the declaration about the dignity of the individual and the tragedy of existence, reminding one on occasion of ... modern existentialism. *Cain* has seemed to us important not because of its solutions, or

5 *Cain* – Zygmunt Molik.

rather the lack of them, but because of the range of the problems it raises. The freedom of the individual and moral dictates; ethical results of knowledge, the awe of irrevocable death; the antagonism between man and society, man and the world – in a word ... the peculiar philosophical climate thanks to which existentialism has had such a resounding career. *Jerzy Grotowski's production, in tackling these problems, proposes solutions decidedly polemical in relation to existentialism and its absolute pessimism.* (Flaszen's italics)

The production transfers the problems of *Cain* from the level of religious revolt ... to the level of purely secular considerations. Hence the place of God is taken by Alpha – the impersonation of the Elements, of the automatism of Nature's forces, which act blindly and relentlessly; the place of Lucifer is taken by Omega, the impersonation of Reason, of the restlessness of human awareness. [409/353]

Flaszen goes on to explain that in their opinion 'the pathos of absolute pessimism' deserves mockery as much as its polar opposite. 'For this reason, the form of the production is changeable, flickering: from seriousness to mockery, from tragedy to grotesque'. [409/353] Although this production for the most part still took place on the theatre's small end-stage, Grotowski was already beginning the experiments

6 *Cain* – Tadeusz Bartkowiak and Zygmunt Molik.

into the actor–spectator relationship. A stage curtain was not used and two of the actors (playing Cain and Omega) made brief and limited forays into the spectator areas, and addressed the audience directly using lines from the Byron text. According to Barba the spectators themselves were designated as descendants of Cain, 'present but remote and difficult to approach' [115/162]

Two professional stage designers worked in collaboration on the décor, which included a triptych altar on stage facing the audience, painted with images in the style of Bosch. There were elaborate effects: the text being used as orchestrated sound played through loudspeakers, to which the actors moved in rhythm; an attempt at representing the cosmos visually with lighting in Act II; the intellectual confrontations between Cain and Omega being physically encapsulated in metaphors such as wrestling, boxing, and at one moment a fencing match using beams of light as swords. Something of the overwhelming variety of tones in the performance comes over in this review:

> Pretty well all known theatrical means are to be found all together in the production of *Cain*. Philosophical dialogue turns into scorn, metaphysical shock into derision, demonism into circus, tragic dread into cabaret, lyricism into clowning and frivolity. In addition there is caricature, parody, satire, vaudeville, an operatic sketch, mime, a little ballet scene, and besides all that – an irreverent attitude towards the text. Each situation is formulated differently. There are continual changes in the acting and a thousand ideas, insistent deafening music, a loudspeaker talking (none too distinctly) in place of the actor on stage, an actor amongst the audience, actors addressing the public, actors improvising during scene changes. A general tower of Babel and confusion of tongues. [327]

As in the preceding production, in the end Grotowski felt the need for his own text to clarify his message. The concluding scene of the performance consisted of an ecstatic dance to celebrate the theme that 'the world is one'. Alpha is revealed to be Omega (shown on stage as Omega asleep) and all of the characters put on Alpha-Omega masks to express unity. In addition, there appeared at the back of the stage, behind the final dance, a placard bearing Grotowski's epilogue: it celebrated again the unity of the world and its intrinsic polarity 'which means from Alpha to Omega'. It was in a stylized dialect, written in a childish scrawl, and decorated with naive drawings of a cat's head, flowers, heart, moon, a pair of spectacles (Grotowski) and the sun.

It seems quite understandable from the present perspective that, with as yet no well formulated and matured method of training and acting, Grotowski's creativity at this early stage should have found expression in both intellectual manipulation and a profusion of effects. The production evoked a wide variety and extreme of response: one reviewer, Jan Pawel Gawlik, specifically criticized Grotowski for his 'spontaneous use of form, at times without order or sequence, for the sole purpose of achieving richness without regard for the possibilities of the actors'. [256] However, he concludes his review, with a certain degree of insight, by suggesting that despite all the 'cool, calculating material of intellectual struggle', Grotowski's

7 *Cain* – Tadeusz Bartkowiak and Zygmunt Molik.

work as evinced in this production is in fact predominantly non-intellectual and spontaneous, 'operating in the field of emotions, reactions, symbols ... the spontaneity of form, sometimes irrational and nebulous and yet – as it were – total and sensual, has turned out to be stronger than all intentions and designs'. [256]

MYSTERY-BOUFFE (MISTERIUM BUFFO) after Mayakovsky
Premiere: 31 July 1960

Mystery-Bouffe was the final production in the first Theatre of Thirteen Rows season. In the programme notes Flaszen pointed to the affinities between the experimental attitudes of Meyerhold, Mayakovsky and Grotowski, not least of which was the fact that Mayakovsky treated his own texts as scenarios, advising subsequent adaptation to suit the ideological and theatrical requirements of the

8 *Mystery-Bouffe*: Rena Mirecka and Zygmunt Molik.

times. Mayakovsky in fact described this play in a preface as

> a high road – the high road of the revolution. No-one can predict with certainty
> how many more mountains will have to be blasted away by those of us who are
> travelling that high road.... In the future, all persons performing, presenting,
> reading or publishing *Mystery-Bouffe* should change the content, making it
> contemporary, immediate, up to the minute. [343/39]

No more appealing invitation could have been offered to a director of Grotowski's
inclinations, and he took full advantage of it (although, as Flaszen pointed out in
the programme notes, Grotowski did not on this occasion manipulate the text in
order to engage in polemic with the author). In fact he combined *Mystery-Bouffe*
with Mayakovsky's *The Bath-House*, and characters were freely shifted about
between the two plays. The original *Mystery-Bouffe*, as the title suggests, in formal
and stylistic terms had humorous allusions to a folk or mystery play, and Grotowski
extended the parallel by including fragments of Polish medieval mystery plays as

a Prologue and Epilogue. As with previous productions the degree of textual manipulation by the director invited severe criticism. But in this respect Grotowski was acting strictly in accordance with the author's instructions and with Meyerhold's precept that 'the art of the director is the art not of an executant, but of an author – so long as he has earned the right'. [171/209]

The production was staged in emblematic form, with debts to both medieval drama and Oriental theatre. The entire material at Grotowski's disposal comprised six actors, a few shields painted to represent individual roles, a tin tub, a black painted bench and the theatre's microscopic stage, conventionally divided from the audience. Underlining the medieval theme, the stage design was painted in the style of Hieronymous Bosch, provoking, according to Flaszen, a comparison with 'popular folk forms of art where terror is intertwined with the grotesque, and characters take on a permanent form which is schematically and naively defined'. [100] In contrast the characters in Grotowski's drama underwent lightning changes in which the shields played a key part:

> The actress who begins her part as the Lady, will return in a moment as the rebellious Unclean; she will also be the Devil, and the Angel, then a Secretary, and at the same time . . . a typewriter and a telephone. A tin bath-tub, according to its position on stage, can perform the function of the ark, a desk, a table in the theatre foyer, as well as an element of the 'time machine'. It is enough to

9 *Mystery-Bouffe*: Theatre of Thirteen Rows Company.

turn around and grasp the shield, which serves to present characters in a certain way, and it becomes a rifle or a painter's palette. When the passage of time is to be marked, for instance a night that has passed, the shields are swayed rhythmically over the prostrate actors, to signify their sleep.... [239]

Although Grotowski can be seen here already formulating the concept of 'poor theatre' (albeit through necessity and somewhat simplistically), the atmosphere of alienation – and the separation of actor from image – is still a long way from the synthesis of the concept of 'holy actor' which was to be born in following years. In fact Flaszen said of the approach used in this production, perhaps not altogether seriously, that it 'permits in a provocatively literal manner the application of one principle of modern acting technique, according to which the actor does not entirely impersonate the performed character, but rather acts as if 'beside' the role. And – of course – it extricates us – with the small size of our group – from the problems of a play with such an excessively large cast....' [100]

SHAKUNTALA (SIAKUNTALA) after the drama by Kalidasa
Premiere: 13 December 1960

It is quite possible that one of the reasons Grotowski selected *Shakuntala* at this stage in the Theatre of Thirteen Rows' work, was for its alienatory qualities in his exploratory treatment of literary text, and his search to free the actor from litera-

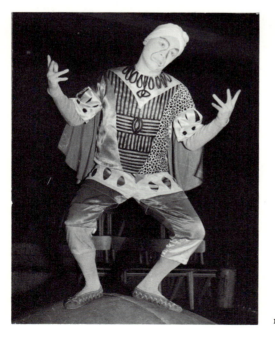

10 *Shakuntala* – Zygmunt Molik.

ture's overpowering influence. M. K. Byrski, in an article entitled 'Grotowski and the Indian Tradition' explained that Grotowski

> was searching for a score that could be performed by the team with complete freedom to 'instrumentate' ... and of course *Shakuntala* in its original intention is undoubtedly a score ... its character, and its awkward translation into Polish, strengthen the strangeness of the fable atmosphere. It permits a loose, flippant treatment of text. [202/86]

Shakuntala itself is a drama from the 4th or 5th century A D, and it first appeared in the West in 1789 in an English translation. Grotowski made extensive cuts to the original, inserting fragments from ancient Indian ritual texts, including the *Kāma-Sūtra*.

In the usual pamphlet issued as an accompanying programme to the production, there were included two pages of 'Viewing Regulations for the Spectators and in particular Critics' written by Ludwik Flaszen. It is worth extensive quotation, in view of the formulation it contains of Grotowski's approach at that time:

> The text of the play, according to the usual practice of this theatre, has been used by the director as a canvas for his own contents and scenic invention....
>
> In the original version *Shakuntala* is somewhat naive, a poeticized story of love. In dealing with love the director has introduced a duality, the dialectics of extremes. In the course of the production there is repeated confrontation between the sublimated poetry of love and the plain prose of ritual injunctions, customary laws and the sexual code....
>
> The performance is to some extent a visible demonstration of the sources from which the style of our theatre is drawn. For the theatre of the East is one of ritual, where the performance constitutes a ceremony communicating with the spectator through conventional signs, and in which the division between stage and audience does not exist. The ritual theatre is the opposite of the theatre of illusion, in which there is portrayed on stage an ostensible picture of life, while the spectator views apart. All of Grotowski's productions carry into effect the principle of ritual, not only *Shakuntala*.
>
> In view of its secular content, the ceremonial aspect of the performance should not be taken completely seriously. It's an invitation from the director to a game. Here we are – concretely – playing at oriental theatre. More precisely – pseudo-oriental. Through a convention of gesture, a way of talking, through the creation of an entire alphabet of conventional scenic signs, it is in some way aiming at a synthesis of oriental theatre (or rather a parody of the usual concepts of the theatre of the East). The director uses as material not only the forms of Eastern theatre – but also certain of the more common Indian notions. On the one hand life is shown as some kind of trance, a reverie, a dream; whilst on the other – as a conventional ceremony, the expression of human demeanour in conventional form, etiquette.... This brings about the double rhythm of the

11 *Shakuntala*
– Zygmunt Molik
and Rena Mirecka.

production. The phase of 'trance' is shown in immobility, composed of a grotesque adaptation of yoga postures. The 'conventional' phase is movement ('graceful, formal'). . . . The interchange and succession of these phases creates the rhythm of the production. . . . The scenic word is treated very conventionally. It has to be not only the carrier of meaning and intention, the transmitter of the contents, but must also act with its own sonoric value, become sound, act artificially. . . .

The main task of Grotowski's staging is not however a pure game. Through game it aims to break certain intellectual habits. It tries to bring home to the spectator the ancient, but eternally valid paradoxes of love. And at the same time mock the naive and commonly held truisms about the East, which is no longer today a giant sunk in age-old slumber, but an important element in the fortunes of the modern world. [101]

Nearly seventeen years later, Flaszen described the production more graphically in the following terms:

We chose it because of Grotowski's weakness for India, doubtless. In this play, we deal with the extreme mysteries: strange sounds and dances are made. The sense was that we were all naive, child-like, vis-à-vis these mysteries. And so the costumes, for example, were actually made by children. We had a friend who was a teacher; he asked his pupils to paint a Knight, a Prince, a Lady. The resulting costumes were extremely colourful, a little primitive, somewhat Oriental. This was how the young saw the Orient. The room was designed so that the audience sat on two sides, with a construction on the floor in the middle. It was a round, organic shape, covered with sack-like fabric, and with a protruding column. It was simply a phallic symbol; but this was in 1961, before the great sexual revolution (at least in Poland!) so it was a kind of joke; after all, it *was* a play about love. . . . The whole movement of this performance was, for the first time in our theatre, extremely precise and dance-like. Likewise the whole score of sound. The sense was rather parodistic and sometimes malicious. For example, the hero has great love-monologues. We had him stand on his head. At that time we were at a cross-roads. Something crystallized then – we were looking for a purer theatre where one could not tell content from form. We wanted pure form – movement. This change was of tremendous consequence. The need of exercise suddenly appeared: just in order to be able to do it! Our relation to the physical world was still uneasy as if eroticism or physicality was not acceptable. It was a primitive animalism, the result of the male-female schism. Important in Grotowski's perception of the world then was the non-acceptance and mockery of nature as something unpleasant. These were strong motives. [143/321]

12 *Shakuntala*
– Zygmunt Molik and Antoni Jahołkowski.

The play was presented on a centrally arranged stage, with the audience divided into sections facing each other. There were two additional stands placed behind the spectator areas where 'yogi-commentators' sat above the heads of the audience to interpret the action. The original text contained 34 characters, whereas the action was presented in Grotowski's version with only seven actors. However in this production, again, the spectators were assigned roles, this time as hermits and courtiers within the play, and were treated as 'participants' with lighting used alternately on the stage and audience area.

There were already in evidence in *Shakuntala* many of the elements which were in time to become significant features of Grotowski's philosophy of theatre, which is why the production is historically of relevance: the fascination with ritual; the experiment with architectural space and the actor-spectator relationship; the insistence on the spectators' participation. It was with the abolition of the conventional end-stage in *Shakuntala* that the young architect Jerzy Gurawski joined the company to collaborate with Grotowski on an exploration of space. Furthermore it was for this production that Grotowski's acting company first undertook investigations into a theatrical 'system of signs', and the necessary actor training. In terms of the aesthetics of the performance there was a further development of the 'poor theatre' concept, with Grotowski attaching greater importance to the achievement of scenic effects through the actor's physiology, particularly in terms of utilizing natural and vocal sound effects. And there was the beginning of Grotowski's dialectical approach to aesthetics – contents and form – as can be perceived in Flaszen's introductory notes.

It is also evident, however, that these elements were not yet functioning in a coherent, unified whole. There was a noticeable ambivalence, particularly in terms of the attitude towards the spectator, and towards the 'ritual' aspects of oriental theatre. The play seemed to be presenting at the same time the potential for 'communication through ritual', and the potential for alienation. It was as if two incompatible techniques were being put to the test, which could only ultimately cancel each other out. It is hopefully not too much of a presumption to suggest (based on Flaszen's reference above to the 'non-acceptance and mockery of nature as something unpleasant') that the dichotomy was one that belonged to the creators of the performance and was yet to be resolved. One contemporary review, whilst praising the physical agility of the actors, concluded:

> He has filled the little stage in the round with truly theatrical movement, a curious architecture of forms, colours, sounds, languages and songs. However, in the end this beautiful Indian tale of love reaches us rather in the form of a philosophical treatise, an intellectual game, it doesn't touch upon other regions of the theatrical experience. There is here too much of mathematics, of conceptualism, and too little poetry. [334/8]

DZIADY (FOREFATHERS' EVE) words by Adam Michiewicz
Premiere: 18 June 1961

Dziady is the principal and most frequently performed play from the Polish
Romantic period. It was also the first Polish play that Grotowski directed at the
Theatre of Thirteen Rows with his new company (there had been murmurings in
the press about the previous dramatic works having originated in France, England,
Russia and India). The publication in 1823 of parts I, II and IV of *Dziady* led to
its author Adam Mickiewicz being imprisoned for 'spreading nonsensical Polish
nationalism'. Part III, containing what is known as the 'Great Improvisation' scene
was written in exile (1832). The title (trans. *Forefathers' Eve*) refers to an ancient
folklore tradition of recalling the dead, which Zbigniew Osiński briefly describes:

> A peasant ritual called Forefathers' Eve takes place in a village chapel, in the
> depths of Lithuania, assembling all the main characters of the drama. Mickiewicz
> makes the folk ritual the basis of a dramatic structure. . . . The revolt of a romantic
> individual is demonstrated through a love which is rebellious and contrary to
> prevailing convention. Among phantoms and ghosts, Gustaw appears as a silent
> vision, and later recounts the story of his childhood, love and personal life.
> [360/20]

Part III of the drama, which was influenced by the defeat of the Polish November
Uprising (1830–1831) changes the emphasis of the play and causes the romantic
lover (Gustaw) to transform himself into a national rebel and poet:

> Gustaw is transformed into Konrad – poet and seer – who, by the power of
> poetry, sees into the future and assumes responsibility for the entire nation. In
> this way, Gustaw's personal drama transforms itself into national drama, per-
> sonified in Konrad. [360/20]

The play's popularity in the past and in present day theatre is due both to its poetic,
fragmented form – by which it is a perfect vehicle for experiment in theatrical
technique – and because, having been written partly in exile during the Partitions
of Poland, it is intensely patriotic. In the Improvisation scene the main character
challenges, in Promethean fashion, God's handling of his country's past and
present, and, claiming his patriotism as his 'cross', demands cosmic rule over
Poland's future. In another section of the poem/drama, Poland is represented as
a 'Christ among the Nations of the Earth', an innocent victim crucified by foreign
powers:

KONRAD: I love a nation, and my wide embrace
        presses the past and future of the race to my deep breast
        Both friend and lover, spouse and father, I;
        And I would raise my country high upon the crest
        Of joy, for all the world to glorify. [348/103–104]

Dziady appealed to Grotowski in that its loose form permitted a creative, rather

13 Poster for *Dziady*.

14 *Dziady*
– Theatre of
Thirteen Rows Company.

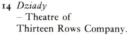

than representational response. He has talked of how he responded to the text of Mickiewicz: 'It was a fascination not completely subordinated to the text and was expressed not so much in dedication, but rather in the attempt to exploit its possibilities'. [15]. One of these possibilities that Grotowski explored was that of audience participation. According to the Polish critic Jan Błoński

> The Romantics . . . attached the greatest importance to audience involvement in a performance: it was a dream of art penetrating into the reality of life. . . . It strove in its highest achievements towards mystery, to a union with the viewers, if not in ritual, then in a common sacrifice, in a gesture which would shake the world. That gesture was a collective celebration, as it were, of the dreamed-of act, which must finally be made flesh. [161/144]

Grotowski himself has cited his own fascination with the ritual aspects of the play: 'It is a question of a gathering which is subordinated to ritual: nothing is represented or shown, but we participate in a ceremonial which releases the collective unconscious'. [15]

To this end Grotowski completely abolished the conventional stage (stating categorically that it would never be returned to) and collaborated again with Jerzy Gurawski on the construction of scenic space. Spectators were dotted about the room in 'islets' of chairs, seemingly at random. Action took place directly behind spectators, or confronted them, and their observation of the other spectators' reactions to confrontation was intended to contribute to their own reactions and experience of the play. Flaszen:

> Directing a performance, unlike in the traditional theatre, concerns two companies. The director constructs his performance not only of actors, but also of spectators. Theatrical ceremonial is created at the intersection of these two ensembles. [360/14]

This was Grotowski's first attempt at a total spatial integration of actors and

15 *Dziady*
– Theatre of
Thirteen Rows Company.

spectators, and the partial elimination of the intellectual division, by treating the audience as actor/participants. The actors and spectators were designated as 'participants on the first and second levels' and the attitude of the actors was that of an invitation to participation in ceremony.

The attempt at active involvement of the audience was not repeated to the same extent until much later, with the earliest versions of *Apocalypsis Cum Figuris*, which also explored more deeply aspects of a theme touched upon in *Dziady* – namely the significance of 'play'. Grotowski:

> We want to expose the relationship between ritual and play: the actors begin the magic lore as a kind of entertainment. From amongst the circle of spectators and actors they 'number out' – according to the Mickiewicz text – the first leader of the chorus.... This game grows into something sacral, the participants call up the dead and immediately take their parts. [15]

There were other elements of the production which maintained this theme of 'play'. Characters wore bedspreads, quilts or window curtains in place of romantic cloaks and dresses, like children in a game of 'make-believe'.

16 *Dziady*
– Theatre of
Thirteen Rows Company.

This was just one aspect of a 'specific theatrical dialectic' Grotowski was striving for in *Dziady* – 'the play and the ceremonial, tragedy and the grotesque, quixotry and "sacrosanctity"'. [15] Through play to an involvement in secular ritual, Grotowski was aiming to release and confront within his audience the symbolic and mythic images springing from its own culture. And, of course, the peculiarly national character of *Dziady* made it a fertile subject for confrontation with myth – a theme that was to be developed in subsequent productions. Grotowski described how the production treated the Improvisation scene:

> The long soliloquy has been changed into the Stations of the Cross. Gustaw-Konrad moves among the spectators. On his back he carries a broom, as Christ carried his cross. His grief is genuine and his belief in his mission sincere. But his naive reactions are shown to be those of a child who is not aware of his limitations. Here the director used a specific dialectic: entertainment versus ritual, Christ versus Don Quixote. The meaning of the production becomes clear in this final scene, where the individual revolt aimed at effecting a radical change is shown as hopeless. [115/156]

Such a handling of this most sacred of national dramas naturally provoked some confusion and hostility. Spectators and critics were well aware of the political implications contained in the representation of Konrad, moving in mystic pride among the spectators and weighed down by a broom. But Barba explained that 'the artificiality which Grotowski strives for must stem from reality, from the organic necessity of the movement or the intentions'. He refers to one instance from *Dziady*: 'In the Improvisation. . . . Gustaw-Konrad is exhausted and drips with sweat. He does not try to hide it. His gestures suggest that it is the blood Christ sweated'. [115/163] Thus the intellectual, dialectical approach was already being balanced, in the performance techniques, by attentions to actor training and a dependence on the organism of the actor.

It was in fact from a review of *Dziady* (by the critic T. Kudliński, who had attended nearly all of Grotowski's productions since Ionesco's *The Chairs* in 1957) that Grotowski took the phrase: 'the dialectic of apotheosis and derision'. This was to become a familiar motif in subsequent productions at the Theatre of Thirteen Rows, particularly when Grotowski was dealing with his national Romantic dramas. It was evidence, on an intellectual level, of one of Grotowski's most abiding characteristics – the dialectical approach – which was a heritage both of his Marxism and his interest in Eastern philosophies. But in the following few years this principle came to be applied in physical terms also, in the training and performance techniques of the actor, and it was only then that the work of Grotowski's actors began to be recognized as truly innovatory.

CHAPTER THREE
The Laboratory Theatre

The first play of the third season of Grotowski's Theatre of Thirteen Rows was not presented to the public until 13 February 1962. *Kordian*, by the great Polish Romantic poet, Juliusz Słowacki, was significantly the second Romantic drama Grotowski and his group had worked on and it was an indication that Grotowski's early concepts concerning ritual, myth and collective participation were beginning to concentrate themselves in a specific, ultimately fruitful, direction. It had been eight months since the preceding premiere (of *Dziady*) and this length of time is equally relevant, for it indicates that in their acting research and theatrical practice also, the group were becoming more focused and stringent. This development was acknowledged externally by a change of title: from 1 March 1962 the Theatre of Thirteen Rows became the Laboratory Theatre of Thirteen Rows (Teatr Laboratorium 13 Rzędów).

Nearly six months after the premiere of *Kordian*, at the end of July and beginning of August 1962, Grotowski went to Helsinki for the 8th World Youth and Student Festival as part of the Polish delegation. Here he had the opportunity of addressing an international public concerning the work of his small, experimental company. Amongst those present was the French drama critic Raymonde Temkine, eventually the author of one of the first books to be written about Grotowski: 'I gathered that he belonged to the avant-garde, and was so far ahead of the theatre I knew that I did not understand what he told me of his.... There were many hours of conversation and, since then, the dialogue has never ceased'. [415/37] Almost immediately after the Helsinki visit, Grotowski went to China for one month, until the middle of September 1962, as the delegate of the Polish Ministry of Art and Culture.

Less than a month after Grotowski's return to Opole came the first presentation of Version I of *Akropolis* (words by Stanisław Wyspiański). Directed by Grotowski in collaboration with the stage designer Józef Szajna, and with Eugenio Barba as assistant director, it was the most highly stylized of all Grotowski's staged works. It was to remain in the theatre's repertoire for almost eight years (in five different versions), being taken on almost all of the company's major international tours. Following this production, and as a result of the curiosity that Grotowski had provoked during his visit to Helsinki, there began a steady increase in the attention from the West focused upon the small experimental group in Opole. More students began to arrive for periods of apprenticeship, articles appeared in the Western press, and the first tentative steps were taken towards making Grotowski's work accessible outside Poland. But this was unfortunately being off-set by indifference or even hostility at home – a state of affairs that was to continue for many years. And the international acknowledgement by no means brought immediate security or increased resources for the work. Osiński quotes Grotowski from this period, complaining that 'every detail, every step, every blunder requires an absurd degree of effort and risk' [361/112] and an article in a local paper published at the beginning of 1963 reported:

> The group is working in very difficult conditions. Their subsidy does not cover the renovations and improvements necessary for the work. And the difficult working conditions are matched by the difficult living conditions of the members of the group.... At this moment the Theatre of Thirteen Rows receives the lowest subsidy in the country for its activity. It does not meet the needs of the theatre in the sense of securing its harmonious activity.... [308/110]

1963 clearly emerges, in retrospect, as the turning point in international terms of the Laboratory Theatre's fortunes. In December of the previous year the company had already begun rehearsals for Christopher Marlowe's *The Tragical History of Dr. Faustus*, and this work was continued during the spring months in the context of a steady development and crystallization of Grotowski's practical methods of training for his actors. Michael Kustow, who visited Opole that year and saw the actors at work, reported on his return:

> There is a long, low room, about 40 by 15 feet, bare, its walls painted black. Two long rostra, like trestle tables, run the length of the room.... eight actors are lined up on the tables. Grotowski, still in black, sits silent in the corner. The actors are performing their exercises. Every morning at ten they come, and for three hours work on breathing, voice, balance and acrobatics.... Voice work aims at discovering extra resonators, rarely used by the European theatre. Oriental techniques and Meyerhold's biomechanics help the actor to divide effort between parts of his body, and, like a conjuror, force the audience's attention on one part at the expense of the rest. 'The actor is a sorcerer, doing things beyond the spectator's means, affecting his subconscious. His face can express heroism, hands doubt, and his feet panic.' Grotowski is trying to build a resolutely *artificial* theatre-language. Naturalism is left behind: vocal and physical 'compositions' (as in the Japanese theatre) are yoked to a developed sense of irony to create a style of playing which, not literally, but by association and allusion, calls up responses deep-rooted in the collective imagination. [332/12]

Most of the actors concerned remember this as the period in which emerged the 'Exercises' proper, for which the Laboratory Theatre team were to become renowned (as opposed to the elaboration of specific techniques to be used in a particular production, as with the vocal work for *Shakuntala* or the mime and 'facial mask' techniques in *Akropolis*). In practice individual actors, encouraged by Grotowski, began to focus on those areas of training for which they had a natural

17 Training session at Theatre of Thirteen Rows.

disposition or particular knowledge, and evolved their own specialized fields which were then applied to the rest of the group and later, in workshops, to students. For example Rena Mirecka became an instructor in the area of the *'exercises plastiques'*, Zygmunt Molik in vocal-respiratory exercises, Zbigniew Cynkutis in 'rhythmic' work and Ryszard Cieślak – who had joined the company in October 1961 – developed particular skill in the area of acrobatics and 'mastery of the body'. (These basic demarcations of interest were perceptible in the work of the individual actors throughout their time in the company, and their influence could still be detected in the later, post-theatrical work.)

The production of *Dr. Faustus* (premiere 23.4.63) was particularly significant in the company's theatrical history. In its realization there could be seen a major progression in the evolution not only of the actor's physical training, but also of Grotowski's theatrical aesthetic and ethic. In broad terms this could be described as the gradual coalescing of the different strata of Grotowski's artistic credo into the central motif of 'sacrifice': in this the elaboration of the themes of the drama are inextricably linked with its aesthetic realization in scenic terms, and the ethical demands placed on the actor both within the production itself and in daily life. (Grotowski: 'It can be said without exaggeration that each "laboratory" premiere is bought at the price of the hard – one might almost say "convict" – labour of the team of eight' [19/58]).

But *Dr. Faustus*, unhappily, was also significant for its public and critical reception. It crystallized a particular, painful dichotomy: of recognition, and eventually adulation from outside its own country and particularly from the West; and of indifference and even hostility (with notable exceptions) from the Polish theatrical fraternity and the public. This hostility was often – it must be said – exacerbated by the success in the West. According to Osiński there appeared, after the premiere of *Dr. Faustus*, about one hundred reviews, essays and studies in Western publications: 'all this was in glaring contrast to its reception in its own country. The Opole press passed over it in complete silence, and no reasonable treatment appeared in any Polish periodical'. [361/117]

The fact that *Dr. Faustus* was the first of Grotowski's productions to be seen by many influential members of the Western theatrical world was due to particularly fortuitous circumstances: namely, that from 8-15 June 1963 the Tenth Congress of the International Theatre Institute took place in Warsaw. The participants were treated during this period to a full programme of the theatrical events taking place in Warsaw – while the Laboratory Theatre was on tour in Łódź presenting *Dr. Faustus*. It was in fact solely owing to Eugenio Barba's energy and determination that these facts in the long run were turned to Grotowski's advantage. Barba attended the Congress in Warsaw, and according to an English critic from *The Times* who was present, he drew attention to the theories at that time being developed by Grotowski by speaking up in a discussion on the merits of intellectuality amongst actors, proposing the idea that actors need only be virtuosos of the voice and body. [420] Subsequently Barba persuaded a group of those attending the Congress to visit Łódź by private car (paid for out of his own pocket) to see *Dr. Faustus*. The following day, according to Alan Seymour who was at the Congress, there were 'controversial and heated' reports, which attracted a large enough number of delegates to visit Łódź on an arranged coach trip to see the theatre's next performance. [387/33]

As a direct result of these events the Laboratory Theatre was invited to perform in Belgium, Holland and at the Theatre of Nations Festival in 1964 and 1965 in Paris. These visits did not materialize, however. It appears, according to Kazimierz Braun, that the Polish authorities were not convinced at that stage of the relevance and value of the Laboratory Theatre in international cultural terms and sent other, more official theatres instead. [173/155]

The following year, 1964, was a period of extreme existential uncertainty for the Laboratory Theatre. In their practical work a significant change of direction was becoming more perceptible. Less time was being devoted to the preparation of a conventional repertoire as the company continued to turn their attention more forcefully to research and experiment. Of at least four major productions proposed for the 1963/1964 season (a dramatisation of a Polish story; Dante's *Divine Comedy* directed by Barba; Shakespeare's *Hamlet*; Ibsen's *Peer Gynt*) only the *Hamlet* achieved any final form, and even that was not an official performance, but an 'open rehearsal'. Of this period Osiński says:

> *The Hamlet Study* was prepared in exceptionally difficult circumstances. The institute's future fate was unsure. The directors and actors had, for instance, no guarantee that they would receive a salary the following month. Some quite simply could not withstand this situation psychologically and left the Group. Only thanks to the heroic obduracy of Grotowski, who infected his colleagues with his own attitude, did there emerge finally, after several months of extra-ordinarily intensive and feverish work, a public presentation of a 'rehearsal' on 17 March. [361/120]

In the event *The Hamlet Study* was not considered a great success, even in retrospect, although Osiński himself feels the experiment to have been crucial in terms of the group experience and their later explorations. In all it received just twenty presentations, confined to the Opole public, and owing to lack of money there was neither the usual extensive accompanying pamphlet nor photographs.

Finally, the uncertainty as to the theatre's future, fuelled by its critics in Poland, was resolved in a highly propitious way. The proposition was put forward, and agreed upon in the summer of 1964, that the theatre should move from the small provincial town of Opole (considered 'not suitable as an environment for such shocking research' [361/124]) and take up residence in Wrocław, a large industrial and university town in the East of Poland (formerly the German Breslau). Grotowski and Flaszen obviously felt no hesitation in accepting. In a discussion between the directors of the Wrocław theatres published in 1965, Grotowski admitted to his theatre having benefited at the early stages of its development from the lack of pressure, but now welcomed the move to an academic centre such as Wrocław. There they could make contacts in specialized fields and explore con-temporary developments in peripheral areas such as cultural anthropology, psychology, psycho-analysis and physiology. [21/32] It would probably also be accurate to say that they welcomed at least in equal measure the increased security that this move would bring.

The transfer to Wrocław, to a tall, three-storied building in the very heart of the central market-place, officially took place on 1 January 1965. On 10 January there was the first performance in their new home – a presentation of *Akropolis*, reserved for the student population. Less than a week later came the official inaugural presentation of the same production for the public, thereafter performed regularly every weekend for the next three months. In their private work, however, the company were continuing their research into actor training and the exercises, and most particularly concentrating on the rehearsals (which had already commenced in Opole the previous June) for their next production: *The Constant Prince* (written by Calderon de la Barca and translated and adapted by the Romantic poet, Juliusz Słowacki). This production had its premiere in April 1965 (there was a 'closed' premiere on 20 April, and the official opening five days later). With Ryszard Cieślak in the central role, the production came in time to be seen as the pinnacle of the

18 Entrance to Laboratory Theatre from Wrocław Rynek.

theatre's acting technique expressed in performance, and for five years was taken on international tours as a demonstration of their achievements.

In the late spring of 1965 Grotowski began to travel more widely in Europe, sometimes accompanied by one or two of his actors, to attend festivals and seminars and to give practical demonstrations of the theory. At the end of April and beginning of May Grotowski was a member of the international jury of the 2nd World Festival of Student Theatre in Nancy (for the second year running), and led a two-day seminar with demonstration of work by Rena Mirecka and Ryszard Cieślak. Directly afterwards the trio gave a similar seminar in Paris as part of the University of the Theatre of Nations season, and at the end of May and beginning of June Grotowski and Cieślak travelled through Italy, leading courses on the theatre's approach to acting method. In August Grotowski came to London, at Peter Brook's invitation, and after a showing of a documentary film on *Dr. Faustus* (shot in Łódż in 1963 by an English student at the Film School there) there was a lecture and discussion with English directors, actors and critics. And in September 1965 Grotowski published in the Polish magazine *Odra* his short manifesto: 'Towards a Poor Theatre'. [20] Although it drew from the Polish press some adverse critical response, it still remains to this date the most concise and rich statement of his theatrical intent.

1965 and 1966 also saw the institutionalizing of the annual courses held at the theatre for visiting foreign students. These visits had already been taking place during the theatre's time in Opole (Barba being a notable example) and an article in a local Wrocław paper in 1965 comments on the arrival of more students (including Elizabeth Albahaca from Venezuela):

> This annual migration of theatre people to the Thirteen Rows is certainly known about, but not recognized or institutionalized. And yet people are beginning to say openly that knowledge of this theatre's technique and practice is all but inaccessible to actors who don't attend in person. Maybe it's time to institute officially at the Theatre of Thirteen Rows an acting studio, from which students in our country and neighbouring nations can also benefit. [422]

These comments highlight a particular problem relating to the dissemination of the practical results of the Laboratory Theatre research, which has been significant in the long run for the troubled relationship between the Laboratory Theatre and the Polish theatrical world. From the moment that his work had begun to be noticed, discussed and written about, Grotowski had strongly resisted any attempt to categorize and 'package' the results into a method to be placed alongside those of Stanislavsky or Brecht. He saw any fixed framework which could be externally adopted by a developing actor, rather than emanating from personal, organic research, to be ultimately stultifying. A consequence of this can be detected in the

19 Zbigniew Cynkutis in rehearsal with student.

tone and content of his theoretical writings. Although rich and inspirational when discussing attitudes towards work, conditions of work, and the theoretical and metaphysical bases for work, it rarely provides anything substantial in the way of a concrete 'method' of work, such as may be extracted and applied independently. The only way that interested students could really discover and explore the theatre's work was to become participants. This was possible if they were lucky enough to belong to an establishment Grotowski was visiting, or alternately, they could go to Poland. This attitude on Grotowski's part did not spring exclusively from a gratuitous desire for secrecy and elitism, as has sometimes been imputed, but had other motives. One was quite simply that much of the Laboratory Theatre work was not only non-verbal, but did not lend itself easily to conceptualization. Flaszen, recalling the earlier years of work with the actors, has talked of this:

> Grotowski... didn't want them to be intellects at work.... In the actor's work, there is no room for intellectualisation. If you want something, a lofty discussion won't accomplish it. One must act, think, do. So we 'discussed' through our actions.... For example, when language must be used in the work, either by Grotowski or among the actors themselves, it is a language of images, not the language of naming things by their names.... It is a search for such a language which in itself is a chain of associations that don't refer to the mind, but the whole of our being. [143/305, 316]

The 'inaccessibility' of Grotowski's work, then, had the effect of putting a block between what was essentially a non-intellectual function, and the hunger of a language-orientated critical world for verbal formulation. It was not so much that Grotowski decried the desire to verbalize – he was more than ready to make use of the process when it suited his ends. But he was perhaps simply too aware that, if not carried through with the real understanding that comes from direct experience, it can easily lead to the glib formulae he considered so destructive to the delicate growth of actor training. Nevertheless this attitude, perhaps not surprisingly, has also had undesirable results: on the one hand it has led precisely to that outward imitation by those wishing to emulate his work, that he was attempting to pre-empt. And it has also earned for him a reputation of non-cooperation, the implications of which (in terms of his relationship with his Polish theatrical colleagues) will be examined later in this chapter.

At the beginning of December 1965, the Laboratory Theatre company began rehearsals for their next production – a work based on Juliusz Słowacki's *Samuel Zborowski*, a drama that had figured in Grotowski's thoughts as early as the summer of 1959, when he had been setting up his new theatre in Opole. But in reality, during the next couple of years, the energies of Grotowski and the group were patently in other directions. On the one hand, internally, there was still the work directed towards the Laboratory Theatre acting 'method' and the exercises. And in terms of their public activities the theatre began a series of international theatre tours, which were to absorb much of their time and effort during the years 1966–1970,

20 Members of Laboratory Theatre in Mexico.

and to leave little, apparently, for either familiarizing the public in their own country with their work, or for any overt determination to supply the public with a new production.

The Laboratory Theatre's first foreign tour took place in February and March 1966. Its realization owed much to Eugenio Barba's energy and organizational activities: encompassing Sweden, Denmark and Norway, it included performances of *The Constant Prince*, seminars, demonstrations of practical work and a television programme about the theatre filmed earlier in Wrocław by Swedish Television. The second foreign tour took place in June and July of the same year and included appearances with *The Constant Prince* at the 10th Theatre of Nations Festival in Paris, and in Amsterdam for the Holland Festival of 1966. The appearances in Paris provoked a storm of response, some adulatory, some outraged – but whatever the tone, the general opinion, according to Raymonde Temkine, was that the Laboratory Theatre's *The Constant Prince* had been the 'event' of the season. [415/25]

And so the tours continued over the next few years: Holland again, Belgium, Italy, Yugoslavia, Great Britain, Mexico, France and the United States. Osiński says with some pride that in each country 'the Laboratory Theatre was welcomed ... as a group with a sure reputation, and its role was compared to that of the Berliner Ensemble in Brecht's lifetime or the French group of Jean Vilar'. [361/156] In the meantime, on 1 September 1966 the 'Laboratory Theatre of Thirteen Rows' became the 'Laboratory Theatre – Institute of Research into Acting Method'

(Teatr Laboratorium – Instytut Badán Metody Aktorskiej), which provoked the following response from one Polish journalist:

> The Theatre of Thirteen Rows was always a theatre so weary of itself that in reality it never wanted to be a theatre, although as a theatre it considered itself superior to all other theatres existing in Poland. . . . At present it is no longer in fact a theatre, but an educational institute! [361/152]

This educational inclination, so disparaged by the writer, was during the years of the theatre's foreign travels given as much if not more emphasis than their strictly theatrical activities. In 1966, 1967 and 1968 Grotowski, in collaboration mainly with Cieślak, gave courses for actors in Holstebro in Denmark (where Eugenio Barba now had his own centre), and in August 1966 they were invited by Peter Brook to conduct a workshop for the actors of the Royal Shakespeare Company. (It was during this visit that Grotowski met Joseph Chaikin, invited to London for collaboration on Brook's *US*.) For some of this time Grotowski also had a continuing collaboration with the Centre National Dramatique in Aix-en-Provence, and the École National Supérieure, which had made a policy of applying the Grotowski 'method' in their teaching process. In November 1967 Grotowski travelled with Cieślak – by now the recognized exponent of the Laboratory Theatre's almost perfected artistic technique – to the United States for the first

21 Ryszard Cieślak

time. There they directed a four week seminar at New York University. From New York Grotowski went directly to France (for consultations with Peter Brook, and also to the École National Supérieure in Aix-en-Provence) and on his return to his own country he spoke of a diminution in the theatre's international activities:

> We have decided, for one year, to discontinue foreign travel as a group, not only because we are preparing a new premiere, but in order simply not to be uprooted or thrown from the natural course of work. The new premiere? Speaking in the most general terms, it will be based around motifs of The Gospels. [39]

This premiere based on The Gospels, re-scheduled for January 1968 and again not realized, was in fact the same for which rehearsals had commenced as long ago as December 1965. At that time the production envisaged had been Słowacki's *Samuel Zborowski*, but in the course of unproductive work that theme had been abandoned, and some work had evolved based on motifs from the New Testament. The apparent lack of conviction in the work demonstrated by the changing theme and the length of time in production gave rise to further attacks in the Polish press:

> Jerzy Grotowski has ceased to goad the sturdiest of his opponents, or to give his followers anything to hold onto. He is no longer either an inspiration or an irritation in theatrical life: he is exploiting his previous work (for a year there have been regular presentations of *The Constant Prince* and we are waiting for the new premiere of The Gospels at the limits of our patience). . . . It's becoming difficult to avoid the conclusion that Grotowski has found himself in a 'state of recognition' and become settled, since he's achieved what he set out to achieve and can now quietly export his goods and enjoy the benefits. From a creative and restless artist he is slowly turning into a lecturer and teacher. [219]

The slightly aggressive and highly sceptical attitude towards Grotowski evinced by this journalist was by no means unusual. Despite the support and credence of many influential individuals in theatrical and artistic circles, and despite the fact that between 1967 and 1970 Grotowski received three State awards for his achievements, there was in general a distrustful reticence in Poland in response to Grotowski's statements and artistic achievements that for many years was manifested by a lack of serious response on the critical and literary levels. The major books on Grotowski's work during the 1960's (by Eugenio Barba and Raymonde Temkine) were written in Italian and French respectively (Temkine's book was published in an American translation in 1972, but neither book has been translated into Polish). And Grotowski's own book, *Towards a Poor Theatre*, has still not been printed in Polish, despite a world-wide distribution. The Polish critical fraternity was only too aware of this omission: in a review in 1968 Jan Pawel Gawlik pointed to the anomaly of a book by a Polish theatre director being published in English by a Danish company on the initiative of an Italian, finding it typical of the 'characteristic distrust with which the traditional Polish theatre, and its even more

traditional circle of intellectual elite received Grotowski's radical and uncompromising doctrine of methods'. [257] Those few writers in Poland who were
prepared to give time and space to a serious treatment of the work of the Laboratory
Theatre consistently pointed to the disparity of response compared with the West.
Jan Błoński, who wrote (in 1969) one of the few considered and balanced essays
in Polish in that decade, summed up the situation then:

> Besides essays by Flaszen and Grotowski I was only able to find various
> reviews, mostly enthusiastic, some of them penetrating, and some only
> snobbish. . . . Yet nowhere is to be found a concise but comprehensive introduc-
> tion to the Laboratory Theatre, or an interpretation of its ideas, not to mention
> a history of that theatre. That's a poor showing, indeed, considering the impor-
> tance of the company's work. [161/150]

This paradoxical situation was due in part, as has already been pointed out, to the
equivocal attitude in the Polish theatre world to the concept of a 'Grotowski
Method', and the questionable applicability of the Laboratory Theatre techniques.
From the principles of the statute drawn up when the theatre acquired the status
of Institute of Research into Acting Method in 1965:

> The aim of the Laboratory Theatre is to examine by way of practical ex-
> perience the technical and creative problems of theatre with special attention
> given to the art of acting. The purpose of the analysis is to improve the actor's
> work in the theatre and to achieve a general development of the acting craft. . . .
> The Laboratory Theatre functions through (a) studies in the area of acting
> technique with special attention to creative training (b) productions of an
> experimental acting and staging nature: these are the working models on which
> the actors test the effects of the elements of technique and training that have been
> discovered (c) documentation of tested elements of technique by producing
> written descriptions of exercises for actors as well as of other elements useful in
> creating roles (d) instruction for trainees from other theatres and theatrical
> centres (including foreign centres) within the limits of actual need and the
> theatre's capabilities. [408/147-148]

On reading this, a critic could be forgiven for expecting something very concrete
from the experiments of the Laboratory Theatre, and it is apparent in some of the
theoretical and publicity material emanating from the Institute that these expectations were actually being encouraged. In an American-English programme for the
second version of *The Constant Prince* (premiere 14.6.65) Ludwik Flaszen wrote:
'Apart from training the actors of its company and apart from improving their
techniques, the Laboratory Theatre is also working on an acting method. The
general outlines are now ready'. It may well be that such statements arose from
a need, on the political/administrative level, to justify subsidy for non-product work
(i.e. work not resulting in a theatrical 'product', or production), but the general
effect was one of ambivalence and confusion. At the same time, however, Grotowski
was attempting in his own statements to clarify the increasingly transcendent nature

of the processes that he and his team were investigating. He wrote in an article in 1967:

> An institute for methodical research is not to be confused with a school that trains actors and whose job it is to 'launch' them. . . . We take away from the actor that which shuts him off, but we do not teach him how to create. . . . For it is precisely in this 'how' that the seeds of banality and the cliches that defy creation are planted. . . . I am speaking of the surpassing of limits, of a confrontation, of a process of self-knowledge and, in a certain sense, of a therapy. Such a method must remain open – its very life depends on this condition – and is different for each individual. [73/97, 99]

Although, strictly speaking, the Laboratory Theatre could be said to have conformed to the letter of its principles quoted above, it was obvious that it was this question of 'how' that was confounding its critics. (In an early review Grotowski was criticized for being 'a talented creator whose problem of *how* is subordinated to the problem of *why*'. [378])

In an article in 1971, purporting to examine Grotowski's impact on the Polish theatrical scene, the writer was forced to conclude that this was minimal in the fundamental matter of actor's technique, and that the influence could only be detected in 'superficial imitations of purely external features'. [309/9] Another reviewer referred to 'plays with incoherent content full of shouting and rolling about on stage, and actors wearing white sheets instead of costumes' [277/33–34] (as can be seen from Grotowski's 1968 interview in France, quoted on page 99, Grotowski considered this form of imitation to be no flattery at all).

Examining more deeply the question of 'method' at the Laboratory Theatre in his article in 1969, Jan Błoński speculated whether, in so far as it has any meaning at all, it is not intimately connected with Grotowski's own personality. He postulated an interpretation of the process in which the resultant role comes from a 'spiritual drama' between the 'master and his disciple' and is in fact the actor

> re-shaped by the director. . . . Therefore, we may never be able to gauge to what extent the director in fact simply guides the actors to a discovery of the artistic forms that are already in them (. . . such a view is a major tenet of the Theatre's doctrine) and to what extent he imposes them on the actors. [161/143]

And in his interview the actor Zbigniew Cynkutis was even more explicit about this process:

> Everything that we did that was any good was not even made by Grotowski, but was *born between* me and Grotowski, Grotowski and me; Cieślak and Grotowski, Grotowski and Cieślak. It was the strong, direct relationship between Grotowski and each actor that enabled that actor to express something – something that originally may very often not have been the actor's own but that in time came to belong to him. That is why there is such a huge valley between Cynkutis the man, with a 42 year old mind, when we take away everything that

I got from the work with Grotowski – and Cynkutis after the work with Grotowski. Because so many things, thoughts, experiences, which to begin with were even strange to me and didn't belong, after long practice and investigation found their place, in my bloodstream, in my respiratory system, in my muscles.

This shamanistic view of the processes involved in the work of the Laboratory Theatre is of fundamental relevance to the question of Grotowski's antagonistic relationship over the years with the critical establishment. Helmut Kajzar is a young Polish theatre director who was once an admirer of Grotowski. In a conversation with Katharine Brisbane reported in *The Guardian* in 1969, Kajzar admitted to having become 'disenchanted with [Grotowski's] demands for a holy aesthetic'. [175] And in an article in *Teatr* in 1968 Kajzar rejected the 'imposed faith' of Grotowski's doctrine. In a phrase that was still being quoted many years later, he wrote of his 'resistance against fascination'. What he was referring to was the degree to which he was psychically affected by the experiences within the Laboratory Theatre productions. But, as he said, from a perspective of time:

> I remember *The Constant Prince* as I do other magnificent works of theatrical art. . . . You cannot change the theatre into a liturgy – I keep on reminding myself – above all these productions are works of art, they are not creating a new religion, they are not regenerating my subconscious, they are not purifying me, they are not freeing me from the weight of my complexes. [290/9]

In this fervent denial lies the very basis of the personal rejection of Grotowski by so many of his colleagues. What they are rejecting is not a personality, a method or an 'imposed faith', but quite simply the almost superhuman demands springing from a vision of the dynamic spiritual possibilities inherent in the process of acting. (After the 1969 New York season Robert Brustein commented: 'American actors do not have the self-denial demanded by Grotowski's technique. To create this theatre, you must believe in something greater than theatre'. [361/171])

In this debate concerning 'method' and Grotowski's role at the Laboratory Theatre Błonski has isolated what he believes to be the truly revolutionary aspect of Grotowski's work – the fundamental belief that theatre can in fact change both the actor and the spectator. Grotowski rebelled against the banality of the actor's conventional position and found it unacceptable that after so much toil and conviction the spectator should be 'allowed the luxury of returning to his former self. The same applies to the actor'. That is why, Błonski states, Grotowski dislikes the word 'role' and prefers 'process . . . which assumes authentic transformation'. [161/144, 145] This is a fundamental distinction. The reciprocal and transformative nature of the latter interpretation surpasses in some respects the conventional artistic demarcations of actor and director (and indeed spectator), and illuminates the transcendent nature of the Laboratory Theatre experiment – that of a group of actors working together over a prolonged period, even permanently, for the deeper exploration of self.

And it is precisely the validity of this exploration, and the 'authentic transformation', that Kajzar, and so many others, were rejecting. Kajzar was reminded by Grotowski of 'a scientist who wants to establish that sensitive frontier between pretence and possession', an investigation Kajzar considers to be 'verging on the pathological'. [296/9] Błoński summed up the resistance to the Laboratory Theatre doctrine, which he called 'inconvenient, and actually unpopular.... First of all it dooms the theatre to the necessity, or perhaps the blessing, of small audiences ... (and) it opposes the ways of an age which prefers to change conditions rather than attitudes, circumstances rather than souls.' [161/145]

CHAPTER FOUR
Kordian to The Constant Prince

The productions documented in this chapter belong to the historical period covered by the preceding chapter, i.e. 1962–1968. They are *Kordian*, *Akropolis*, *Dr. Faustus*, *The Hamlet Study* and *The Constant Prince*. With the exception of *Akropolis*, they all deal with the image of one individual, isolated from the surrounding environment and social milieu because of a particular set of ethics or a principle adhered to – and the ultimate sacrifice through death of that individual. This focus on the individual, sacrificial act was indicative of the shift that took place in theatrical terms within this period of Laboratory Theatre work. Although in *Kordian* (and to a slight extent in *Dr. Faustus*) there was still a confrontation of the spectator by the actor, they gradually abandoned the attempt to manipulate the spectators' reactions in any of the performances. They were still assigned a nominal 'role', but all that was expected of them was that they be silent witnesses.

The focus of the Laboratory Theatre research process became the actor. Grotowski said in a talk given in 1968:

> Gradually we abandoned a manipulation of the audience and all the struggles to provoke a reaction in the spectator, or to use him as a guinea pig. We preferred to forget the spectator, forget his existence. We began to concentrate our complete attention and activity on, above all, the art of the actor. [46/70]

With the concentration upon the actor, the notion of 'poor theatre' became more refined and rigorous, including an increasingly peremptory and assertive use of text. Grotowski in time undermined completely the supremacy of the discursive level within the plays he utilized, the notion of an intellectual exchange of ideas on the verbal level, and emphasized instead the central characters and themes (the 'myths') and the poetic language to be used non-intellectually as sound or music. And, as will be seen, the experiments with theatrical space (still conducted with the architect Jerzy Gurawski) were also influenced by the change of emphasis. It became not so much a question of spatially orchestrating the two groups, actors and spectators, but rather of creating the conditions for a concentration upon the process of the actor: the conditions, finally, within which the spectator could best witness what Grotowski came to call the 'total act'.

KORDIAN after JULIUSZ SŁOWACKI
Premiere: 13 February 1962

Kordian was written in 1834 by Juliusz Słowacki, a poet of the same era as Mickiewicz, but judged by many the greater Romantic poet. As a drama *Kordian* was conceived in reaction to *Dziady* part III, a reaction against the apotheosis of Poland Mickiewicz had displayed. In the main character, Kordian, Słowacki attempted to present the psychology of the contemporary Polish character – in which the desire for greatness and the realization of ideals is off-set by indecisiveness, scepticism and pessimism.

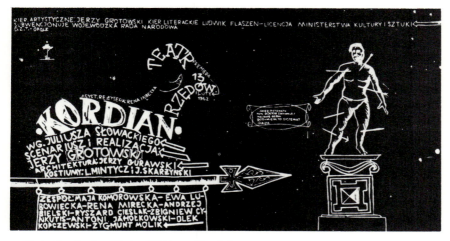

22 Poster for *Kordian* (Design: Waldemar Krygier).

Kordian is a man who has dedicated himself to a search for ultimate truth and experience. In the midst of his travels, while he is in fact on top of Mont Blanc, he receives the revelation that this can be realized through sacrificing himself to his country. He returns to a beleagured Poland and participates in a plot to assassinate the Tsar, taking upon himself the responsibility for this action. The plot fails but the Tsar, in leniency, sends him to an insane asylum, where his desire for self-sacrifice is mocked and placed on the same level as a madman who thinks that he is Christ. Ultimately, however, Kordian is judged sane and condemned to death.

Grotowski used the scene in the insane asylum as the key to the production. He expanded the concept of this scene to incorporate the action of the entire play, which unfolds with Kordian as a patient, being administered to by doctors, and a prey to his own fantasies and anxieties. In the programme notes Flaszen has suggested that this manipulation of the text was justified by the Romantic poet's

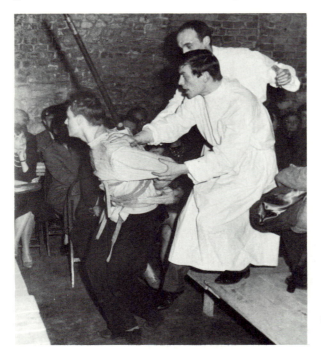

23 *Kordian*
  – Zbigniew Cynkutis
  and Ryszard Cieślak.

own attitude of irony in the asylum scene, and was used in order to 'secure a necessary contemporary distance'. [106] Any intellectual distance, however, was undermined paradoxically by the intricate staging devised by Gurawski and Grotowski. The actors and audience were again spatially integrated, but within a far more structured arrangement than in *Dziady*. The floor area was on several levels, while the 'scenery' took the form of metal-framed hospital beds – single, double or treble tiered – which filled the entire scenic space. The beds were used by the actors as a performance 'platform' and also assisted in the acrobatic acting style (Barba has drawn an analogy with the circus, with simultaneous action taking place throughout the space). Spectators were either seated on chairs amidst the beds, or seated on the beds themselves, with the action taking place in direct proximity. Again, spectators were provoked or compelled into response – as in one scene when, having ordered all present to join in a song, a Doctor identified and threatened anyone not doing so. There were no costumes as such, and props were either mundane (connected with the hospital) or very theatrical (connected with Kordian's fantasies).

The spectators, although generally passive witnesses were designated as patients or inmates of the asylum and, as such, enemies of the controlling doctors/mani-pulators. Thus, claimed Flaszen, the actors were in fact simply 'more active

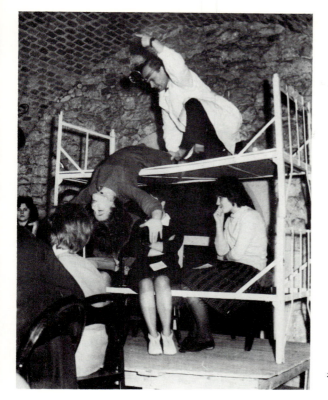

24 *Kordian*
– Zygmunt Molik.

patients' together with the audience. To Raymonde Temkine, however, judging
from her own experience, it seemed that

> ... the spectator, plunged into this unusual universe, would instinctively seek
> out his place, either among the sick people, or among the normal people, and
> absorb the psyche of one group or the other. But who is mad? And where is
> health? One's choice would be subject to continual reconsideration. [415/87]

Grotowski was here experimenting, as he indicated later, with what he called the
'unities' of the performance. Flaszen explained:

> This performance is conceived as the interpenetration, an interplay of reality
> and fiction: The action takes place on three simultaneous levels, as it were.
> Reality is the theatre in its literal sense: the room where spectators assemble in
> order to see a performance. Superimposed on that theatrical reality is the first
> level of fiction: all spectators, not only actors, have the roles of patients of a
> psychiatric clinic imposed on them. While from the hospital reality yet another
> fiction is emerging: the proper action of Słowacki's *Kordian*, interpreted as the
> collective delusions of sick people. [360/24]

Flaszen further clarified Grotowski's aims: 'The director analysed the meaning of an individual act in an era where collective action and organization are the guarantees of success. Today, the man who tries to save the world alone is either a child or a madman'. [115/157] Employing again the 'dialectic of apotheosis and derision', Grotowski continually juxtaposed his own images against those of Słowacki. The most vivid example was probably from the key scene of the drama, in which Kordian declaims his monologue of self-sacrifice on top of Mont Blanc. In Grotowski's production, Kordian falls into a coma, and delivers the monologue as if in a state of delirium.

25 *Kordian* – Antoni Jahołkowski, Zygmunt Molik and Zbigniew Cynkutis.

> The orderly binds his right wrist with a rubber band and stands still, holding a bowl for blood at the ready. The Doctor raises his lancet and stands for a while, aiming with precision at the patient's vein. The cool, matter-of-fact actions are in contrast with the desperate euphoria of Kordian who is now making the most important choice of his life. [360/24]

At the precise moment that Kordian is solemnly offering his blood for Poland and Europe, the Doctor's lancet strikes in a blood-letting. The rest of the speech takes place while the orderly prosaically tidies up the instruments:

> 'The great scene of the individual's self-sacrifice has been counterpointed by the prose of a medical operation. Literal blood mixes with metaphorical blood; imaginary suffering with real suffering; the physical with the spiritual; drastic body functions with poetic sublimity. [360/24-25]

AKROPOLIS words by STANISŁAW WYSPIAŃSKI
Premiere 10 October 1962

Akropolis (first published 1904) was written by Stanisław Wyspiański, playwright, poet and Symbolist painter. It is probably the most formally stylized of the Laboratory Theatre productions in conventional theatrical terms, and one of the first to be seen and recognized internationally.

The play revolves around the tradition that on the night of the Resurrection, the characters from the sixteenth-century tapestries on the walls of the Wawel (the Cracow Royal Palace) will come to life and re-enact classical and biblical scenes. In a letter, Wyspiański stated his intention of revealing the sum total of all civilizations' contributions to humanity, and confronting this with contemporary experience in what he called 'the cemetery of the tribes' (i.e. the Wawel). Grotowski, with the same symbolic insight that produced the complete metaphor of the *Kordian* staging, took Wyspiański's own key phrase 'the cemetery of the tribes' and transferred the action to the Auschwitz extermination camp, where our century has had to measure its values. Flaszen: 'The ancient myths and motivations are played by the fragments of humanity on the fringes of experience to which we have been driven by our twentieth century'. [159/6]

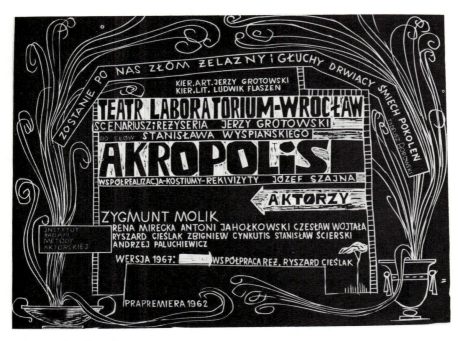

26 Poster for *Akropolis*

Flaszen has said, more recently, about the work on the text:

> Grotowski took Wyspiański's drama and fashioned a montage, with frag-
> ments, scenes, and with the concentration camp. So, there *was* a script of sorts,
> although this script made no sense as a drama, because the whole structure was
> destroyed in it. [143/318–319]

The two phrases 'our Acropolis' and 'cemetery of the tribes' were isolated and
obsessively repeated in the performance, becoming focal points. In addition inspiration was taken from the stories of Tadeusz Borowski, an ex-inmate of
Auschwitz and a writer who died while still a young man. Two lines from a
Borowski verse became a motto for the production:

> It's just scrap iron that will be left after us
> And a hollow, derisive laughter of future generations. [360/25, 32]

The characters of the Laboratory Theatre drama represented the Auschwitz dead,
resurrected from the smoke of the crematoria. The audience were the living,
witnessing or dreaming a world they could not experience. Around the verbal score
Grotowski and his actors built up an entire score of actions through improvisational
work in rehearsal. The scenes of mythic re-enactment (the Trojan war, Paris and
Helen, Jacob and the Angel, the Resurrection) were constructed in work with
Grotowski and represented a dream-like reality. These were interspersed with
scenes of hard labour and rhythmic movement which represented the reality of the
concentration camp (worked on with Eugenio Barba, assistant director for this
production). It was as if the strong discipline and structure of the 'work intervals'

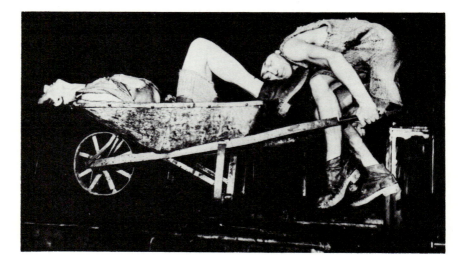

served to waken the actor-prisoners to the harsh world of their concentration camp reality.

Here again, as in *Kordian*, there were presented layers of super-imposed reality – the theatrical reality/Auschwitz dead/the scenes of mythic re-enactment. But there was in *Akropolis* no attempt to make direct contact or elicit response from the audience. There were deliberately created effects of rejection and alienation, the psychological imposition of the initiated upon the uninitiated. The actors sought to give the impression that they lived in another world. Flaszen:

> They are two separate and mutually impenetrable worlds: those who have been initiated into ultimate experiences, and the outsiders who know only the everyday life; the dead and the living. The physical closeness on this occasion is congenial to that strangeness: the audience, though facing the actors are not seen by them. The dead appear in the dreams of the living odd and in-comprehensible. As if in a nightmare, they surround those living on all sides. [360/32]

This psychological barrier was an effective way of preventing conventional catharsis. Raymonde Temkine (who saw *Akropolis* in Opole in spring 1963) wrote:

> The spectator would be relieved if a real contact could be established, a communion through pity; but he is rather horrified at these victims who become executioners . . . and who repulse or frighten more than they evoke pity. [415/126]

The spectators of *Akropolis*, seated on raised platforms, had before them in the middle of the room a huge box, on which was piled a heap of metallic junk – stove pipes, wheelbarrow, tin tub. From these objects alone the actors physically constructed during the course of the action the dynamics of the play. The stove-pipes, hung on ropes, were man-handled into an intricate architectural arrangement: 'By the end of the production the entire room was filled, oppressed, by the metal. . . . We didn't build a crematorium but we gave the spectators the association of fire'. [42/42] The claustrophobic spatial dimensions of the production have been interpreted by one American reviewer as demonstrating what he called a 'crisis-of-space':

> Actors move in and out of one another's space in demanding physical ways, but they never violate *our* space, or even look at us, though missing us by a hair's breadth. We are reminded, in this structural metaphor, at what close quarters we live, how narrowly we are missed or stricken by disaster or love. [429/108]

Flaszen has indicated that, in architectural terms, the production was a deliberate demonstration of the principle of 'poor theatre':

> The production was constructed on the principle of strict self-sufficiency. The main commandment is: do not introduce in the course of the action anything which is not there from the outset. There are people and a certain number of objects gathered in a room. And that material must suffice to construct all

circumstances and situations of the performance; the vision and the sound, the time and the space.... The poor theatre: to extract, using the smallest number of permanent objects – by magic transformations of object into object, by multi-functional acting – the maximum of effects. To create whole worlds, making use of whatever is within reach of the hands. [360/32–33]

Irving Wardle, who saw *Akropolis* at the Edinburgh Festival in 1968 wrote:

The execution is of extreme beauty. Its basic property is iron precision. If you stopped the action at any point, you would have a fine plastic composition; equally, while in motion, you notice its rhythmic delicacy under the brutal surface. Inside those rough clogs, for instance, the feet move with the fastidious-ness of Noh actors. Every movement has the definition of strictly stylised choreography.

28 *Akropolis*
– Ryszard Cieślak, Rena Mirecka
and Antoni Jahołkowski

This result evidently follows a prolonged period of inward preparation. The discipline of the company may be rigorous, but what it conveys is an intensely private sense of what it feels like to be at breaking point. [426]

Eric Bentley on the other hand, during the 1969 New York season, considered the production to be 'over aesthetic and therefore distressingly abstract' and accused Grotowski of formalism. He compared *Akropolis* to Peter Weiss's *The Investigation*, in which the young Auschwitz guards were dressed up in 'senility and business suits':

Those who disliked Weiss's show complained that its subject was too unpleasant. Those who liked yours praised the various technical devices.

In New York, thousands of whose families lost relatives in the extermination camps, you show us an Auschwitz that is of technical interest to theater students. If that isn't an example of a deplorable formalism, what would be? [157/1]

Despite Bentley's concern, it should be remembered that this *Akropolis* was created only sixty miles from the original Auschwitz, and, in Grotowski's words 'was influenced by the nearness, both in time and place' of the camp. [332/11] Grotowski has described at length, in interview in 1968, the company's concern that their subject matter was not compromised theatrically:

We did not wish to have a stereo-typed production with evil SS men and noble prisoners. We cannot play prisoners, we cannot create such images in the theatre. Any documentary film is stronger. We looked for something else.... No realistic illusions, no prisoners' costumes. We used plain costumes made from potato sacks, and wooden shoes. These were close to reality, a reality that is too strong to be expressed theatrically. [42/42]

For the costume and design, Grotowski had collaborated with Józef Szajna, a theatre designer and old friend and supporter from the early days. Szajna also happened to have been an inmate at Auschwitz from 1940–1945. His vision was stark:

The costumes are bags full of holes covering naked bodies. The holes are lined with material which suggests torn flesh; through the holes one looks directly into a torn body. Heavy wooden shoes for the feet; for the heads anonymous berets. This is a poetic vision of the camp uniform.... The actors become completely identical beings. They are nothing but tortured bodies. [73/64]

Moreover, during the actor training for *Akropolis* special emphasis had been given to the use of face as mask, by manipulation of facial muscles. Classical mime techniques were initially used as a base for the training, in a search, as Flaszen has stated in conversation, 'for a basically non-emotive form of expression'. Grotowski:

Each actor kept a particular facial expression, a defensive tic which was elaborated with facial muscles without make-up. It was personal for each, but as a group it was agonising – the image of humanity destroyed. [43/43]

In the programme notes Flaszen has also described how vocal means of expression were explored in this production:

> ... starting from the confused babbling of the very small child and including the most sophisticated oratorical recitation. Inarticulate groans, animal roars, tender folksongs, liturgical chants, dialects, declamation of poetry: everything is there. The sounds are interwoven in a complex score which brings back fleetingly the memory of all the forms of language. [73/69]

This is language used ritualistically, the word (according to Barba) as 'more than a means of intellectual communication. Its pure sound is used to bring spontaneous associations to the spectator's mind (incantation)'. [115/163]

29 *Akropolis* – Final Scene.

Wyspiański's drama concludes with the resurrection of a Christ/Apollo figure, who leads the progression of hope for Poland and Europe. It is an effigy of the nation's aspirations. In Grotowski's version of the drama there was no hope, and the Christ/Apollo was a corpse that the inmates had mistaken in their hysteria. Raising it reverently aloft, they led their mock procession of hope and progress, singing a well-known Polish anthem, to the crematorium – like a phoenix returning to the ashes. The American writer, J. Schevill, wrote after seeing *Akropolis* in New York in 1969:

> At the climax of ecstasy, the Singer shrieks jubilantly, opens a hole in the box in the centre of the stage, and drags the corpse of the Saviour into it. The prisoners follow him, singing their frenzied, messianic discovery. The cover slams down. I have never heard a silence like this. Abruptly, quietly, a voice is heard ... 'They are gone and the smoke rises in spirals'. This message I don't need to understand. I know now why there is a strange joy as well as terror in crematories, and I will never escape this revelation. [386/299]

30 *Akropolis* – Final Scene.

THE TRAGICAL HISTORY OF DOCTOR FAUSTUS (TRAGICZNE DZIEJE DOKTORA FAUSTA)

words by Christopher Marlowe
Premiere: 23 April 1963 (Polish premiere)

31 Poster for *Dr. Faustus*.

A textual montage of this production has been published in *Towards a Poor Theatre* [73/71–79] in which it is explained that, without changing a single word of Marlowe's text, the episodic structure of the play was re-arranged. The production commenced with the final hour of Faustus' life on earth, before being called to eternal damnation: it took the form of a Final Supper, at which were served up episodes from Faustus' life.

A reviewer from *The Times* who saw the production in Poland in 1963 expressed a rather naive surprise at finding such 'considerable interest in diabolical forces' [420] in Marxist Poland. Yet Grotowski has long had a fascination with the myth of Faust: he produced Goethe's play for the Polski Theatre in Poznań during his directorial apprenticeship, and his reading of Thomas Mann's novel had some oblique influence during the work on *Apocalypsis Cum Figuris*. But Grotowski's treatment of Marlowe's Faustus, as of the religious aspects of all his productions, was one facet of his preoccupation with the concept of sacrifice. Faustus represented for Grotowski an archetype – that of 'the shaman who has surrendered to the Devil and in exchange has received a special knowledge of the universe'. [115/155]

In this production Grotowski again adopted a polemical attitude to the original text, and made of Marlowe's Faustus a saint. Grotowski's Faustus became in effect a lay martyr – a seeker after truth so pure that he must accept the penalty of eternal damnation for rejecting the catechismic compromise. (This theme was returned to in *Apocalypsis*, and confronted through the text of Dostoyevsky's Grand Inquisitor speech.) In the case of Marlowe's text Eugenio Barba has defended Grotowski's treatment by referring to Christopher Marlowe's own life – claiming that although the word may have been traduced, the spirit was better served. Renée Saurel responded to this claim by paraphrasing Dumas: 'On pourrait dire que, s'il les viole, du moins leur fait-il un enfant'. ('Although he commits rape at least it brings forth a child'.) [384/761] Michael Kustow, who saw the production in Poland in 1963 (it was never taken abroad on tour) wrote in a review of an

awareness of theatrical irony and counterpoint. . . . Remembered passages of the play appeared in strange forms. Faustus treated his studies of law and theology as sins; black magic became a saintly pursuit. Mephisto, dressed in a monk's robe, appeared as a double, played by an actor and actress. They also took the roles of the Good and Bad Angels. Understanding began to glimmer. Devil, Good and Bad Angels are all *agents provocateurs* for God, against whom Faustus, a Saint against God, a lay saint, rebels. He embraces necromancy with the fervour of a man who cares about his soul so much that he won't submit it to the Divine Blackmail. [332/13–14]

The scenic arrangement was of a more rigidly contained form than that of any previous production. There was a three-sided table arrangement, as in a monastic refectory. Faustus sat at the smaller top table, which represented the present, and the audience sat at the longer side tables, on which were enacted past episodes of

32 Scenic arrangement for *Dr. Faustus*.

Faustus' life. The whole was enclosed in a wooden box-like structure. In this
production, as in *Akropolis*, there was demonstrated a rigour of threatening, but
disciplined scenic manipulation. Kustow:

> There is one terrifying sequence in which the Emperor's servant goes berserk
> and rushes around dismantling the rostrum-tops (inches away from us) and
> leaving only the skeletons of the tables. The world, for a moment, seems to be
> coming apart. [332/14]

The atmosphere of the production was heavily religious. The setting was monastic,
the characters dressed in habits of different orders – Faustus in Dominican white,
the double male/female Mephistopheles in Jesuit black. Again, there was a development towards a less compromised realization of 'poor theatre', with a complete
absence of props: in one scene where the Pope is at dinner, the double Mephistopheles is both the chair he sits on and the food he eats. And sound is again used
and explored only through the actor's physiology. Alan Seymour, who also saw the
production in Poland in 1963, described one effect:

> At one climatic moment voices in harmony rose softly right behind us,
> obviously from actors behind the partition, the closeness wrapping us in the
> atmosphere in a way 'background music' in a proscenium rarely does. [387/34]

33 *Dr. Faustus.*

34 *Dr. Faustus* – Zbigniew Cynkutis, Rena Mirecka.

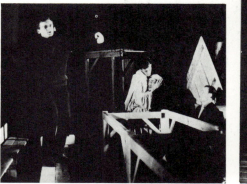

As mentioned earlier it was about the time of preparation for *Dr. Faustus* that the very intensive research, daily training and use of specialized exercises were undertaken by Grotowski and his acting team, with the assistance of Eugenio Barba. This work had noticeable results, as Seymour again noted: 'Their voices reached from the smallest whisper to an astonishing, almost cavernous tone, an intoned declaiming, of a resonance and power I have not heard from actors before.' [387/34]

Similarly, in work on the face (also undertaken for the previous production):

> They use no masks or make-up, but they are keenly aware of the power of expression of each muscle in their face. Moreover, their intensive practice enables them to make these muscles express anything they wish. They manage to create natural masks and can draw from a vast repertoire of faces. For example, Cynkutis, though very young, can go through a whole range of expressions from the luminous face of Faustus welcoming friends to the convulsed face of Faustus surrendering his soul to the devil. [116/184]

More conscious researches were also being conducted, within the context of the productions, into actor/spectator relationships. At the beginning of the production, Faustus greeted each member of the audience as an invited guest. In the audience were planted two actors (Alan Seymour called this 'the only shop-worn device of the evening' [387/34]) who took the farcical roles and lines. It is they who, near the beginning of the production challenge Faustus to justify his life and his decisions, and tempt him into a recounting of the past. This recounting turns the banquet into a confessional, and the spectators from guests to confessors. At times the actors directly confronted the audience, and according to Grotowski this proximity facilitated a study of the mechanics of human reaction within a theatrical context:

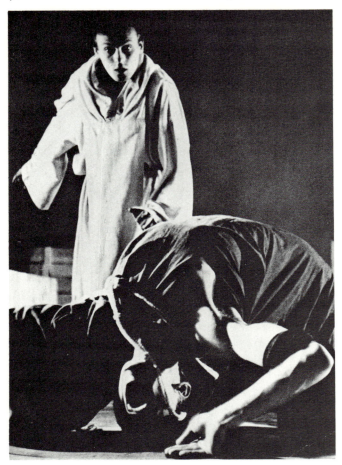

35
Dr. Faustus –
Zbigniew Cynkutis
and
Ryszard Cieślak

Distance between the spectators and actors can be measured literally in inches, and it happens sometimes, that the actor turns directly to the spectator and his own reaction depends on the reaction of the spectator.... And so we are facing human reaction, we are witnessing what happens between people and what happens within them. [19/57]

However, several years later Grotowski acknowledged in retrospect the manipulative aspect of this device:

A spectator in the face of a certain kind of aggression on the part of the actor has at his disposal, let us say, five or six kinds of reaction, and so for every production we prepared in advance several versions of the actors' behaviour towards the spectator, according to the reaction of the latter. [46/65]

Alan Seymour has described how the total experience aimed at by this 'magic and sacrilegious theatre', in which the spectator is placed in the physical context of the drama, can inhibit rather than encourage involvement. He found himself embarrassed by his British reserve when confronted by an actor 'kneeling on a table before you, lowering his face towards yours, and whispering a no doubt compelling passage at you in Polish'. [387/34] He confessed to a surfeit of 'Polish emotion' which had an alienatory effect. But despite such reservations, in both method and ethic Grotowski could be seen to be moving closer to the realization of what was eventually to crystallize into a recognizable system. He was already narrowing the field of his laboratory study to the processes made visible within the actor, and in *Dr. Faustus* could be seen for the first time the glimmerings of that sacrificial, total act; of the individual against God, the individual against society, an actor before an audience:

> Now thou hast but one bare hour to live.... Faustus is in ecstasy, literally possessed, a lay saint behaving like a religious fanatic. As his body freezes in a triumphant trance, menacing *Pater Nosters* and *Aves* break out, and the double Mephisto, in priest's costume, picks him up like an object and takes him off. Out of his mouth comes a piercing scream, and inhuman, inarticulate noises. Faustus is no longer a man, but a sweating, suffering animal caught in a trap, a wreck who screams without dignity. [332/14]

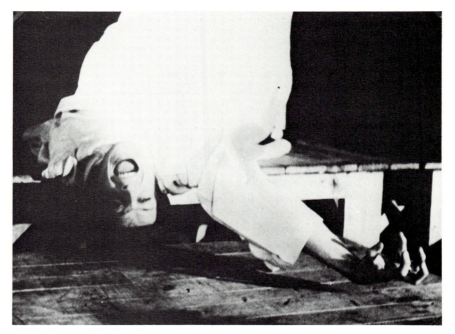

36 *Dr. Faustus* – Zbigniew Cynkutis.

THE HAMLET STUDY (STUDIUM O HAMLECIE)
from the texts of William Shakespeare and Stanisław Wyspiański
Premiere: 17 March 1964

37 Poster for *The Hamlet Study*.

The title, *The Hamlet Study*, was taken from an essay by Stanisław Wyspiański, in which he analysed and commented upon some of the key scenes from Shakespeare's play in the light of his own theatrical theory. Wyspiański, like Grotowski, measured all that was of value in theatre through the presence of the actor: 'In the conception of man and theatre created by Wyspiański, the inner purity, truth and commitment of the actor are in general the condition of the existence of an authentic theatre'. [419] But the Laboratory Theatre version, according to Flaszen speaking on behalf of the group in the programme notes, was intended to portray neither the classical, Shakespearian Hamlet, nor one based upon Wyspiański's suggestions. They used extracts from both sources but presented their own 'history of the Danish Prince: variations on selected Shakespearian themes. The study of a motif'. [113]

The motif was basically that of the 'outsider'. Hamlet, played by Zygmunt Molik, was associated with the image of a Jew – most specifically 'a bookish type, rattling off smart phrases, a gesticulating intellectual, a faint-hearted and cunning casuist, a strident and jumped-up Jew'. Hamlet, the individual, is placed in the social context of the Court at Elsinor, and the parallel drawn here is with the Polish Populace. The Populace (in Hamlet's eyes) is 'a collection of primitive, thick-skinned individuals, acting through physical strength, who only know how to fight, drink and die in a sullen frenzy'. [113] But the production was not intended – again, in Flaszen's words – as a treatment of anti-semitism. Anti-semitism is but one form of prejudice, arising from social superstition and judgements based on stereotypes. The Laboratory Theatre production was intended as a study of the superstitions and stereotypes, and the resulting situation of conflict, and therapeutic overtones. For the superstitions will always exist, on the psychological level: 'We draw these out from the depths of the unconscious with the aim of healing'. [113]

The performance took place in a completely empty room, with spectators seated around the walls, and it consisted of 'scenes from the life of the Populace, amongst whom hangs a strange, eccentric Job'. [113] The setting and enactment of each scene was designed to emphasize the contrasts in attitude and behaviour between Hamlet and the Populace and the resulting alienation. The wedding of the King and Queen was celebrated in a public house and the death of the Queen-Ophelia character (played by Rena Mirecka) was staged in a heavily sensuous bath scene – in which Hamlet 'with inappropriate formality clings on to his "otherness" by remaining fully clothed'. [113] There are martial and political overtones in Hamlet's relationship to the King, and his dreamt-of act of revenge becomes the act of an insurgent. In the concluding scenes as the troops set out for war 'marching through a sad landscape, singing perennial holy war songs', [360/35] Hamlet is shown as a humanitarian, trying to hold back the inevitable slaughter. At the very end he is seen, a weakling in comparison to the crude strength of the Populace and Soldiery, yearning for a solidarity and fraternity in the extremity of the battlefield. Józef Kelera wrote in his review:

> In such a treatment it is not important who Hamlet really is, but how Hamlet is seen through the eyes of 'others' – mystified in their vision, deformed by their pressure. And what those 'others' are – deformed, mystified altogether through Hamlet's vision – is also important. The error is on both sides – the director and the company suggest. [360/35]

It has already been pointed out in the preceding chapter that this production was prepared and presented in uncertain and difficult circumstances for Grotowski and his group. The degree of disapproval, incomprehension and even animosity that their work evoked in certain quarters was severe enough to cast doubt on the continuing survival of the theatre as a subsidized institute. Instead of compromising and preparing a suitably acceptable production, the group continued to develop the research aspect of their work: *The Hamlet Study* was in fact the only new public performance presented in 1964, and according to Osiński it was never intended as a full production, but as an 'open rehearsal'. It was also innovative for the group in that it was a purely collective piece of work. Flaszen:

> The director suggests the basic themes, but only in order to stimulate the actors' creativity. During the course of rehearsals the actors explore and im-

provise entire scenes, stimulating equally their own and the director's creativity.... This is the second meaning of the word 'study' in the title: a study on the theme of acting method and collective direction. [113]

The critics at the time were almost unanimous that *The Hamlet Study* was the least 'successful' of Grotowski's productions. From a present perspective, Osiński contends that it was a significant piece of work and an important precursor of *Apocalypsis Cum Figuris* in the relinquishing of theatrical convention and the attempt to create a 'collective "total act"'. The fact remains, however, that there were only about 20 performances (to a total of about 630 spectators), all of which took place in Opole. More significantly, *The Hamlet Study* has never been referred to in any of the published statements of theory and history originating from the Laboratory Theatre. Neither Grotowski nor Flaszen, when mentioning that period of work, make any reference to it, and one can only assume that they are happy for it to be forgotten. This is perhaps not surprising since the alienation which was the subject-matter of *The Hamlet Study* almost undoubtedly had personal relevance for the group, and specifically Grotowski, at that time in their history. In a series of retrospective talks given by Flaszen in 1977, he has talked about a particular Polish myth, the 'myth of the intelligentsia'. Although he made no direct reference to *The Hamlet Study*, his words may contribute to an understanding of the production:

> When our country didn't have its own existence, the population grew passive throughout the nineteenth century. The intelligentsia fought for and created a new culture and a new awareness: *they* kept the nation alive despite its lack of political existence.... The myth is that by carrying the culture, *we* redeem the others.... So our very theatre experience is based on the same motif. Thus, the dual myth of martyr and intelligentsia was not abstract for us – it was directly connected with our experience. [143/312]

THE CONSTANT PRINCE (KSIĄŻĘ NIEŁOMNY)
words by Calderon-Słowacki
Premiere: 25 April 1965

The production of *The Constant Prince*, based on Juliusz Słowacki's adaptation of the Spanish playwright's text, was of considerable significance in the Laboratory Theatre's development. Although work on the production had commenced nearly a year before, in Opole, the premiere took place in their new home, in Wrocław's Rynek-Ratusz (market-place). It marked the beginning of a period of both greater practical security and greater public acclaim and acceptance. It was also the first piece of work in which Ryszard Cieślak became prominent as the principal exponent of the Laboratory Theatre approach to acting. The production has been seen by many as the summit of Grotowski's acting method, the synthesis of all that Grotowski had attempted to achieve in his years of research. Flaszen, in the

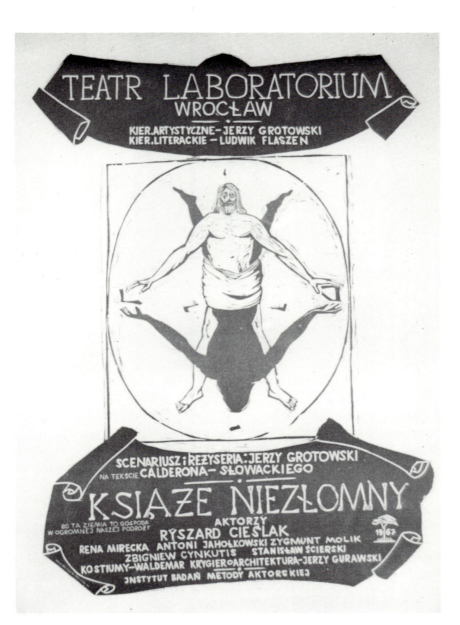

38 Poster for *The Constant Prince*.

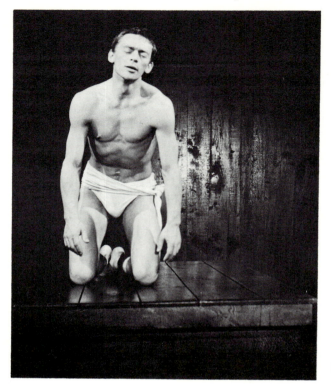

39 *The Constant Prince
– Ryszard Cieślak.*

programme notes, described it as 'a kind of exercise that makes possible a verification of Grotowski's method of acting. All is moulded in the actor; in his body, in his voice and in his soul'. [73/83] On this occasion, from the evidence of press reviews both in Poland and abroad, it would appear that at last the majority of critics were in harmony with Flaszen.

The Constant Prince was also the last production that had as its basis a conventional theatrical text, although one that had already passed through the filter of another artist's consciousness (in the Słowacki adaptation). The production owed to Calderon the barest outline of a scenario, stripped of the more subtle geographic or national characteristics. There was a group of persecutors and the First Prisoner (the Moorish court and Don Henri). Once symbolically castrated, he acquiesced and melted into the group (Don Henri was released to carry the Moors' demands for the Spanish Island of Ceuta). In contrast the Second Prisoner, Don Fernando (Don Henri's brother) refused all compromise on the matter of the island, even though he was being held a hostage in exchange. In the face of the Moors' manipulations he passively opposed his humiliation and persecution with purity and love. Fascinated by his inner strength, the group was driven to

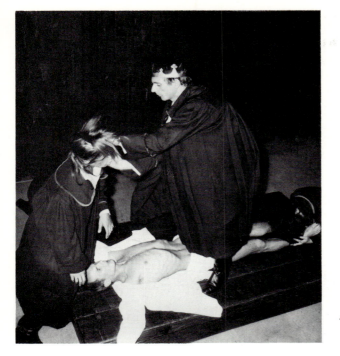

40 *The Constant Prince*
 – Stanisław Scierski,
 Antoni Jahołkowski.

ever greater acts of cruelty, which found their culmination in the Constant Prince's tormented death. Gone were the elements of scepticism and despair, discernible in the sacrificial motifs of earlier Laboratory Theatre productions: this was a hymn to the inspirational strength of the individual act. The Prince's death represented a martyrdom of purity and love to the brutality of unrelenting social order and blind authority, of the individual against the group.

As far as the treatment of this text was concerned, Eric Bentley concisely expressed the reservations of those who resent what they see as Grotowski's dismissive handling of literary masterpieces:

> In your notes on *The Constant Prince* you congratulate yourself on catching the 'inner meaning' of this play. Cool it. The inner meaning of a three-act masterpiece cannot be translated into any one-act dance drama. Its meaning is tied indissolubly to its three-act structure: otherwise Calderon himself would have reduced it to one act – he was a master of the one act. [157/7]

Bentley did, however, alleviate somewhat the rebuke contained in these words, and went on to acknowledge the validity of Grotowski's treatment in theatrical terms for a modern audience; in particular he praised the spatial arrangement, which he said led him to an understanding of the meaning of environmental theatre.

41 Scenic Architecture for *The Constant Prince*.

42 Scenic Architecture for *The Constant Prince*.

Once again, scenically, there was a rigid structure for this production, but with the spectators being physically cut off from the action. They looked down, over four wooden walls, on to the square of the stage, which had as its centre a slightly raised dais serving as a bed, an operating table, an executioner's platform and a sacrificial altar. The spectators therefore assumed the role almost of clinical observers, although the spectacle they witnessed had all the mental and emotional blood-letting of a bull-fight. In the programme notes the association was made with the surgical operation in Rembrandt's 'Anatomy of Dr. Tulp', and Grotowski has made clear retrospectively that the spatial arrangement for *The Constant Prince* was the result of conclusions drawn from their earlier architectural experiments:

> When for example you wish to give the spectators the opportunity for an emotive participation, direct but emotive – that is the possibility of identifying with someone who bears the responsibility for the tragedy taking place – then you must remove the spectators from the actors, despite what may be the assumption. The spectator, distanced in space, placed in the position of an observer who is not even accepted, who remains exclusively in the position of observer, is really in a position to co-participate emotively, in that he may eventually discover in himself the primitive vocation of spectator. [46/66]

The first international viewing of *The Constant Prince*, at the Theatre of Nations Festival in Paris in 1966, provoked a storm of reaction, as the festival spectators and critics sought to verbalize, condone, rationalize or simply minimize their reactions to the emotional assault. Temkine, who was herself present, recorded some reactions: 'shamefaced participants' … 'communing in uneasiness' … 'voyeurs, shameful accomplices, looking at one another mutually looking at something they shouldn't be seeing'. [415/26, 30] Temkine attempted to make some sense, in her book, of the confusion arising from the need for verbal categorization of the human response, and was primarily concerned with what she felt to be the condemnatory use of the word 'voyeur': 'That is condemning oneself.... One is not a voyeur when one is primarily a participant'. [415/31] But being a participant in this sense – a party to a set of reactions, being acted upon oneself – is not an extenuation of voyeurism but its main constituent element, which was precisely the painful aim of the production.

Textually, the poetry of the production belonged to Słowacki. Despite popular misconceptions regarding Grotowski's mistrust of words, it was as much for the poetry as for the mythic content that Grotowski repeatedly turned to the great works of literature, especially those of the Polish Romantic period. What Grotowski was happy to dispense with was the purely intellectual or ideational aspect of text, as something to be preserved and represented. The poetic aspect of text, as also the mythic association, served his concept of theatre being primarily a non-intellectual, emotive, and thus transgressing and transforming experience. It was for this reason that he chose to work on the Słowacki adaptation: 'In our *Constant Prince* the word melts with the melody that is contained in Słowacki's text'. [44] Peter Feldman endorsed the description:

43
The Constant Prince
Laboratory Theatre
Company.

> I did not expect that words would be so important in the Laboratory Theatre's work. I expected a theatre of body image, with strange cries in the night, not a chamber orchestra of rippling Polish. The effect of this theatre's unique use of vocal rhythm, pitch, dynamics, tonality and careful orchestration is to enhance the word, to restore it from idea to image. [243/193]

The use of costume, props and sound in *The Constant Prince* extended and crystallized the theatre's aesthetic in this direction in the same way as the staging had crystallized Grotowski's spatial explorations. The persecutors wore cloaks, breeches, top-boots and in one case a crown – all symbols of power. The Prince on the other hand wore the white shirt of purity, a loin-cloth symbolizing nakedness, and a red cloak of martyrdom, which was to become a shroud. There was an almost total absence of props. A Polish reviewer wrote:

> When this young man in the person of The Constant Prince faces the crowd of dark, angular and uniformed characters, we recognise him as the anointed one, even though he wears no crown or any other sign of power. He towers above the others in his simplicity. He is the Lord of Creation: he is a human being. [280]

44
The Constant Prince
Laboratory Theatre
Company.

Jan Błonski, examining in his 1969 article the 'act of faith in the profound universality of myth' that justifies the Laboratory Theatre doctrine, proposed the often voiced opinion that Grotowski

> shows one and the same thing, namely the death of Christ, over and over again.... A similar fascination occurs on several levels of the Laboratory Theatre work.... It is a fascination with salvation through sacrifice. [161/147]

But if it is indeed the 'death of Christ' we see, then it is a Christ who conforms in symbolic clothing only to the mythic Saviour we are familiar with through Christian heritage – a Christ re-crucified, in the manner of Dostoyevsky's Grand Inquisitor, by that very catechismic heritage. In Temkine's opinion, 'Moors and Christians merge because they belong to the same order, the temporal persecutor of the spiritual.... It is not the reign of the crescent that is flouted but much more that of the cross'. [415/135] In this respect Jean Jacquot, in his introduction to Serge Ouaknine's very detailed study of the production, has pointed to the significance of Słowacki's literary intervention in the textual confrontation:

> Let us not forget ... that the text used is that of Słowacki. If the Oriental atmosphere of the work could enthrall the interpreter ... it is also natural that,

in the context of Poland's history the theme of non-violent resistance to oppres-
sion, rather than that of religious confrontation, was a significant factor in
Słowacki's choice. [285/29]

The visual analogies with our Western civilization's images were, however, strong
and purposeful, embodying yet again the familiar principle of blasphemy and
devotion. They were also unequivocally Polish, as a reviewer from a local Wrocław
paper pointed out after the premiere: 'Fernando, posing as a folklore saint, is not
only the Little Polish Christ, but at the same time all that is embodied in Konrad
and Kordian'. [154] The illustration following shows Fernando sitting on the dais
and listening to the confession of Fenixana. His eyes are closed: he appears to be
drained of strength and hope, yet overflowing with gentle patience and love. The
image is that of 'Christusik Frasobliwy', Christ suffering, the Little Polish Christ
– it is to be found everywhere in Poland from roadside shrines to tourist souvenirs.

45 *The Constant Prince* – Ryszard Cieślak and Rena Mirecka.

The Constant Prince also carried one step further an association evoked in the preceding *Hamlet Study*. The group of persecutor-Moors in *The Constant Prince* view Fernando as a strange, incomprehensible creature – his refusal to conform to their world evokes as much curiosity and fascination as it does cruelty. In the course of this drama the 'outsider' aspect of *The Hamlet Study* is taken to a sadistic extremity: they manipulate and torture him physically since they cannot affect him spiritually. From the programme:

> While they are able to do anything with him – wielding supreme power over his body and life – yet they can do nothing to him. The Prince, yielding with apparent submission to the sick manipulations of those around, remains separate and pure – to the point of ecstasy. [117]

It is tempting at this stage to carry the Hamlet/Grotowski analogy, alluded to at the end of *The Hamlet Study* treatment on page 74, further into *The Constant Prince*. It could be said, extending Flaszen's own association, that Grotowski (and his group) saw themselves as the 'outsiders' in the face of the insensitivity of the Populace (the Polish public and press). They explored this alienation in *The Hamlet*

46 *The Constant Prince* – Laboratory Theatre Company.

Study with the aim, as Flaszen said, of healing the rift. But the sense of alienation and rejection did not lessen: Osiński clearly documents in his history that the aversion was strong enough in some quarters as to be directed at the closing of the theatre. *The Constant Prince* could be said to show the theatre's response. In the production was seen the image of constancy and total self-sacrifice in the face of those trying to enforce conformity, even to the point of torture and death. The attitude of the Constant Prince – of non-resistance to the annihilating forces of those who, through fear of his otherness try to make him conform – is seen as the only possible, uncompromising course of action.

In the event it brought the Constant Prince – and the Laboratory Theatre acting team – apotheosis. There were of course still those who reserved full approval and maintained scepticism, but for the most part critics both in Poland and abroad were tempted into superlatives. Kelera:

In my profession as a theatre critic I have never yet felt the desire to use that

47 *The Constant Prince*
   – Laboratory Theatre Company.

48 *The Constant Prince* – Ryszard Cieślak and Rena Mirecka.

dreadfully banal and overworked expression which, in this particular case, is quite simply true: this creation is 'inspired'. [299]

Similarly, in another recantation of former doubts that amounted to a public confession, the respected and respectable Polish actor Jan Kreczmar (who died 1973) described 'living through one of my strongest emotional experiences in post-war theatre':

> I want to draw the attention of all actors to the importance of what is happening, and the need for all with strength, health and the desire to enrich his art to refer to Grotowski and what is happening in his Laboratory. It is a life-giving current to the actor's art, and one that could restore its relevance and somehow repair its failing dignity. [324]

It was to be three years before the Laboratory Theatre presented another premiere to the world. The years 1965 to 1968 were filled with international tours, and assiduous preparation for the next production. When *Apocalypsis Cum Figuris* was finally shown in July 1968, it was realized in retrospect that *The Constant Prince* had marked the end of one stage of work for the Laboratory Theatre, a period in which the force of their experiments had been centred on the theatrical processes of the actor in the given limited structure of a production. *Apocalypsis Cum Figuris* was a collective and continuing search through the levels of response, and the implications of responsibility, of the Laboratory Theatre members as human beings within the overall structure of their theatre, and in relation to their audience.

CHAPTER FIVE

Apocalypsis Cum Figuris

By the beginning of 1968, with yet another deferred premiere of the new, awaited production from the Laboratory Theatre, there was again an atmosphere of impatience and scepticism in the Polish press (see page 49). And it was true that, after their few years of stabilization in Wrocław and their sudden and overwhelming successes abroad, the Laboratory Theatre now appeared to be at a new point of crisis. It would be easy to conclude that Grotowski's creative drive had indeed been blunted by his theatre's success, as was imputed, and that energy had been dissipated through their numerous international appearances. Or, as one Polish journalist later suggested in an article entitled 'The Hero is Weary', that Grotowski was now beginning to yearn for the time when he was unknown and unfollowed, and the creativity of those years of solitude and silence. [340] Even further, to suggest that in keeping with the 'sacrificial' and 'martyr' motifs of his theatrical ethic, he was finding it difficult to create from a position of success.

It is, however, probable that this period of creative difficulty was born of nothing so obvious, but instead owed something to inner changes that were taking place inside the man, and to a fundamental questioning of his commitment to an artistic and creative path; and that this questioning was not resolved until his departure from the strictly theatrical confines of his work in 1970. Be that as it may, the particular period of crisis in 1967/1968 was still to bear theatrical fruit: *Apocalypsis Cum Figuris*. Ludwik Flaszen recalled the process some ten years later:

> I should say first that such a crucial crisis may be a creative one. The most fundamental one occurred in the course of creating *Apocalypsis....* A moment occurred about a year after we started working on it, when it seemed that nothing could be created. What we were doing was The Gospels, which lapsed, naturally, into a repetition of what we already knew. We were playing out illustrations of the myths.... This was a 'void' beneath the zero point. I think it gave birth to *Apocalypsis*. This terrible dead hole which had swallowed all our work was the womb in which the work was born. [143/323]

In many ways *Apocalypsis Cum Figuris* occupies a curious position in theatrical history. It is, almost unquestionably, one of the great theatrical productions of the twentieth century. It was also exemplary of a particular convention of theatrical construction which was widely used in the seventies, particularly amongst small groups in Europe and America who were attempting to base their work on

49 Poster for *Apocalypsis Cum Figuris.*

Laboratory Theatre principles. Yet the performance itself has been seen by comparatively few people and, by virtue of its method of construction, has no objective relevance outside the small group of people who created it. And although it was in the repertory of the Laboratory Theatre for twelve years, for most of that time it was performed as the only theatrical piece of work undertaken by the company, who were concurrently devoting most of their time and energy to the investigation of post-theatrical forms.

The process of the production's genesis, which lasted nearly three years, was complex and erratic, and in all probability impossible to unravel accurately from an external perspective. We know from retrospective statements made by Flaszen and other members of the company that work based on Słowacki's *Samuel Zborowski* was initially undertaken. This text was Słowacki's last dramatic poem, written 1844/1845: Ireneusz Guszpit, in an article on the Laboratory Theatre production, said of Słowacki's work: 'In scenes of *Samuel Zborowski* we can discern a particularly accurate understanding of the phenomenon which the contemporary term 'archetype' defines as the collective experience of humanity, housed in the individual subconscious'. [274/125] But *Samuel Zborowski* was completely abandoned in the course of improvisational work, leaving not a single textual trace. Work had also been planned, and undertaken, on The Gospels – specifically, as Grotowski said in interview at that time: 'the New Testament, which we are producing in latin: this is planned as a new, theatrical *Life of Jesus* of the kind written by Renan'. [25]

From recent talks given by Grotowski (in 1979 and 1980) containing more intimate biographical material, we know that he read Renan's work, which was on the Catholic Church's Index, as a child: it was a gift from his mother, who attached great significance to Renan's human portrait of Christ. Renan denied the Nazarene's divine descendance, and portrayed Jesus very much as a Palestinian conditioned by his times and environment, but full of charm and power and motivated totally by the value and ideal of love: 'But whatever the mysterious future hides in its bosom, nothing will be greater than Jesus. His cult will be continually renewed; his legend will always bring tears to the eyes; his suffering move the most noble heart; all ages will bear witness, that in the whole of the human tribe the greatest man was Jesus'. (Renan) [274]

It was this emphasis that conditioned the work after the abandonment of *Samuel Zborowski*. In interview the actor Stanisław Scierski recalled the progress of the preparation from this stage:

The progress of the collective search was in Grotowski's hands. He helped the 'studies' to develop, respecting our right to take risks; he selected them; very often he inspired them in their entirety; in short – he watched over the collectively emerging outline. And it must be stressed that many 'studies' were improvisational in nature. This was how a production with the working title of *The Gospels* came into being. There were even a few closed performances. After one of them, together with Grotowski, we came to the conclusion that while what we had done was an entirely new structure, the general area was nevertheless familiar to us, and – roughly speaking – there was discernible in it elements of our earlier work. So we decided – whilst retaining whatever was fertile for ourselves – to abandon it. It was then that we came across something that was vital for us, which was to lead in time to *Apocalypsis*. From the 'studies' which we had presented to Grotowski, and from those he created with us from the outset – he built a new structure. For those parts which were not based on text but were obviously in need of them he made suggestions, in collaboration with us. [139/83]

As a production *Apocalypsis Cum Figuris*, therefore, contained no intrinsic life of its own. After abandoning *Samuel Zborowski*, there was no original dramatic text with which the actors were able to interact creatively, as in previous productions, and neither was there allocation of roles which the actors were able to use as a 'springboard'. (We have it on Ludwik Flaszen's authority that 'in all performances before *Apocalypsis*, roles were divided more or less as it happens in other theatres'. [143/322] The performance therefore arose exclusively from improvisational style work and formed in totality an objective network of interwoven myths, historical events, literary fable and everyday occurrences. But without the actors who performed it, it ceases to exist: for on one level it was drawn uniquely from the experiences of the actors involved, and the levels on which it operated were so completely interdependent that destruction of any single level results in collapse of the whole. Grotowski:

> In *Apocalypsis* we departed from literature. It was not a montage of texts. It was something we arrived at during rehearsals, through flashes of revelation, through improvisations. We had material for twenty hours in the end. Out of that we had to construct something which would have its own energy, like a stream. It was only then that we turned to the text, to speech.' [350]

The text was established, in fact, only in the very final stages of rehearsal. Latin was rejected, except for some of the more liturgical phrases, the use of the New Testament was broadened to include the whole Bible, and there were passages from Dostoyevsky's *The Brothers Karamazov*, T. S. Eliot, and Simone Weil. In its final form the production lasted one hour. (I have included a full translation and account of *Apocalypsis Cum Figuris* in the Appendix.)

Because of the nature of their training, there has probably never been a group of actors better prepared for, or more skilled at creative work based entirely on improvisational material. But as any group using this technique knows, there are inherent dangers and problems, which it would appear that the Laboratory Theatre encountered in the course of their preparation for *Apocalypsis Cum Figuris*. The most obvious is that of the actors falling into stereotype responses in the course of improvisation. The quality and nature of the stereotype will of course depend on the level of skill and experience in the group: for the Laboratory Theatre actors, the problem was their tendency to revert to a representation of the Judaeo-Christian myth which characterized so much of their former work. To repeat Flaszen: 'What we were doing was the Gospels, which lapsed, naturally, into a repetition of what we already knew. We were playing out illustrations of the myths'. [143/323] The resolution of this crisis, the group discovered for themselves, was in finding a particular contemporary significance in their characteristic use of the myth. They had to re-discover the Gospels, as Scierski says, 'as they were present in each of us, not in a literary or religious sense, but as they were alive in essence in us, just as time is alive in us, in a human way'. [139/82] In other words it was necessary that they place more emphasis on the 'reality' aspect of the creative theatrical equation. Flaszen:

> I think the problem was that we had escaped from ourselves. We had allowed the myth its own autonomy. By presenting the Gospel, we had withdrawn ourselves. The solution was to depart from the myth to discover a point of reality – this being the awareness of the consequence of the myth. What would have happened to Christ if he revealed himself nowadays? In a literal way. What would we do with him? How would we see him? Where would he reveal himself? Would he be noticed at all? With the help of these questions, the crisis was resolved. And then it turned out there is a passage in the Gospel: 'I have come and you haven't recognised me'. [143/324]

The other major problem in the improvisational process that the Laboratory Theatre group were undertaking concerns the relationship between the actors and the director. The director can become creatively authoritarian and manipulative, since the actor's work is wholly subjective and is relying on the director to be the 'external eye'. Without even an objective text as a guideline, the director can use the actors as passive creative material, rather than serving and encouraging their own process. Avoiding the danger of over-manipulation involved for Grotowski another shift in attitude, towards his work, his actors, and himself as a director. This change was both a significant development for the company in the preparation of creative work and was an early indication of the radical developments that were to take place over the following few years. Flaszen again:

> I remember, also, in the course of *Apocalypsis*, Grotowski discovered another way of work and who he was in the work. The basic method of his activity was no longer the instruction of the actors, but rather expectation. He sat silently, waiting, hour after hour. This was a very great change, because previously he really was a dictator. At that point there was no more theatre, because theatre to some extent requires dictatorship, manipulation. [143/324–325]

Osiński refers us to Thomas Mann's *Doctor Faustus* as the source of the eventual title for the performance. He quotes from Mann's own notes on the writing of the novel, concerning Adrian Leverkühn who, 'as a man of thirty-five, under the influence of the first wave of euphoric inspiration, composes his main work, or first great work, *Apocalypsis Cum Figuris*, to fifteen woodcuts by Dürer, or directly based on the text of the Revelations, in an uncannily short time'. [360/57] Osiński draws a parallel between Leverkühn and Jerzy Grotowski, who was 35 years old when the first open rehearsal of his own *Apocalypsis Cum Figuris* took place on 19 July 1968, saying of Mann's work: 'There was in it the implication that it was the last work, to be followed by something like madness, an entirely new way. Lever-kühn, as we know, went into madness, while for Grotowski an entirely new horizon of creative life was opened'. [360/57] Grotowski himself, however, in recalling that period, has referred to 'the feeling that leaving the confines of a classically recognized discipline was madness and bound to come to ill'. [76]

These kind of doubts were not however in evidence when *Apocalypsis Cum Figuris* received its official premiere on 11 February 1969, and was seen and reviewed at home and during international tours. Few critics, apart from such staunch opponents as Helmut Kajzar, were able to deny that it was a theatrical creation of extraordinary power – or that, within its context, each of Grotowski's actors was able to reach her or his own, personal 'total Act'. Certainly each actor, when questioned about the production, has talked of the experience in terms beyond those usually applied to theatrical performance. The actor Zygmunt Molik, in interview with me in 1981, has said: '*Apocalypsis* was never like a performance for me. It was like a time in which I could live a full life ... in another world for a while, and this can give you the power to endure everyday life'. Similarly Stanisław Scierski has said: 'It was all an overwhelming and dramatic experience for me, involving an awareness of that particular community in which closeness can provide unexpected hope and strength – and I could in no way relate it to "theatricality", even in its most honest form, or to an "artistic experience"'. [139/84]

For several reasons an objective, definitive description and interpretation of *Apocalypsis Cum Figuris* is not possible. On the one hand there is the factor that during the twelve years it was presented to the public it underwent continual transformation and evolution, so that the performance finally witnessed in 1980 was vastly different from the 1968 closed premiere both in external, structural features and in terms of inner content and feeling. (Details of this evolution will be given later in this chapter, but for the moment it is worth noting that the version I myself became closely familiar with dates mainly from the year 1975, although I also attended performances in 1972, 1976, 1977 and 1978).

Far more difficult to describe, however, was the structural density of the production: as an art form it was possibly closer to poetry than anything else. There was a poetry of body complementing a poetry of sound, in which the reverberations of each action or word were inexhaustible. Associations were condensed into rich metaphors or naked imagery, and a response from actor or audience did not necessarily operate on the conscious level. Eric Bentley, in a review addressed to Grotowski, during the 1969 New York season, pointed to the importance of the production's spatial dimensions:

What you insisted on in New York was the Washington Square Methodist Church ... in addition to clear outline, you wished your image to have many, delicate, shifting details which would get lost in a larger place ... you have created the conditions in which you can achieve a theatrical equivalent of modern poetry. [157/7]

And Margaret Croyden has remarked that Grotowski's empathy with T. S. Eliot's poetry was not just limited to the sentiments but encompassed the aesthetics:

... the poet's method of compressing central metaphors, his utilisation of myths and history, and especially ... Eliot's principle of the 'objective correlative', his search to concretise an emotional state in his poetry. [213/158]

On one level *Apocalypsis Cum Figuris* was a parable of the Second Coming, but with neither a sense of total acceptance, nor denial. A Christ-figure was certainly evoked, and the final words spoken to him in darkness were 'Go, and come no more'. But when the lights came on at the end of the action and the room was discovered empty, it did not necessarily mean that he was gone – or that he had been. The room had simply returned to the state it was in when the first spectator entered.

So what *has* been witnessed? A group of ordinary people, in everyday clothes. Actors and audience together, without pretence and on equal footing, enter the playing area: the ones to give and present, the others to receive and witness. The room is long, with a high vaulted ceiling, and bare except for two spotlights against one wall which illumine the rough brick walls. The tall windows are boarded over, giving a faintly claustrophobic feel to the space. The audience are seated on the floor against the walls, two or three deep. The actors have been entering one by one at the same time, taking up their own positions without any attitude of performance. Once all are positioned, there is a roughly elliptic space left in the centre as the playing area. The doors are closed, and after a few moments of waiting silence, the words and action commence.

The starting point for the action is a situation in which a handful of contemporary individuals, waking up jaded and with hangovers after some revelry, find a tramp or idiot, and decide to engage in play-acting at his expense. Roles are assigned amidst mirth, and assumed, rejected, fought against. But each role, once assumed, possesses whoever is trapped within it: finally they are drained by the excesses with which they have fulfilled or denied it.

There is a Simon Peter, calculating, intellectual, head of the temporal church mouthing the twentieth-century revolt of Dostoyevsky's Grand Inquisitor. A John who, animal-like, is consumed by the excesses of the body, and taunts the Christ-figure with his physicality. A Mary Magdalene who, procured by John, becomes the bride of the Son of God and makes an irrevocable reality of his humanity. Judas – mocking, trivial, often aloof – parodies the episodes from the sidelines. Lazarus, passed over at the beginning of the game as a prospective 'Saviour', undergoes a reluctant Resurrection during the course of the action, and in return hurls in the Saviour's face all the most violent accusations spoken by Job in the Bible.

And finally, there is the Simpleton. His name in Polish (Ciemny) means 'The Dark One' and has associations of a touched innocence, a medieval idiot unknow-

50 *Apocalypsis Cum Figuris.*

ingly holding powers of light and dark. He is drawn, an unwilling victim, into the group's games and is elected to be their Saviour. Desperate for their love and acceptance, he is gradually consumed by the power of his own role, and struggles helplessly towards the final extinction. His agonies produce in his tormentors pleasure, rage, pity and final acceptance.

For a period towards the end of the action the room is plunged into darkness. The actors are scattered around the playing area, exhausted by their games. Then the room is gradually filled with flickering light as Simon Peter re-enters, carrying candles. From this point the action moves swiftly, following more nearly the Gospel sequence of events. The actors are finally acquiescent in their roles. The Last Supper, the Betrayal, Golgotha, and at last the Crucifixion. At the very end only Simon Peter is left with his academic arguments to confront the Simpleton. To these the Simpleton has no logical response, and the second and final crucifixion at Simon Peter's hands is a cold, intellectual verification of the earlier emotional one. The Simpleton, in a state of agonized delirium, flounders on the floor. From his lips there comes his final response – a latin hymn, a prayer in the ritual language of organized religion. It deepens and soars to envelop the darkening room, as Simon Peter stealthily circles towards him, extinguishing the candles one by one. The final image before total darkness is that of a helpless moth, pinned to the floor, still yearning towards the last rays of light.

A textual base for the work was not the only thing dispensed with in the course of preparing *Apocalypsis Cum Figuris*. In contrast to the richness of action and possible interpretation, the production represents in its most obvious external

51 *Apocalypsis Cum Figuris* – Ryszard Cieślak.   52 *Apocalypsis Cum Figuris* – Ryszard Cieślak.

manifestation an extension of the 'poor theatre' concept, taken over the years to its limit. Costume – to begin with simple and symbolic – was eventually abandoned, and properties used were limited to the most basic and elemental of objects: bread, knife, white cloth, candles, bucket of water. Lighting, also, was deceptively simple, with two spotlights and candles being used to full and dramatic advantage. But it was in terms of the scenic space – with which, during his earlier productions, he had been most adventurous – that Grotowski was most uncompromising in his final production, leaving the playing area to be defined solely by the actions and relative positions of the actors and audience.

This process of elimination was not taken to such ascetic limits as to call in question its function in the aesthetic realm. Although stripped of the conventional technical and material resources, the aim was still, through an almost magical talent, for the actor to achieve scenic effects. In fact Helmut Kajzar has called the formulation of the 'poor theatre' concept the 'coquetry of the rich', pointing to the sophisticated composition of materials, the conscious play of light and sound, and the symbolic use of costume. Similarly, Leonia Jabłonkówna has written in a review of *Apocalypsis Cum Figuris*:

It is true that Grotowski's ascetic approach reaches its limits here... And yet in spite of the poverty the spectacle dazzles with a richness of visual effect (in the best sense). The circumstances, gestures and movement have a dynamic intensity and a fascinating precision of detail.... Each gesture, however insignificant, each movement of the hand or sway of the body has expressive power.... The actor is like an instrument capable of registering a variety of tones and octaves. He could take the place of a powerful symphony orchestra, and himself perform the symphony. [281]

Neither did Grotowski abandon his characteristic use of blasphemy and profanation in the confrontation with the mythic substructure of our social beings. If anything, his employment of these was less equivocal and certainly less intellectualized than in former productions. The most fundamental and universal of religious myths became incarnate in a brutally literal manner. Indeed, the opening words of *Apocalypsis Cum Figuris*, taken from the traditional Christian ritual of the Mass, presaged both physical acts undertaken in the course of the production, and the underlying spiritual parasitism of the theme: 'He who eats my flesh and drinks my blood will have eternal life'. Similarly, the central Christian miracle of Godhead, for love of humanity, becoming incarnate in Christ, was portrayed literally in the physical acts of love between Mary Magdalene and the Simpleton.

This particular aspect of Laboratory Theatre aesthetics has, predictably, provoked strong reactions. In his 1969 article, Jan Błoński attempted to reinterpret the doctrine and fashion it into a more acceptable format. Where Grotowski uses the words 'blasphemy' and 'profanation', Błoński replaces them with 'test' or 'initiation'. Blasphemy, he claimed, can only stimulate the sacred very temporarily, before de-fusing it and destroying the mystery. In order to be strengthened, the sacred must be put to a test, from which it will emerge victorious.

Applying this interpretation, Błoński saw *Apocalypsis Cum Figuris* as a contemporary passion play. The modern tragedy, in Błoński's definition, revolves around the idea of doom as moral evil, an ethical translation of the classical paradigm in which doom is a disintegration of cosmic order, releasing internalized dark forces. Therefore in *Apocalypsis*, the blasphemy is nightly taken to the extreme of showing us God's death before our eyes, and almost by our own hands, and thus rekindles in us a 'feeling for the sacred' and a 'nostalgia for the specific eternal values it embodies'. The contemporary existential condition of doubt and abandonment is cathartically exploded and values strengthened. Błoński questioned whether Grotowski was simply failing to recognize the conventional cathartic process in the reactions evoked in his audiences:

> What strikes me in this theatre is the understanding of the profound mechanism of the tragic experience, though its creators seem to use other terms, which sound like substitutes for the real thing. [161/149]

Błonski's arguments, although cohesive, may be misdirected. Catharsis presupposes a fundamental inner belief, possibly subconscious, in an ordered model. This belief is ultimately strengthened through the dramatic tragic experience, and it is thus a process that endorses the status quo. Grotowski, on the other hand, believes that

Today there are many half-truths – a Tower of Babel – so it is impossible to find this primordial ritual. One can stimulate external phenomena ... but it's not a deep, authentic participation. It's only the participation of the common mask. [42/40]

His aim, therefore, is to bring us momentarily into contact with the deepest levels within ourselves, deeper than those engaged within the order of forms, through incarnate mythic confrontation. If we succeed, through the shock of exposure, in touching those depths, we are changed for ever. The process does not involve release: it is rather a re-awakening, or a re-birth, and in consequence potentially painful.

Whether or not one chooses to attach importance to categorizations such as 'tragedy', the significant factor to be borne in mind is Grotowski's continual submission to the real possibility of *change* within the work and performance processes (for actor and spectator). Joseph Chaikin, discussing Brecht's epic theatre, makes the familiar point that it 'asks for a removal of pity by the performers and audience, since pity is a response to that which cannot be changed'. [206/35] This could be said to be one of the few genuine links between Brecht and Grotowski – a rejection (in their very different ways) of the old concept of catharsis, involving terror and pity, which inhibited real change.

Apocalypsis was the last theatrical production Grotowski was to undertake with his Laboratory Theatre group in Wrocław. It was played periodically for about twelve years (with occasional lapses, once for as long as a year) both in Poland and on tour abroad, even after *Akropolis* and *The Constant Prince* had been abandoned and the company had ceased their strictly theatrical activities. As the last production, even in its inception it was an indication of radical changes that were fermenting at the Laboratory Theatre, and which were to become apparent in the following months and years.

In July and August 1968 Grotowski was present at another training course at the Odin Teatret in Holstebro, organized by Eugenio Barba, and principally for the benefit of Scandinavian actors and directors. There were, however, American groups and observers present, and during the course of the work Grotowski made a direct attack on certain aspects of American group theatre work, which provoked a heated debate. Margaret Croyden, who was present, later reported in *The Drama Review*:

He felt that Americans never follow through their own techniques and when they try to do this, they can't keep the techniques pure. ... American work was too mechanical, the creative work depended too much on techniques foreign to American sensibility. He criticised all the groups present for using his exercises without the images to support them, reducing them to acrobatics, to zero. [212/181–182]

It was, perhaps, the first overt indication of a gradual disillusionment on Grotowski's part concerning the possibility of changing the accepted ethics of theatre practice. At the same time in Holstebro there appeared the first edition (published in English) of Grotowski's book *Towards a Poor Theatre*, with its concluding 'Statement of Principles':

> The main point then is that an actor should not try to acquire any kind of recipe or build up a 'box of tricks'. This is no place for collecting all sorts of means of expression. The force of gravity in our work pushes the actor towards an interior ripening which expresses itself through a willingness to break through barriers, to search for a 'summit', totality. [73/218]

In September 1968, after appearances at the Edinburgh Festival and the Cultural Olympics accompanying the 19th Olympic Games in Mexico City, the Laboratory Theatre were refused entry visas to the United States for their first New York season. An open letter of protest signed by 60 American artists (including Arthur Miller, Edward Albee, Walter Kerr, Jerome Robbins) was sent to the State Department and published in the Sunday edition of the *New York Times* 18.9.68. The Laboratory Theatre, however, at the invitation of Antoine Bourseiller went instead to France and for two months gave performances of *Akropolis* in Paris and Aix-en-Provence. In addition they visited London for a few days at the end of October to work on a television film of *Akropolis* at the Twickenham studios. The film was made by American television and broadcast 12.1.69, to a cool reception (there is always a painful disparity between the reality of the Laboratory Theatre work and any filmed representation).

In October 1969, after nearly one month's tour of Great Britain including appearances in London, Manchester and Lancaster, the Laboratory Theatre finally realized their New York debut. The tour had been announced the previous summer by the Brooklyn Academy of Music in association with Ninon Tallon Karlweiss and Ellen Stewart (founder of La Mama) and had been due to last five weeks. In the event it lasted over two months, with 48 performances instead of the planned 34 (of *Akropolis*, *The Constant Prince* and *Apocalypsis Cum Figuris*), all of which took place at the Washington Square Methodist Church in Greenwich Village. This delayed appearance was attended by a hysteria of publicity and adulation that seemed to make a mockery of the company's declared asceticism. Eric Bentley: 'I would call your Poor Theater *elemental theater* to avoid those jokes about poor theater at 200 dollars a seat, which is what your tickets were selling for on the black market'. [157/7] It would perhaps again be an over-simplification to say that an experience of this nature contributed in a direct way to Grotowski's subsequent withdrawal from a theatrically committed path – but it is certainly true, as Grotowski later verified, that this period proved to be a turning point in his life.

Perhaps what distressed him most in his relationship with the theatrical world was that despite his conscientious efforts to prepare and explore an individually creative path towards self-discovery for the actor, and his repeated emphasis on the essentially autonomous nature of this journey, there were few actors, directors or groups who had the discipline or dedication to follow with integrity. The majority, as Grotowski had pointed out in the Holstebro seminar in 1968, sought merely for the easiest formulation of external manifestation, avoiding the essential inner commitment. In an interview during the theatre's stay in France in the autumn of 1968, Grotowski gave full voice to his despair:

> Hence it is so much easier to yell, cry out and make uncoordinated movements than to truly accomplish certain acts which involve us in our totality. It is easier in performance, for the actor and for the spectator, to put oneself in a state of hysteria than to truly confront oneself with the problem of one's life, to question oneself (oneself and not another) ... Without any responsible system of training, without any technique which could permit true research of a creative act, a conjunction between the significative structure of a role and the process which reveals our own life in its palpable matter.... easy and immediate success is sought. There are many people who do that in my name.... and I don't wish to be embroiled in a dance of whores. The whole world is in search of a New Theatre. Conventional theatre is a dead frog which presents itself as full of life, but the theatre called new theatre is that same frog galvanised, with certain superficial symptoms of life. [45]

In February 1970, just over two months after the Laboratory Theatre's return from their highly successful New York season, when the group could perhaps be said to have been at the very peak of their theatrical career, there was a press meeting organized in Wrocław between Grotowski and theatre critics who arrived from all over Poland. Grotowski spoke of the current situation at the theatre, hinting at fundamental, unprecedented developments in the nature of the work ahead, and speaking also of the need to enlarge the working team at the theatre:

> Numerous artistic journeys are at present impeding us in our work. These travels must be curtailed. Concentration is demanded.... We are living in a post-theatrical epoch. It is not a new wave of theatre which follows but something that will take its place. Too many phenomena exist on the basis of custom, because their existence is generally accepted. I feel that *Apocalypsis Cum Figuris* is, for me, a new stage of our research. We have crossed a certain barrier. [50]

In June and July of that year Grotowski and Cieślak were once again in Aix-en-Provence, conducting a workshop at the Centre Dramatique National. At its conclusion on 10 July Grotowski departed directly from France for India and Kurdistan. It was his third visit to the area and lasted for six weeks.

In the meantime the Laboratory Theatre departed on their sixth and last purely theatrical tour abroad – to Iran, Lebanon and Berlin. When, however, the company went to meet Grotowski at Shiraz airport in Iran after his solitary journey in India, they found he had completely changed in outward appearance: 'even his closest associates did not recognize him – so much had he changed in that short time: he looked quite a different person from the one whom they had known under that name before'. [360/95] He had lost a considerable amount of weight, abandoned his familiar black businessman's suit in favour of casual clothing, and grown his hair and a beard. From Shiraz Grotowski himself went to the Festival of Latin America in Manizales, Colombia (he was its honorary president), where he made the following highly personal statements to the many young theatre groups gathered there to hear his words:

> This is a two-fold moment in my life. That which is theatre, 'technique', methodology, I have behind me. . . . What was a search in theatre, in 'technique', even in professionalism (but as we understood it – as a vocation) is in some way dear to me. It led me where I am. It led from theatre, from 'technique', from professionalism. It is still vital as a life experience. But already I am breathing different air. My feet are touching different ground and my senses are drawn towards a different challenge. That is where I am heading. I hear your voices, your questions. About theatre. I look back towards it, towards theatre. It is the past. I am speaking about what was. What I sought in that life. [63/111]

Almost simultaneously there was appearing in many popular youth periodicals in Poland, and on Polish Radio, a personal and unusual invitation from Grotowski and the Laboratory Theatre team to the youth of Poland, entitled 'Proposal for Collaboration'. It was addressed to those 'who – because it is quite simply a necessity for them – leave their inner comfort, and seek to reveal themselves in work, in meeting, in movement and freedom'. [48]

After travelling with his group to the 'Polnische Wochen' in West Berlin at the beginning of December 1970 (during which *The Constant Prince* was presented, on 10 December, for the last time) Grotowski went directly to New York where, after the 1969 tour, he had been invited by New York University to present a series of meetings and talks. During the course of these he made a definitive statement concerning his present position vis-à-vis theatre and the pursuit of art, the text of which has subsequently become known as *Holiday*: 'I am not interested in the theatre anymore, only in what I can do in leaving theatre behind. . . . Am I talking about a way of life, a kind of existence rather than about theatre? Undoubtedly'. [64/116–117] Despite distrust, disbelief, cynicism and a total lack of comprehension, Grotowski was to repeat and expand this message in future public debate. Although willing to participate in theoretical discussion concerning the Institute's former theatrical experiments, he was constantly at pains to emphasize that this was past history for them, a closed chapter. The search had been taken to the outer boundaries delineated by theatrical art, and since it was not in the nature of the Institute or its members to remain static, they had simply stepped beyond. It was to be many years before critics were able to recognize this fact.

The evolution of *Apocalypsis Cum Figuris* during the years since its initial presentation in 1968 was an indication of the changing priorities within the Laboratory Theatre company, leading to the final, dramatic 'departure from theatre'. At the beginning *Apocalypsis* was still, in certain respects, a relatively conventional theatre production: there was a clearly defined spatial division, although there was neither a stage nor any form of scenic architecture as in previous productions:

What is essential is the architecture of the room itself, which forms a living part of the performance. Here, our demands are great. It can't be a modern, elegant, neon-lit room, or a gym, etc. It could be a church, basement, attic – whatever, it must be real. No cosmetic changes or artifice are allowed. In other words, we don't pretend it's something it's not. [143/310]

In the performance space in the theatre buildings in Wrocław, there was a bare, windowless room, with five rough benches set against the walls, seating about thirty-five spectators. Two spotlights shone upwards from a corner of the room on the floor, and constituted the only formal scenic effect. Although the actors were dressed in contemporary, unremarkable clothes, they still retained some of the symbolic qualities of costume. They were all dressed in white, with Simon Peter in a white poncho, which later assumed ecclesiastical significance. In contrast Ciemny (literally The Dark One) wore just a black, kneelength raincoat and carried a white stick (which came, Flaszen tells us, from early associational work with Cieślak as a blind man). Flaszen also elaborates on the dramatic intention behind the sparse design:

Because the performance was conceived as a Second Coming (i.e. would He be noticed, today?), it must happen among a few, far-away people in a cellar or attic. Maybe these are the last who can recognize the Second Coming. It creates the feeling of a void, with benches scattered as if at random.... The sense was as if those who were here came by chance, possibly as if these are the last who can be touched and to whom the event might be significant. Especially important was that it happened in emptiness.

This arrangement had a certain sense for our group at that time. We had become a renowned theatre. But in fact we still felt lonely, solitary, almost alien. We lived in tension with the world, or possibly in rebellion, or negation. [143/310, 326]

Between 1971 and 1973 (a period the group spent mainly in closed experimental work on post-theatrical forms) significant external and structural changes took place within *Apocalypsis*: the most obvious of these were in relation to the audience. In 1971 the first performances were presented in which the benches were removed and the increased number of spectators sat on the floor or stood around the walls. These spectators were in the main a specifically young audience, and numbered 100–120. For a couple of years *Apocalypsis* was presented in two versions (one 'without benches' for young audiences, one 'with benches' for more conventional spectators) but in 1973 the benches were removed completely. The reasons for this were two-fold. On a purely practical level, the number of people wishing to see the Laboratory Theatre productions had been steadily increasing. And despite generalized assumptions that Grotowski practised an enforced elitism by rigidly restricting the numbers of spectators, the necessity of turning members of the public away was becoming a pressing problem. Secondly, as *Apocalypsis* evolved internally for the performers, there was a gradual move towards greater physical and psychological closeness with the audience:

> If we have now removed benches in *Apocalypsis* and seat people directly on the floor, we do it not only because this enables us to let in more of them but because now we are not afraid of those who come and are almost in the midst of us. What we are doing is based on the fact of human presence: I am before you. [64/129]

In the post-1973 versions the proximity was perceptible not only in relation to the actor and spectator, between whom incidental physical contact frequently occurred, but also between spectator and spectator. In entering the room one submitted to an experience of intense physical closeness rare in any social circumstance, and this was undoubtedly an element that contributed to the intensity of the audience experience. But a balance had to be maintained between a natural desire to increase the numbers of spectators, and the loss of intimacy that would occur in a larger area. The dimensions finally arrived at (i.e. an audience of 120–130) probably denoted the limits both of physical containment and supportably psychic intimacy.

There were other discernible elements of change within the production –

53 *Apocalypsis Cum Figuris.*

generally in a move away from the aesthetic and the theatrical. In mid-1972 any inference of costume was abandoned by the actors in favour of their everyday clothes (although these were specific outfits reserved only for use in the production). The Simpleton retained his black raincoat, but his white stick was exchanged for one of wood. The spotlights were moved from their visually symmetrical position in the corner of the room to a less emphasized position against a side wall. Similarly, there were changes within the scenes that had used the lights to such conscious, plastic effect in the earlier versions. Where, for example, the Simpleton and Mary Magdalene had performed their love rites in the direct beam of light, conventionally highlighting their own actions and throwing the rest of the room into dark, voyeuristic intimacy, the scene now took place on the dark side of the lights. According to Flaszen, these changes were in direct relationship to the development of the post-theatrical experiments within the group, which were taking place together with the newcomers to the team, recruited since 1970:

54 *Apocalypsis Cum Figuris* – Ryszard Cieślak and Rena Mirecka.

The evolution, then, consisted basically of the following. We tried to take away everything that had to do with 'theatre' or the 'putting on of faces' or precise composition etc. The source of this change was not an aesthetic premise or assumption . . . it was a situation in which it was no longer necessary to establish a wall in relation to others by being an 'artist' behind an objective structure. A factor of *direct* human communication appeared, and we stopped being against those who were coming to us and those not coming to us. And then, *Apocalypsis* began its evolution. With the new sense of directness, we began to remove all that still seemed artificial and theatrical and formal; all that was ready-made beauty; all that was distant, or remote. [143/326–327]

In an interview published in 1975, the actor Ryszard Cieślak has emphasized that these external changes were only significant in so far as they permitted continuing fresh reactions to the roles and score. The essential transformation was in the attempt to open to the possibilities inherent in the physical and psychic closeness of the audience, to the inexpressible that may take place between 'an individual who still is in some part a spectator, and the individual who still is in some small part an actor. Although one yearns that the old "spectator" relic give way to another human reaction.' [140/6] This yearning was a fundamental, almost tangible aspect of the audience experience, which Cieślak described further: 'We do not think of them as the "public". They are much closer to us: we are not indifferent to them but react strongly to their presence with every fibre of the organism and with every nerve. We react with warmth". [140/5] Subjectively there was the sense of a challenge being directly offered – a carnal dare to break through what is mere tangible convention. There were one or two moments within the production when an actor physically confronted an individual spectator (in an objectively unobtrusive manner) to offer a personal challenge. Cieślak stated categorically that any spectator who reacted to this would be accepted into the performance:

> This possibility lies in the very nature of the *Apocalypsis*: it emerged as the idea of the performance developed. *Apocalypsis* is only a title, a certain stream of associations: the rest is open to the unexpected, it awaits, tempts, lures the unpredictable in us and outside of us.... [140/6]

At a meeting in 1971 with participants of a student theatre festival in Wrocław, Grotowski said:

> If one aims at revealing man, as I see it, in every phase of life this revelation should mean crossing a new barrier. It is in this connection that one must be disloyal to the last crossing of the barrier. In *Apocalypsis* this problem seems to us particularly clear and sharp-edged. Already during the preparatory work we realized that potentially there is in it the seed of something different, in a concealed form, a blurring of borders, as it were. [64/127]

It would seem that *Apocalypsis Cum Figuris*, in one sense, was indeed borderline theatre – an attempt to stretch the most fundamental laws of theatrical convention without any compromise in formal structure. Everything that could possibly be done was done to permit the spectator to meet the physical challenge of the actor's gesture spontaneously. According to an article in *Le Monde* in 1973 (based on Grotowski's statements during the company's French visit that year), experimental versions of *Apocalypsis* were presented in Philadelphia earlier the same year, during which spectators were invited to directly participate, with the sole stipulation of not destroying the structure of the performance. 'The aim of this "opening" is to study the conditions under which the spectator, without coercion and in a gentle, almost imperceptible manner, might abandon the role of observer". [264] And there were rare occasions when there was a genuine response: Ludwik Flaszen describes an incident during the Australian visit (in 1974) when 'a girl entered the action with tenderness to console the Simpleton; this lasted awhile, because she did it humanely and softly. It was a Pietà.' [143/310] But the fact remains that, on the whole, the challenge was not taken up. The total act of uncovering, of meeting with one's whole self, remained as one-sided as in the earlier productions.

For the longest period of its life, *Apocalypsis Cum Figuris* played a double role in the repertoire of the Laboratory Theatre. It was, on the one hand, presented as a (relatively) conventional production – an 'artistic product' performed for the spectator-witness. But it also served as a bridge to the post-theatrical experiments – an invitation for those within the audience unsatisfied with the limitations of artistic form to participate in further communal activity. It would seem that, at that stage in their exploration, Grotowski and the members of the Laboratory Theatre felt that they had exhausted for themselves the possibilities of conventional theatrical form. They decided to abandon the framework in an attempt to explore more fully the furthest implications of what they had been moving towards in 'theatre'. The search remained the same – only the territory was unfamiliar.

SECTION II
Theory

According to Peter Brook, 'no-one, since Stanislavsky, has investigated the nature of acting, its phenomenon, its meaning, the nature and science of its mental-physical-emotional processes as deeply and completely as Grotowski'. [73/11] It is my intention within the following three chapters to concentrate upon those investigations into the craft of acting. In doing so I will make no attempt to document in technical detail any physical work (in the way of exercises etc.) undertaken at the Laboratory Theatre. Descriptions and full technical details referring to some of the exercises used at the Institute 1959–1966 are contained in *Towards a Poor Theatre* (pp 101–172) and there is no point in duplicating them here.

Instead, I will attempt to translate and transmit some of the ideas, attitudes and ethics informing the acting process under Grotowski's direction, and to make possible connections, whether in terms of influences upon the work, related disciplines, or simply a more familiar context for some aspects of the philosophy. In describing the evolution of Grotowski's theories during the twelve years or so of strictly theatrical work, I will draw as precise a demarcation as is possible and appropriate between the notion of training and the research connected with it (dealt with in Chapter Six) and the notion of performance, preparation for performance, and the creative process (which belongs to Chapter Seven). This is a distinction that I have noticed is frequently left unclarified in consideration of the Laboratory Theatre work, with resulting confusion. In general I feel that there are, overall, two basic (positive) attitudes towards Grotowski's place in theatrical history. The first admires above all Grotowski's theatrical works of art as aesthetic products and consequently values and emulates the technical path by which the product was achieved (i.e. the actor training, the methods of preparation for performance). The second attitude sets less store by the results as such, but values what Grotowski has contributed in terms of an approach to theatre and an ethical and humanistic context. It should be obvious from these chapters that I hold the second of these viewpoints.

CHAPTER SIX

Training

The overwhelming temptation for actors, indeed for all men, is the search for a prescription. Such a prescription does not exist' (Grotowski) [90/123]

We have already seen, in Chapter Three, how Grotowski's resistance to the process of making his work with the actor available as a 'method' provoked confusion and some hostility amongst the theatrical world in Poland and abroad. The use of the term 'method' has become widespread since Stanislavsky first introduced a more conscious, scientific perspective to the process of preparation for stage-craft. Those who use the term most probably intend to imply a collection of internally coherent techniques for training voice and body, or as performance techniques which, if applied systematically, will be reasonably reliable in producing a recognizable effect or style.

There are without doubt those who would claim to recognize a particular style produced by the application of a Grotowski 'method'. And in the terms within which method has been defined above, then it is certainly true to say that a Grotowski method exists. It is perfectly feasible for an individual to duplicate the exercises and vocal and physical training techniques used by the Laboratory Theatre from 1959–1970, and to follow faithfully their process of construction and preparation of a performance through the application of a recognizably Grotowskian aesthetic. If this were done with a reasonable degree of dedication and commitment there would probably result an impressive artistic product within a Grotowskian style. (This indeed has been a common sight in the work of experimental theatre groups in the past ten to fifteen years.)

According to Grotowski, however, this would be little better, in creative terms, than taking a photocopy. As such it is no more true to the Grotowskian principles than the emotionally indulgent attitude of many supposedly Stanislavskian actors is faithful to the original research of Stanislavsky. For Grotowski, there is essentially no such thing as a Stanislavsky Method either, although Grotowski himself was educated in the State Theatre School according to the accredited Stanislavsky system. In the process he became fascinated by Stanislavsky and by the questions he raised about the technique and motivation of the actor, and Grotowski now acknowledges him without reservation as his first master:

When I became a student at theatre school in the acting department all of my theatrical knowledge was founded on Stanislavsky's principles. As an actor I was obsessed with Stanislavsky: I was a fanatic. I thought that this was the key opening all doors to creativity. I wanted to understand him better than anyone else. I worked hard to learn everything I could about what he said or what was said about him. This progressed – according to psycho-analytic rules – from a period of imitation to one of rebellion, or a striving for independence. In order to play that same role in the profession for others as he played for me. . . . [94/112]

According to Grotowski, Stanisławsky's primary legacy – his 'great service' to the profession – was the establishment of the Western actor's obligation to daily work and training in addition to performance. There are two other qualities of Stanislavsky's work and attitude that Grotowski isolates in particular. One is Stanislavsky's 'concentration on what is practical and concrete. How to touch the intangible? He wanted to find a concrete path towards what are secret, mysterious processes'. [94/113] Secondly (and perhaps principally for Grotowski) Stanislavsky was a man in a state of 'permanent self-reform'. In other words his attitude was one of unceasing research and readiness to question earlier achievements and stages of work. Stanislavsky's research was only brought to a stop by his death, which is why there cannot truly be a Stanislavsky Method. But this did not stop the process of what Grotowski calls Stanislavsky's 'assassination after death' by the vast number of those seeking to crystallize the stages of his research into the perfect 'prescription' for achieving results.

Grotowski gives two specific examples of ways in which Stanislavsky's very precise research has been invalidated over the years by those of his followers in search of the easy solution. The first concerns 'precision of action', whereby through work with real and imaginary objects an action is magnified into micro-scopic movements. According to Stanislavsky this exercise would give precision and expressiveness to an action. But Grotowski contends that in much Stanislavsky-style training this process has been reduced to an emphasis on the sensation and feeling behind action, rather than on the reality of the details themselves, and this is an emphasis which robs the actions of precision. A similar fate attended Stanis-lavsky's work with relaxation and tension. He observed that tension usually has a focal point in the body – different for each individual – which 'contaminates' the whole body. Excess tension can be released by the actor, through discovering and working from this focal point, and thus achieving the feline ideal of 'relaxation with the possibility of immediate mobilization'. But again the precision of these researches became diluted, and relaxation was applied indiscriminately as a general remedy for all problems encountered in acting training. Grotowski:

> One cannot be totally relaxed as is taught in many theatre schools, for he who is totally relaxed is nothing more than a wet rag. Living is not being contracted, nor is it being relaxed: it is a process. [73/176]

Grotowski is vehement in his condemnation of this kind of attitude to actor training:

> When someone has studied a concrete aspect of the craft in order to find a precision, and through this precision a richness, others shelter behind his name

in order to achieve something apparently similar but in reality sterile. You can meet great specialists in this field: they imitate the appearance of things and avoid all the difficulty which underlies it. [89/129]

For Grotowski there is only one possible attitude to one's teacher or master – that of a 'profound betrayal':

If I said once that the technique which I follow is that of creating one's own, personal techniques, there is contained here that postulate of a 'profound betrayal'. If a pupil senses his own technique, then he departs from me, from my needs, which I realize in my way, through my process. He will be different, distant.... Every other technique or method is sterile. [94/119]

The crucial factor in making these demarcations in attitude towards method is the product/process emphasis. If, again, the *product* is given significance, then the application of 'method' in order to achieve a particular style or aesthetic is perfectly acceptable. But if the *process* is emphasized, then a 'method' will be creatively inhibiting, since no one method can be universal and cover all possible needs: each actor would require an individual method:

When I came to the conclusion that the problem of building my own system was illusory and that there exists no ideal system which could be a key to creativity, then the word 'method' changed its meaning for me. There exists a challenge, to which each must give his own answer. [94/112]

And so, does this mean that there exists nothing from the body of Grotowski's investigations into the 'mental-physical-emotional processes' of acting that has objective relevance outside his group of investigator-actors? Are these processes indeed so shamanistic that they rely solely upon the medium of Grotowski as some critics have suggested? One way out of the conflict of attitudes attendant upon the concept of 'Grotowski Method' is to attempt a redefinition, for the purposes of this book, of some of the terms used.

The first point to re-state is that, for Grotowski, only a process of creating one's own method is important. This means that although Grotowski believes that there exists a concrete path of research and training for the actor, the essential condition which qualifies this path or 'method' is that it is individual and personal:

In the final analysis there are no prescriptions. For every individual one must discover the cause which impedes him, hampers him, and then create the situation in which this cause can be eliminated and the process liberated. [90/112]

If, therefore, the only method that deserves the name of the Grotowski Method is that of having no fixed and universal method at all, what are we left with? The answer is: techniques and ethics. Techniques we can understand as the minutiae of method, the practicable directives which, in certain combinations, produce the verifiable results which are usually classed as method. Ethics are what inform the use of technique – the how, when, why and which of technique. What we are dealing with, if we look at Grotowski's training of his actor, is a veritable plethora of techniques, informed by a subjective and continually evolving set of ethics. And what is clear is that while there is a historic and analytic relevance in documenting the training techniques undertaken at the Laboratory Theatre, it is the ethic, or attitude with which they are discovered, researched and performed, that is of primary significance if we are to attempt to penetrate to the essence of Grotowski's approach and work.

Grotowski lists for us in *Towards a Poor Theatre* the major actor-training techniques the company have studied. And there is in fact very little in the way of technique that is in any sense *unique* to the Laboratory Theatre, an objective result of their research to be passed on. (There have of course been valuable objective results in the areas of breathing and vocal training: See pages 123–125. All techniques of actor training have been available in the past to any theatre researcher, although as Grotowski has pointed out, many of them have been derived from non-theatrical areas:

> I do not consider that my work in theatre could be defined as a new method. . . . Neither do I consider that it was something new. I think that this kind of research existed most frequently outside of theatre, although at times it also existed in certain theatres. It's a question of a way of life and of knowledge. [94/119]

It is probably also true that there is no one technique or exercise which had an *absolute* value for the Laboratory Theatre and was a permanent feature of their training. Even the very idea of training itself was abandoned for a certain period when it was found to be losing the quality of challenge for the team. As they progressed from one stage to another of their personal development, and in consequence the metaphysical bases for their work evolved, then certain elements of training inevitably became sterile or inadequate and required adjustment. This of course is another fundamental reason for Grotowski's denials of Laboratory Theatre Method – he found it insupportable that any observer should attempt to so fix or freeze what was a dynamic process:

> If you do not transcend quickly enough that which is perfect – you will fall into automatism. In *Towards a Poor Theatre* you can see how all our exercises evolved – they were never orthodox, but were always in movement and always individualized. If something was becoming perfect there was a need either to surpass it, or return to what was more simple. . . . [92/117]

But Grotowski continually emphasized that the intention was never to train an actor in a collection of skills. He specifically attacked the attitude implicit in the training techniques currently in use in many theatre schools, whereby the application of a wide range of training methods – from fencing and acrobatics to modern dance and mime – is supposed to produce in combination a highly trained actor. This, he claimed, will produce only an actor capable of reproducing skills on stage. It is not that the eclectic approach is to be condemned in itself. After all, it derived from Stanislavsky and was essentially how Grotowski himself worked.

But again, a distinction is to be made in attitude. On the one hand there is the collecting of skills: such an approach instructs 'how to do', that is 'it shows how to arm oneself. We arm ourselves in order to conceal ourselves; sincerity begins where we are defenceless'. [64/121] And on the other hand there is the use of technique or discipline in a revelatory manner, i.e. in order to disclose the limitations and blockages in an actor that are to be transcended:

> He who hesitates before making a powerful somersault, one which carries a certain risk in acrobatics, will hesitate before the culminating point of his role. [89/128]

The most crucial point was that for the Laboratory Theatre members method did not and could not exist as something separate from an individual actor's needs. Since the limitations and blockages in an actor would be personal and individual, then the system of exercises needed to identify, confront and overcome these must also be unique for each.

> In the course of our research it was evident that the difficulties and blockages that emerged were different for each of us. Exercises were of benefit when each person could train using those elements which he found essential; what he acquired from the exercises was, in every case, different. For everyone encountered different obstacles. [63/112]

Furthermore it was these very obstacles that were for Grotowski and his team an indication of the way forward:

> All of the exercises undertaken by us were without exception directed towards the annihilation of resistances, blocks, individual and professional stereotypes. These were obstruction-exercises. To surpass exercises, which are like a trap, you must discover your own blocks. . . . There was never any concept of exercises as being something important in their own right. . . . A personal system of exercises in the true meaning of this term is when one discovers the most difficult exercises, constituting a renunciation of substitution and avoidances, which are only self-indulgence. These exercises are personal, because they function as a test for personal inhibitions. They are therefore considerably more difficult for us than for others. [94/115]

In summary, therefore, we can say that Grotowski considered the only appropriate training programme for an actor to be one in which separate elements are employed or jettisoned according to whether they eliminate the blockages towards spontaneous creativity, necessary for the theatrical act:

> We must find what it is that hinders him in the way of respiration, movement and – most important of all – human contact. What resistances are there? How can they be eliminated? I want to take away, steal from the actor all that disturbs him. That which is creative will remain within him. It is a liberation. [73/16]

The exercises that formed the basic structure of the Laboratory Theatre training programme, then, were the result of a painstaking process of selection, based on the principle of elimination rather than accumulation, and tailored for and by each individual. But when Grotowski initiated his experimental theatre company in Opole in 1959, despite theoretical statements that indicated the future line of his preoccupation with the scenic technique of the actor, there was no training as such for his group. With his first production prepared in only three weeks, and the rest of the 1959/1960 season being taken up with other productions and tours, one can assume that the energies of the company were fully absorbed with the conventional preparation of repertory. It was not until the second season at Opole (1960/1961) and preparation for the production of the Indian drama *Shakuntala* that there began the process of a gradual but systematic application of training techniques. These were in addition to the daily rehearsal work of preparation for performance, but at this stage still very much conditioned by the performance and its aesthetic. In other words techniques were sought for and explored in terms of the effects that could thereby be achieved on stage in performance – an attitude, as we have just seen, that Grotowski was in time himself to condemn.

The production of *Shakuntala* was an indication at that time of two separate, but directly interconnected themes for Grotowski. One was his historic interest in all things oriental, and the other was a preoccupation (at this stage greatly theoretical and intellectual) with the possibility of recreating ritual in theatre, in a way meaningful for our times and our society, as a way of healing the many splits both within an individual and between people. From this arose at that time his image of the actor as sorcerer or magician, capable of far more than the spectator – and the first, groping, theoretical formulations of the actor as shaman/priest, capable of leading those who witness and participate into unknown territory. This was in time to provide rich material for research and the production of *Shakuntala* was but an initial step:

> We wanted to create a performance which would give an image of oriental theatre, not authentic, however, but as Europeans imagine it. And so it was an ironic picture of images about the East, as something mysterious and enigmatic. But under the surface of those experiments, which were ironic and directed against the audience, there was a hidden purpose – to discover a system of signs suitable for our theatre, and our civilisation. What we did was to construct the performance basically from minute gestural and vocal signals. This was of benefit in the future: it was then that we had to introduce vocal exercises in our group, for it is impossible to create vocal signals without special training. The production was presented, and it had an unusual quality. But I saw that it was an ironic transposition of all possible stereotypes and cliches; that each of those gestures, of the specially constructed ideograms, constituted what Stanislavsky called 'gestural clichés'. [46/70]

Grotowski's contact with, and knowledge of Asia, its cultures and philosophies, has already been referred to. And in some ways, not always apparent or acknowledged, this fascination had a profound effect upon him and his work. In an article in 1959 referring to his 1956 visit to Central Asia, he recalled a chance meeting with an old man, Abdullah, who demonstrated for him a traditional 'mime of the whole world', drawing an analogy between the world of form and the art of mime. 'It seemed to me at that time that I was listening to my own thoughts. Nature – changeable, in movement and yet eternally one – always took shape in my imagination like a dancing mime . . . concealed beneath the glittering multitude of gestures, colours and caprices of life'. [361/25] Similarly in a talk given at the first Conversatorium of the 1960/61 season, Grotowski referred to the mythological Indian God of theatre – Shiva, the Cosmic Dancer – who in dancing creates all that exists: 'If I had to define our theatrical researches in one sentence, one phrase, I would refer to the myth of the Dance of Shiva'. He quoted Shiva's words: 'I am the pulse, the movement and the rhythm', saying that this was the essence of the theatre for which they were searching. [361/25]

Apart from Grotowski's own contacts – according to Marian Byrski in his article on Grotowski and the Indian tradition – the members of the Laboratory Theatre team probably made contact with actors from the Indian Kathakali theatre while on tour in Yugoslavia. And Eugenio Barba made a more detailed study during a short visit to India, which he transmitted to the Laboratory Theatre group on his return. Barba states that the purpose of the study was to acquaint himself with 'a special technique and assess the possibilities of adapting it for the training of European actors'. [122/37]

Grotowski has always had the highest praise for the attitude of Asian or Oriental actors, for their hard work, preparation and training. At a meeting in October 1971, in reply to a Japanese actor, Grotowski summed up his response as a respect for 'the morality of their work'. He explained this more fully through analogy with the difference between Eastern and European traditional sports. The traditional European objective is to acquire a skill in order to vanquish the opponent/enemy, whereas for the Oriental it was 'a means to go out of one's self, to meet life; in fact it is life itself, a way of existence. And there was something of that in the Oriental theatre, in their classic theatre'. [60/10]

Byrski, also, has identified this 'morality' as the one quality in which it is reasonable to draw parallels between the Laboratory Theatre work and classical Indian theatre. They both possess a similar quality of intent towards a state of being removed from daily life, and inspired by an exacting sincerity. Similarly, as a consequence of this morality, there exists in both theatres an element of selectivity of the audience, in the need for spectators with certain inherent attitudes. There are also more detailed connections that can be made – in the morality, in the aesthetic and in the training technique – by reference to Barba's study: for example in the use of the facial muscles to construct a mask; different parts of the body interacting with contrasting rhythm and emotion; or even the way in which props and costumes are regarded and used.

Eventually, however, in Grotowski's opinion, the training and techniques from Oriental and Asian theatre probably had minimal effect on the methods of the Laboratory Theatre actors. Despite the respect for the ethic, and the experimentation with Indian text and Chinese Opera training techniques, as well as other techniques such as yoga, Grotowski concluded that 'their aesthetic is completely alien to me. I do not think that we can adopt from them any techniques, or that they could inspire us directly.' [60/10] The basic point of divergence centred on the attitude towards gesture or sign. The classical Oriental and Indian theatres are theatres of alphabetical signs, learnt and passed down through generations. In Barba's words:

> Each gesture, each little motion is an ideogram which *writes out* the story and can be understood only if its conventional meaning is known. The spectator must learn the language, or rather the alphabet of the language, to understand what the actor is saying. [122/38]

In a talk given in 1969 to students at his theatre Grotowski summarized the three-part process of training in classical Oriental theatre as: (i) the memorizing and mastering of hundreds of gestural, corporal and vocal signs, (ii) the acquiring of basic bodily skills so that these signs may be accomplished without resistance and (iii), finally, acrobatic work to liberate the body from 'the natural inhibitions of space and gravity'. In theatre of this nature (and there are analogies with the training in classical mime) it is possible for particularly talented actors to achieve total mastery of their bodies and relative perfection in their craft, attaining practically to the status of sorcerer. Grotowski:

> When I visited the Peking Opera before the Cultural Revolution, I saw their classical production *The Monkey-King*. The same role was taken by the father one day and his son the next. All the elements of the role were identical, because in that theatre everything is codified – the signs are all the same. I did not see any difference. So I asked people why they were so enchanted the first day by the father, and so sceptical of the son the following day. They told me: 'It is because the son perspires under his arms when doing a somersault'. So the son was at the stage where the training was still visible. While the father – who undoubtedly maintained his training constantly – forgot about training during performance.... The father exemplifies the attainment of freedom through technique. [96/12–13]

Although Grotowski always acknowledged the basic lesson of 'sacred' theatre – that 'spontaneity and discipline, far from weakening each other, mutually reinforce themselves' [73/89] – he came to believe that theatre in the West cannot reach this essential balance through recourse to an orchestrated alphabet of gesture, because 'group identification with myth – the equation of personal, individual truth with universal truth – is virtually impossible today'. [73/23] This phenomenon, however, lost to the West through the erosion of religion, is still to a great extent a reality in the East. What is most personal and individual to the actor, therefore, is not revealed but concealed behind costume, make-up, gesture, vocal and bodily signs – all of these separate hieroglyphs being legible to the spectator within a universal frame of reference.

The conviction that such a 'group identification' is impossible in our culture led Grotowski, in time, to strip away everything inessential in a search for what is most basic and empathic in an individual: 'When all that is individual and innermost has been revealed, features of individual behaviour are eliminated; then the actor becomes a paradigm of human kind'. [202/89] In theatrical terms this research led from the construction of an artificial 'system of signs' to the search for an organic 'system of signs'. In an interview I conducted in 1981, Ludwik Flaszen made the semiological distinction between 'sign' and 'symptom' to clarify the transition:

> We can say that in the first period of work (of discipline and spontaneity) the symptoms of life nourished the signs, the construction. Later the contrary held true, and the score was the pretext for the manifestation of the symptoms. During these two phases both elements were present in the activity – but in the transformation a different quality, another hierarchy is created.

This, then, is the underlying principle of the concept of 'poor theatre' based, according to the Polish critic Jan Błoński, on the assumption that by a process of stripping down we will reach a spiritual substance common to all, we will reach 'that which is permanent and common, and thus communicable'. [161/147] This assumption should be borne clearly in mind throughout the rest of these chapters. It forms the basis of a major principle in the Laboratory Theatre work, one which in time conditioned the entire process of training and preparation of the actor.

In comparison with the meticulous preparation and training of the Oriental actor, however, there was little in the way of a tradition of training for the Western actor. Stanislavsky, indeed, attempted to correct the situation, and partly opened up the relevant areas for research, with his emphasis on the psychological disposition and motive of the actor. Pupils such as Meyerhold extended his research in their own ways into the mechanics of physical performance. When Grotowski and his company began to intensify and concentrate their research into actor training in the early years of their work together in Opole, they were prepared to draw upon every relevant source:

> Particular attention is paid in our Theatre to an actor's training and to an investigation of the laws governing the craft. Apart from rehearsals and performances actors do two or three hours of exercises daily.... This work is something like a scientific investigation. We are trying to discover those objective laws which govern the expression of an individual. We have preliminary material from the already elaborated systems of the art of acting, such as the methods of Stanislavsky, Meyerhold, Dullin, and the particular training methods in the classical Chinese and Japanese theatres, or the Indian dance drama of India. There are also the researches of the great European mime artists (e.g. Marceau), and the practitioners and theoreticians of expression; as well as the investigations of psychologists dealing with the mechanism of human reaction (Jung and Pavlov). [19/58]

As late as 1962, during the preparation for the production of *Akropolis*, there was

still evidence of the training techniques used by the Laboratory Theatre being
selected and employed almost exclusively for their potential scenic effect. In the
following extract retrospectively describing the work, however, can also be detected
the first indications of a shift in attitude to the training, whereby the releasing of
inner and personal impulses began to acquire significance:

> At certain moments in *Akropolis* we looked for how to rediscover a human
> expression which would not be sentimental in a tragic situation: that of prisoners
> in a concentration camp. To play that on an emotional level would be shameless
> and out of proportion. And so how to rediscover a bodily expression which would
> be fairly cold as a base? We took certain elements from mime and changed them;
> it did not remain classic mime, but we left the bare elements. They were
> continually transformed from the interior and transgressed by the living im-
> pulses of the actor. That creates a struggle between the structure and the living
> impulses. But to arrive at this point we worked quite a long time to absorb the
> mime exercises. We worked on the signs of the mime to the point where we
> became aware that these signs function as stereotypes blocking the process of
> personal impulses. [89/132]

Similarly Grotowski described the work on the facial mask, also undertaken at this
time for the production of *Akropolis*:

> At the beginning, for example, we even consciously sought a facial mask, by
> use of the muscles, and certain training of movements of different parts of the
> face, the eyebrows, the eyelids, the lips, the forehead, all that: centrifugal
> movements, centripetal movements, extravert-introvert, open–closed. This gave
> us the possibility of calculating different kinds of faces, of masks, but in the end
> it was without a doubt sterile.... We abandoned these researches, although the
> experience stayed with us and we have not hesitated to refer to it whenever
> necessary. As much may be said of many other experiences, other exercises.
> [89/136]

It was during the years 1963–1965, while still at Opole and preparing the productions *Dr. Faustus*, *The Hamlet Study* and *The Constant Prince*, that there began to
emerge and fully evolve the notion of a daily training for the actor. This arose from
the actors' own personal researches, and became completely separate from any idea
of a preparation for performance: it was a work on the *self* to liberate the self
from personal, inhibiting blockages and resistances which hamper the creative
flow. There were three basic categories of work that developed: (i) *exercises
plastiques* (ii) *exercises corporels* and (iii) vocal and respiratory work. There follows
here a brief description of the first two sets of exercises, borrowed from Margaret
Croyden, but the reader is also referred to Eugenio Barba's more detailed
descriptions of the exercises in *Towards a Poor Theatre*, since such a condensation
as follows must necessarily be crude:

> The exercises are divided into two basic categories: the corporeals and the

plastiques. The corporeals are a series of sharp acrobatic-like headstands, hand-stands, shoulderstands, and high jumps, done rapidly, continuously and frenetic-ally. The 'cat', the basic corporeal exercise, is designed primarily for energy and the suppleness of the vertebrae.... The plastiques are fast rotations back and forth of the joints: head, shoulders, elbows, wrists, hands, fingers, chest, hips, torso: also exercises of joints going in opposite or contradictory directions – the head going one way, the shoulders another for example. The exercises represent neither a formula nor a system; they are merely an approach, a way of leading one to find one's biological impulses. [213/163]

Croyden also quotes an American student who worked with Grotowski:

The exercises are designed to stress our capacity for balance, plasticity, fluidity and extension. Their purpose, however, was *not* that we develop physically, but that we learn, organically rather than cerebrally, 'essential things' about our bodies, such as resistances and points of balance. [213/163]

Of the *exercises plastiques* Grotowski has said:

In the body movements there are fixed forms, details that one can call forms. The first essential point is how to fix a certain quantity of details and make them precise. Then, how to rediscover the impulses, personal to us, which may be embodied in these details; to be embodied – that is to change them. Change them, but not to the point of destroying them. How at the beginning to improvise solely the order of the details, improvise the rhythm of the fixed details and then change the order and the rhythm and even the composition of details, not in a pre-meditated way but in the sense of a flow dictated by our own body. How to rediscover that 'spontaneous' line of the body which is incarnated in the details, which encircles them, which surpasses them but which, at the same time, preserves their precision. This is impossible if the details are 'gestural', that is if they involve the hands and legs and are not rooted in the totality of the body. [89/132]

What the Laboratory Theatre team were seeking in these particular exercises, then, was the possibility of an organic response, *rooted in the body*, and realized in accomplishment through precise details. Grotowski in fact went so far as to locate the organic source point of the reactive impulse – in the area of the body called in Polish 'the cross'. This, which Grotowski called 'the organic base of bodily reaction', is located at the base of the vertebral column including the lower pelvic area of the abdomen. There is a connection here worth noting, with *kundalini yoga*: according to this tradition there is a concentration of life energy, represented as a serpent coiled three and a half times, which is dormant at the base of the spine. But Grotowski has qualified this slightly:

The vertebral column is the centre of expression. The driving impulse, however, stems from the loins. Every live impulse begins in this region, even if invisible from the outside. [73/159]

Grotowski warns against the indiscriminate application of this piece of technical knowledge. Not because of the conventional caution with which the use of *kundalini* power is regarded (he has never acknowledged the connection), but because it is what he calls a 'relative truth'. It is something to be 'relatively' conscious of in order to 'unblock' the impulses, but never to be manipulated in exercises or during creative work, as this will inhibit the operation of what Grotowski calls 'body-memory'.

This title serves an associational function within the Laboratory Theatre work to facilitate a process that does not lend itself easily to conceptualization: that is, the activation of the motive and inspiration for reactive bodily impulse. According to Grotowski, we do not *possess* memory, our entire body *is* memory, and it is by means of the 'body-memory' that the impulses are released:

> If you begin to utilise precise details in the *exercises plastiques* and you tell yourself: now I must change the rhythm, now I must change the order of the details etc ... the 'body-memory' will not be liberated, precisely because you are giving yourself commands. But if you preserve the precision of the details and let the body dictate the different rhythms, all the time changing the rhythm and the order, taking another detail as if out of the air, at that moment who gives the command? It is not thought, but neither is it chance, it is related to our life. We do not even know how, but it is the 'body-memory' which is in command, related to certain experiences and certain cycles of experience in our life. [89/133]

There is a connection, of course, with Stanislavsky's 'emotional memory', the main function of which was to arouse inspiration, reaching towards the subconscious by means of the conscious. But Grotowski attempted to eliminate the 'conscious' as a distinctly ideational or analytic aspect of the process. In this respect he distinguished 'association' from 'thought' by a deliberate emphasis on the body:

> What is an association in our profession? It is something that springs not only from the mind but also from the body. It is a return towards a precise memory. Do not analyse this intellectually. Memories are always physical reactions. It is our skin which has not forgotten, our eyes which have not forgotten. What we have heard can still resound within us. [73/185–186]

The formulation of this approach owes a debt to William James's 'bodily sounding-board' and his insistence on the bodily nature of all emotive reaction to perceived stimuli. James experimented on himself and concluded that it was the automatic body response to a situation which constituted the emotion itself, rather than the mental perception of the experienced emotion. This was expressed in the famous example: 'I saw the bear, I ran, I became frightened'. (Interestingly enough James also avoided any formalized theory or system. According to Mel Gordon in an article in *The Drama Review*, James believed 'that while certain patterns of muscular activity elicited certain emotional states, each of these states varied with the individual body and were, therefore, infinite and unclassifiable' [266/77]). Grotowski at one stage made a study of developments in reflexology, the methodological extension of James's basic precept, and Meyerhold of course also made use of the researches being undertaken in Russia in the early decades of this century, in his experiments into the actor's state of 'reflex excitability'. [141/76] In fact Flaszen has stated that this was one of the most important aspects of Meyerhold's influence:

> For us, Meyerhold was important not as the formulator of concrete exercises or techniques, but as the inspiration of the theme that 'Biomechanics exists in the fact that behind each gesture of the actor, the whole of his body stands'. This formula was a major discovery. [143/314]

To return to Grotowski: the response of the actor in the exercises, he says, will not be organic if memory is conceived of as a function of the controlling intellect and not rooted in the body. The application of memory through mental command will not release the body-memory, and the resultant act will be divorced from its physiological roots and will not be wholly and fully accomplished. This concept is of course by no means unique to Grotowski and his work with the actor. It has had a revolutionary effect on psychiatric theory and practice this century, through the work of such radical thinkers as Wilhelm Reich, for example. The American, Arthur Janov (creator of the theory of Primal Therapy), has extended Reich's work, and in a book presenting his own theory he has said (in relation specifically to 'neurotic' needs):

> The need, then, is not just something mental stored away in the brain. It is coded into the tissue of the body, exerting a continuous force towards satisfaction. That force is experienced as a tension. We may say that the body 'remembers' its deprivations and needs just as the brain does. [287/62]

Similarly M. Feldenkrais, in a book based on a series of lectures he gave in the forties, wrote in the summary of his theory:

> Every emotion is, in one way or another, associated and linked in the cortex with some muscular configuration and attitude which has the same power of reinstating the whole situation as the sensory, vegetative or imaginary activity. [242/150]

The comparison with contemporary psychiatric theory is by no means far-fetched. Grotowski has frequently referred to the Laboratory Theatre actor-process as a form of analysis, or therapy for the actor, and by implication the spectator. In a manner reminiscent of an analytic psychiatrist Grotowski examines the states of being of his actors; the relationship of these to functioning social conditioning; the reciprocal effects of action/conditioning; and the effects of past and memory upon action. Similarly, Grotowski's theories relate to some schools of contemporary psychiatric practice in the central thesis that cerebral functioning has been over-emphasized in the past as a medium for comprehending the human condition.

To move on now to the *exercises corporels*: the area of work opened up by these was one that primarily concerned the crucial relationship of actors to their bodies.

This research, also, implied an analysis of states that are conventionally regarded as belonging in the province of psychiatry. According to Grotowski, actors find it difficult to accept their bodies, despite the conventional view of the actor as narcissistic. (In fact narcissism is an inherent symptom of the inability to accept one's body. It is easier to display the body once it has been objectified.) This condition involves more than just a primal shame in relation to the body – the body is, through a process of compensation, held responsible for the shortcomings in life, it becomes an 'intimate enemy'. This 'divided' or schizoid state (in extremity the classic schizophrenia) entails loss of security for actors in relation to the body, which objectively is the instrument of their craft. (C.f. Flaszen's comments concerning the preparation of *Shakuntala* on page 31.) Such a condition is antipathetic to the state of being required for creative work, which demands psychic unity and trust. But, in Grotowski's terms, the state of self-acceptance and wholeness necessary for creative work is paradoxically only possible by transcendence of both self and the body. The *exercises corporels* provided the basis for this area of work.

The *corporels* were, in an obvious sense, more physically demanding than the *exercises plastiques*. Many of them were based on *hatha-yoga* and there was a gymnastic element which gave them a quality of challenge. It was in confronting this challenge and being triumphant, Grotowski believed, that the actor transcended the ordinary, everyday 'self'. Grotowski described this as attaining to a condition of 'primal trust', in which we are led by our natures (and there are interesting parallels here with Taoist philosophy):

> ... when you perform a somersault in space which you are usually not able to do because it seems impossible, you regain some trust in yourself. How do you do that somersault? To discover that somersault, that crossing of the impossible – that is what the individual exercising has to do alone, in his own way, taking his own risks. Only then will it be useful. You have to discover the unknown, and the secret is revealed by the very nature of the one in action.... It is not knowing how to do things that is necessary, but not hesitating when faced with a challenge, when you have to achieve the unknown, and do it leaving the 'way' (in so far as this is possible) to your own nature. [63/112]

As usual, Grotowski cautioned about the attitude with which one confronts this process – it can never be a voluntary, active attitude, which is the result of intellectual control and perpetuates the split condition:

> Some actors, in the so-called *exercises corporels*, torture and martyrise themselves. This is not transcending, because it is active. Transcendence is a question of not defending ourselves in the face of transcendence. There is something which we must do which surpasses us; even a simple somersault in the *exercises corporels*, with certain limited but real risks that we must take; there may also possibly be pain – it is enough not to defend ourselves, to take the risks. [89/134]

What is necessary is what Grotowski called a 'non-active process' or 'via negativa'. This was a guiding principle of all the physical training. In terms of the exercises it demands an emphasis on the elimination of the muscular blockage that inhibits free, creative reaction, rather than a positive, methodical acquisition of physical skills. 'The result is freedom from the time-lapse between inner impulse and outer reaction in such a way that the impulse is already an outer reaction.' [73/16] This is an empirically verifiable proposition, and a familiar precept in, for example, the training of a gymnast. In an article in *The Drama Review* on 'Zen and the Actor' (which will be returned to in more detail in the next chapter), David Feldshuh further elaborates on this point:

> In Zen there is a word for the division between mind and activity. It is *suki* which means 'a space between two objects' or 'a slit or split or crack in one solid object' (Alan Watts, *The Way of Zen*). All separations between thinking and acting are forms of suki and result in a stopping that breaks up the flow of creativity and responsiveness.... On the level of physical movement, *suki* imposes an overlay of thought that may hinder expressive and spontaneous movement. [244/83]

Apart from its physical application this attitude also has an ethical application, and this is the key to what elevated the *craft* of the Laboratory Theatre actor to a transcendent *art*. Grotowski stated categorically that the process is 'not voluntary. The requisite state of mind is a passive readiness to realize an active role, a state in which one does not *want to do that* but rather *resigns from not doing it*'. [73/17] Grotowski also refers to this as 'internal passivity'. It is not a comfortable concept for the Western mind, which tends to prefer positive, intellect-guided action, but it has direct parallels with the Taoist principle of *wu-wei*. This translates literally as 'non-action', and Joseph Needham (in his massive and authoritative reference work on China) elaborates it as 'refraining from action contrary to nature.' He also quotes from Chuang-Tzu: 'Non-action does not mean doing nothing and keeping silent. Let everything be allowed to do what it naturally does, so that its nature will be satisfied'. [355/68–69] Lao Tzu, in Chapter 48 of the Tao Te Ching, puts it more succinctly: 'By non-action everything can be done'.

The above principle – of 'refraining from action contrary to nature' – can be said to apply perhaps with most effectiveness in the area of the vocal and respiratory work. Vocal, as much as physical research is something that the Laboratory Theatre is renowned for, and it is in this area that they have achieved what are probably the most spectacular 'results' (in terms of discovery). But when talking about their vocal and respiratory work it is not the discoveries (such as the 'resonators') that Grotowski emphasizes. Rather, yet again, it is the principle of the via negativa, non-interference, the discovery of blockages, the discovery of the 'natural voice' and the 'natural respiration'. In a talk given to students at his theatre in 1969, Grotowski summarized the company's work on the voice. In this summary he claimed that the majority of problems in vocal and respiratory work arise either (i) from a conscious interference in and manipulation of respiration or (ii) from a blockage of the larynx, often brought about by artificial vocal training techniques in schools (such as exercises for prolongation of breath, or exercises stressing consonants):

... if the actor has no problem with air, if at the moment of action he inhales as much as is needed, this must not be meddled with, even if according to all theories he is breathing incorrectly. If he starts to interfere in his own organic process, the problems begin.... We must not control our own process of respiration; instead it's necessary to know our own blockages and resistances, and that's another matter entirely.... There is no ideal model of respiration, there exists instead something like an unblocking of natural respiration. [90/110–112]

Grotowski does give indications of how to unblock the 'natural respiration', but with caution, continually emphasizing the 'non-active' aspect of the approach. Similarly, he provides professional and technical information on work with the open and closed larynx (acknowledging a debt to Chinese vocal training techniques). But here he is even more cautious. There may well be a value in artificially producing an 'unblocked' voice from an actor by various techniques to open the larynx, but such conscious work carries dangers both on the obvious physiological level, and on the level of the actor's own process of self-liberation:

> The initial danger has arisen again, that the actor repeating this exercise begins to observe himself and to manipulate his own vocal apparatus. Thus his larynx may remain open, but his voice will not be organic. [90/115]

Grotowski lists in some detail the practical researches they drew upon: Chinese classical opera; Louis Armstrong recordings; African singing; Italian Opera; *hatha-yoga* respiratory exercises. But in the end these were rejected as being too conscious and manipulatory. Grotowski fell back upon much simpler and more 'organic' directives:

> Undoubtedly the outbreath carries the voice. And undoubtedly that is a physical act and not some kind of metaphor or something imperceptible.... But to be able to carry the voice, it must be organic and open. The larynx must be open. And you don't get this through some kind of technical manipulation of the vocal apparatus. Maybe there exists on this point only one piece of advice which can be given to actors: not to economise on air.... They must then be told: it's precisely the air that carries the voice. Use the air. Don't economise. Take air when it's necessary, and afterwards don't economise on it. It is that that works, it's not the vocal apparatus but the outbreath.
>
> If you want the voice to carry far use the air, all the way as far as this imaginary, maybe even fantastic point, since it is so incredibly distant, yes, that's it, throw the air out with the voice, breathe out. Don't economise it. [90/117–118]

Finally, Grotowski also describes in great detail their discovery of, and research into the 'resonators' of the body – those focal points of the body where the voice may be amplified and given particular added qualities. The discoveries progressed through personal, associational work – e.g. occipital resonator = Chinese language; abdominal resonator = Buddha belly/cow; vertebral resonator = cat. But once again, Grotowski realized in time that the work was becoming too conscious, which only recreated blockages. Further research disclosed that the way to free the process, and restore the spontaneous, creative value was initially to work with physical echoes:

> By the simple fact of acting in different directions in real space, different resonators begin to work by themselves. The voice is not automatic, it is neither hard, nor heavy. It is living. The whole attention is directed towards the outside: an echo is created – an external phenomenon, and the echo is heard – from the outside, which is natural. Because the actor cannot avoid the tendency to listen closely to himself, he can therefore listen to his echo. And in this case the process can be organic. [90/120]

This was reinforced by associational work, implicating again the use of 'body-memory': 'Everything which is associational and directed in space frees the voice. It frees – particularly in studies – not some cold impulse, but researches in the field of our own recollections, our body-memory. This creates the voice'. [90/121]

This description of the different categories of training developed through research at the Laboratory Theatre, and some of the principles informing their application, has of necessity been only a brief summary of what is a very rich and complex area for study. But hopefully it has served to underline the central direction the researches were taking, within the theatrical phase of work (i.e. until 1970). Grotowski's propositions indicate that this research was based on certain assumptions: firstly – that there exists something in the nature of a natural, organic flow of impulse towards action, sound and expression in the individual human being; and secondly – that this flow, if released, is in some way 'creative' and forms the material for artistic expression (see again Błoński's comments, page 117).

This flow of impulses tends to be impeded or inhibited in the individual by psycho–physiological blockages. Although Grotowski only ever talks in very generalized terms about what these blockages are, one can infer from compatible psychological and spiritual theories that they relate in some way to an individual's past conditioning. The Laboratory Theatre training programme, as it evolved in time, was concerned on an individual level with the eradication of these blockages and the freeing of the impulses. The evolution of this training indicated a transference of emphasis from the 'end result' (i.e. the final artistic product on stage) to the 'means' (the work upon the actor's self.)

In a talk given in New York in 1978, Grotowski emphasized this final point yet again:

> You can say a thousand times that the work is constructed as a process, and not as a product resulting from a process, that, for example there is no division in the work between phases of rehearsal and performances, and still there will be questions posed concerning the results, the product, the production.... In the context of contemporary civilisation it is difficult to understand that the

experience of a process may be important – and not its product, its result. . . . There are not enough words to stress this. [84/95]

The exercises and training that were part of this process, then, were to liberate the actors from the learned and conditioned blockages that belonged to them – in other words to transform them by a psycho-physical process. This was indeed very far from any concept of 'acquiring skills' which is the normal application of actor-training, and is closer, in fact, to psychiatric therapy or a spiritual training. Looked at in this way, it is obvious that the significance and role of the director, as well as the actor, must also change. In this situation it is essential to have a director/teacher with the skill to perceive individual blockages, avoidances and needs and to apply the appropriate course of training. This surpasses by far the conventional role of the director, and refers us back again to the shamanistic view of Grotowski's role within his theatre described in Chapter Three (page 52). It is also obvious that such an approach raises many questions concerning the process of construction of the theatrical product, the performance process, and the director's role in this: these questions will be considered in the following two chapters.

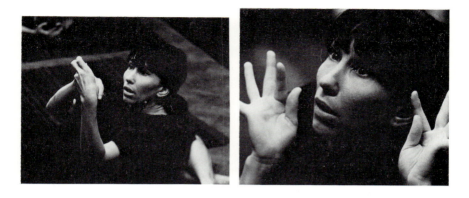

Training
55 Rena Mirecka.

56 Rena Mirecka.

57 Zygmunt Molik.

58 Rena Mirecka
and Zygmunt Molik.

59 Ryszard Cieślak.

CHAPTER SEVEN
Performance

And in order to create, contrary to what is believed, there are no established and infallible rules which permit the transformation from actor to creator, the making of a great actor. There is but one given objective: each actor is the victim of a certain blockage, of psychic or physical origin, which contradicts the creative process. And for each the blockages are different. The method of work consists in discovering and surpassing these difficulties in order to give oneself a liberating technique. And if someone arrives at the point of eliminating the blockages, and the destiny of such an actor is truly to create, then he will be radiant, at centre. [150/250–251]

Few would disagree that all of Grotowski's theatrical work and research can be described as messianic. Throughout his work he has held to the conviction that theatre (including the post- and pre-theatrical forms he has researched) can be a means of changing people – actors and audience. It can improve the quality of life and contribute in some way to the overall development and evolution of the human race. In an interview in 1958 Grotowski described theatre as 'a moral and social mission – built on a core of intellectual values, committed to progress, proposing a new secular and rational ethic'. [9] Such a messianic belief breathes through every word he speaks, and is perhaps not such a strange outcome of his formative years, with the combination of Marxism and a personal fascination with the spiritually-developing philosophies of the East.

How humankind may be changed and the life-experience of the individual improved is also self-evident in Grotowski's words and work. What is required is the healing of the mind/body split (Western society's schizophrenia); the eradication of the psycho-physiological blockages in the individual to permit contact with deeper impulses; a communion with others through spontaneous reaction; and hence a mutual discovery of sources of energy, light and love to enrich daily experience. All of Grotowski's work was implicitly towards these ends, and it is on this level that commentators (such as Planchon) refer to Grotowski's 'means' already being 'ends'. [366] Because what is described above *is*, for Grotowski, the 'acting process' or 'creative process'.

If the act takes place, then the actor, that is to say the human being, transcends the state of incompleteness to which we condemn ourselves in everyday life. The division between thought and feeling, body and soul, consciousness and the unconscious, seeing and instinct, sex and brain then disappears; having fulfilled this, the actor achieves totality. When he can take this act to its limit, he is far less tired after than before, because he has renewed himself, recovered his primitive indivisibility; and there begin to act in him new sources of energy. [46/73]

But Grotowski also foresaw the possibility for this life-enhancing experience to be extended towards the spectator in a shared experience with the actor, and the progress of his work was a continuous exploration in search of this possibility. Initially, he believed that this could be achieved by recreating ritual in theatre:

I was of the opinion that as it was in fact primitive rites that brought theatre into being, so through a return to ritual – in which two groups participate, so to speak: the actors or leaders, and the spectators or indeed participants – may be rediscovered that ceremonial of direct, living collaboration, a particular interaction (rare in our times), a direct, open, free and authentic response ... if the actor through his action in relation to the spectator motivates him, incites him to participation, even provoking him to precise ways of behaving, of movement, song, verbal replies etc., that should enable the restoration of that primitive, ritualistic unity. [46/64–65]

The early work, then, was supposedly directed towards achieving an authentic experience of ritual within contemporary theatre. To this end Grotowski undertook experiments in all the different aspects of theatre: the ordering of theatrical space; the manipulation of the physical and psychological aspects of the actor/spectator relationship; the anarchic use of text and literature:

I had of course certain initial concepts, for example that one must bring together the actors and the audience face to face, as it were, in space – and that one should look for that reciprocal exchange of reaction whether in the domain of language itself, or whether in the domain of theatrical language, and therefore propose to the spectator his participation. [46/64]

At this stage Grotowski believed that if the right theatrical circumstances were only created, ritual – with its unifying and life-giving qualities – would inevitably take place. And so in his earliest productions (described in Chapter Two) Grotowski assumed the conventional director's role with regard to the construction of the performances, preparing his concept of the production in advance of the short rehearsal periods. And even when more time was devoted to the rehearsal phase, the actor's research and training was directed towards the accomplishment of predetermined and conceptualized actions, gestures and scenic effects. Ludwik Flaszen has described this attitude:

When Grotowski began, he had many calculated ideas. It was basic to his way. He approached work with ideas determined *a priori*. He knew what he wanted. The result was as if drawn by him on paper. I observed in his first productions a contradiction between the calculated part of him (his 'constructivism' –

Meyerhold was such a strong influence) and that part which had been unconsciously born in his productions. There was a distinct divergence. [143/304]

What Grotowski was searching for at this point in terms of the physical performance of the actor was (as he stated clearly when talking of the production
Shakuntala, for instance, page 114) a 'system of signs'. This would serve a ceremonial function in invoking the spectator's involuntary, or subconscious participation. He knew full well that the European theatre could not rely upon a system
of ideograms or hieroglyphs in the same way as the Oriental and Asian sacred
theatres – the actors and spectators of those theatres had a mutually accepted and
recognized system of signs based on tradition. Referring, in his chapter on Artaud
in *Towards a Poor Theatre*, to the balance of spontaneity and discipline in these
sacred theatres, Grotowski wrote: 'what is elementary feeds what is constructed and
vice versa'. [73/89] When referring specifically, say, to Kathakali, the 'elemental'
is the numinous network of religious, mythic and cultural beliefs and mores that
find shape and expression in the 'constructed' hieroglyphs. Grotowski's research
at this stage, therefore, was aimed at discovering the 'elemental' in our Western
and European culture, and embodying this within a structure.

To this end Grotowski turned to literary masterpieces of European (and specifically Polish) culture: *Dziady*, *Akropolis*, *Kordian* and *Dr. Faustus*. These, he believed, embodied myths and images powerful and universal enough to function as
archetypes, which could penetrate beneath the apparently divisive and individual
structure of the Western psyche, and evoke a spontaneous, collective, internal
response. This would be the common, shared experience which constituted ritual.
Rehearsal work at this stage, therefore, was directed towards the discovery, with
the actors, of these signs or images:

> We are especially interested in an aspect of acting which has seldom been
> studied: the association of gesture and intonation with a definite image. For
> example, the actor stops in the middle of a race and takes the stance of a cavalry
> soldier charging, as in the old popular drawings. This method of acting evokes
> by association images deeply rooted in the collective imagination. [115/159]

According to all that Grotowski postulated, then, the articulation by signs, constructed consciously in rehearsal work and realized scenically by the actor, should
awaken within us some complementary recognition of sign and symbol, or 'activation of the timeless symbols within our subconscious' [290] as Helmut Kajzar put
it. Grotowski stated explicitly: 'The elaboration of artificiality is a question of
ideograms – sounds and gestures – which evoke associations in the psyche of the
audience'. [73/39] What was being proposed, in fact, was a means of communication
that would exceed the possibilities of verbal expression: a language beyond words
– the dream of every artist (even those who deal in words):

> He must be able to express, through sound and movement, those impulses
> which waver on the borderline between dream and reality. In short, he must be

able to construct his own psycho–analytic language of sounds and gestures in the same way that a great poet creates his own language of words. [73/35]

Eventually, however, Grotowski had to abandon the search for a ritualistic co-participation of actor and spectator. Not only was there the absence of a '"common sky" of beliefs', [73/23] but Grotowski became aware that within their own work they were falling into stylization, in the conscious imitation of mythic images. It is also evident from this perspective that there was a confusion in his work between intellectuality and spontaneity which was most apparent in the attitude towards the spectator. Whilst on the one hand postulating the possibility of participation in healing ritual and ceremony, there was at the same time a sense of distance being created by the treatment of their material and a degree of overt manipulation of the audience. Flaszen specifically says: 'In the early days, the actors attacked the audience and parodied them with malice and unpleasant humour (the best examples are *Dziady*, *Shakuntala* and *Cain*)'. [143/309] This obviously set up an atmosphere of ambivalence which must have undermined the efforts to break through the audience's intellectual conditioning. Within this situation it was well-nigh impossible for any authentic reaction to take place, and it was the lack of authenticity that led Grotowski to abandon this line of research.

Grotowski has made it clear in retrospect that this change of emphasis took place about 1962/1963, after the production of *Kordian* (in which the final conscious efforts had been made at evoking direct response from the spectators) and during the preparation for *Akropolis*, and later *Dr. Faustus*. The spectator was relegated (for the time being) to the role of observer/witness:

> Almost as soon as we abandoned the idea of a conscious manipulation of the audience, I let go of the idea of myself as a producer of performances and consequently – which seems logical to me – I set out on an exploration of the creative possibilities of the actor. [46/70]

In interview the actor Zbigniew Cynkutis was even more specific about the chronology of this development: he said that during the work on the production *Dr. Faustus* (December 1962 – April 1963) Grotowski 'changed totally his relationship towards the actor':

> Up to this point the actor had been a man to be used during performance, manipulated, his solutions suggested for him. But during the work for *Dr. Faustus* he began to listen to the actors. He was listening, watching, trying to fix something almost impossible to fix, points that may not have been aesthetically interesting, but were important as part of the process.

It was also during this phase that the Laboratory Theatre exercises developed, as part of a daily training for the actors that was distinctly separate from a preparation for performance, and functioned rather as work undertaken by the actors on their own selves. What was emerging for Grotowski, was a vision of the actor as an individual capable of divesting her or himself of the social, conditioned layers of the psyche, and revealing themselves at a level beneath the individual or personal. In performance the shock of this exposure should enable the spectator to reciprocate internally. At this point, according to Grotowski, the personal and the collective converge, and the act of exposure functions in the place of the communally-held beliefs of primitive societies which permit ritual to take place. And so the training and preparation work shifted perspective from the construction of the artistic product (the performance) to the process of the actors, to enable them to reach the requisite level of exposure, in what Grotowski called the 'total act'.

To refer back now to the summary made at the end of the preceding chapter, we can say that if the Laboratory Theatre training consisted, in brief, of the liberation of the actor from the personalized inhibitions and blockages that impede the flow of creative impulses, then preparation for performance consequently dealt with the way this flow was (i) stimulated, (ii) channelled and structured and, finally, (iii) effectively and meaningfully transmitted onto the stage on a regular basis for performance.

So what was the work that developed in the Laboratory Theatre as a preparation for and construction of a performance? Raymonde Temkine has described what she calls 'articulation of the role' in Grotowski's productions as a three-part process: initial structuring, performed by Grotowski on an original text; a collective phase of elaboration, involving a great deal of spontaneous creative work; and finally the structured composition of the role into a 'system of signs' [415/111–113] (Grotowski's 'acting score'). Until *The Constant Prince* and even in the early stages of what was later to become *Apocalypsis Cum Figuris* this was always work based upon an original text, most often from the Polish Romantic tradition. Grotowski:

> The initial montage is done before rehearsals begin. But during rehearsals we do additional montage all the time. . . . We eliminate those parts of the text which have no importance for us, those parts with which we can neither agree nor disagree. Within the montage one finds certain words that function vis-à-vis our own experiences. . . . It's a meeting, a confrontation. That's why there must be little interpolation. But there is rearrangement of words, scenes. We organise the event according to the logic of our cues. But the essential parts of the text – those which carry the sense of the literary work – remain intact and are treated with great respect. Otherwise there could be no meeting. [42/44–45]

This crystallized version of some great literary work was then taken into the early phase of rehearsals, where it was used as a reference point, or point of confrontation, for the creative work emanating from the actor. This period of preparatory work, up until the actual fixing of the acting score, could most probably be called the heart of the Laboratory Theatre creative process. Grotowski has stated on many occasions that this was when the most important work took place.

The work undertaken at this stage was clearly improvisational in nature, although Grotowski has rejected the term itself. He came in time to feel that the notion of 'improvisation' had been devalued by being most often associated with the affirmatory and supportive psychology which Peter Brook has called 'the first delusion of the Underground.' [398/80] Grotowski accused those who claim to use techniques of improvisation (and he was most critical of American groups) of looking for emotional security and support in their work. This attitude in turn, he felt, is based on a false understanding of the mechanisms of 'spontaneity': work is undertaken on the premise of the existence of a 'natural spontaneity' which is supposedly evident in the rituals of more 'primitive' societies. This leads, Grotowski claimed, to the most chaotic and hypocritical of performances, with actors imitating 'primitive' behaviour. In an interview in 1969 with Marc Fumaroli, he defined the danger in a working situation of

> confusing my comfort with the free development of my nature. If, as an actor, comfort became my main care, I would forget that rehearsals are for the creation of scenic facts, and that all my work should be determined by the necessity of arriving at those facts.... My efforts, or rather, the by-products of my inertia would have only one end – to identify what is *personal* and what is *private*. This is called 'improvisation'. Once, perhaps, this word meant something. Today it is no more than a pretentious word serving as a substitute for work. [47/173]

Rejecting the term 'improvisation', then, Grotowski called the preparatory work sessions at the Laboratory Theatre 'studies' or 'sketches'. What he postulated for these, as an alternative to what he saw as the corruption of the improvisation principle, was a return 'to the experience of my own life, towards my own life in person, flesh and blood, external and internal intimacy'. [47/173] This must be attended by the same detailed precision that Grotowski demanded in the exercises and training: 'I am obliged to create very precise sketches which have surged up from the concrete facts of my personal experience.... I am obliged to be precise in my work'. [47/174] In this, the creative work at the Laboratory Theatre followed more closely Peter Brook's definition in that it

> aims at bringing the actor again and again to his own barriers, to the points where, in the place of new-found truth he normally substitutes a lie ... If the actor can find and see this moment he can perhaps open himself to a deeper, more creative impulse. [181/126]

The distinctions here, so far as they can be drawn theoretically, are subtle, implicating as they do both attitude and technique. For, despite Grotowski's attempts to disassociate himself from 'improvisation', both attitudes to work are based on the theory that by liberating the creative impulse from the physiological and psychological blockages and healing the mind/body split to permit spontaneous response, the actor is freeing the psychological riches of the unconscious (or even Jung's 'collective unconscious') as the material of a creative representation. But for Grotowski this is only part of the equation, because this process must be linked to consciousness and structure, and this is where he feels so many groups using improvisation go wrong. All primitive rituals appear to be based exclusively on spontaneity, but for the true participant, says Grotowski, there also exists a 'very precise liturgy':

> There exists a primitive order, a certain line prepared in advance, distilled from collective experience, an entire order which becomes a base. It is precisely around this liturgy that variations are woven: thus it is at the same time spontaneous and prepared in advance. [46/71]

This again, then, is Grotowski's 'true lesson' of sacred theatre, that spontaneity and discipline strengthen each other. He called this paradoxical relationship '*conjunctio oppositorum*', and it remained the single most important principle of performance work at the Laboratory Theatre. It was a principle that Grotowski felt no Western director had previously fully grasped. He claimed that neither Stanislavsky 'who let the natural impulses dominate' nor Brecht 'who gave too much emphasis to the construction of a role' understood it, and in a similar over-simplification, he juxtaposed the ideas of Stanislavsky and Meyerhold:

> Meyerhold based his work on discipline, exterior formation; Stanislavsky on the spontaneity of daily life. These are, in fact, the two complementary aspects of the creative process. [73/177]

The Polish critic, Jan Błoński, drew a similar comparison between Brecht and the Living Theatre: he saw the two companies as being on opposite sides in the struggle to resolve the basic theatrical contradiction – which theatre reformers are constantly seeking to resolve – 'between art and reality, engaged in battle for the theatrical spectacle'. [161/146] This recalls Martin Esslin's definition of drama as a fusion between reality and illusion, which 'compared to other illusion-producing arts . . . contains a far greater element of reality'. [236/86] It is precisely in the actor, Esslin pointed out, that these elements of reality and illusion meet. He also referred to the Living Theatre, whom he described as having 'developed a technique which made reality and illusion merge in new ways'. [236/93] He was referring to the Living Theatre practice of consciously involving the authentic reactions of spectators: 'Here theatre veers away from fiction and becomes a manipulation of reality'. [236/93]

This polarity of reality and illusion takes the form for the actor of Grotowski's *conjunctio oppositorum* – the contradiction between spontaneity and discipline. The actor brings the reality/spontaneity of her or his experience and humanity to the discipline/illusion of the stage role. Grotowski is perhaps rare amongst theatre reformers in his aim not to 'resolve' this conflict, but admit it as a fundamental and necessary interaction of theatre, and utilize the resultant tension of the balance. Flaszen has said that the Laboratory Theatre actor 'can be compared to a metaphor in contemporary poetry, where you cannot separate the meaning from the sign, because between these two values there exists a continuous interacting of energy, tying them together'. [269] Other reformers have attempted to give prominence to one or the other side of the conflict – Brecht towards intellect-orientated discipline, the Living Theatre towards life-like spontaneity, but in both cases something is lost. Only by acknowledging and engaging in the conflict can the power be released (as electric current flows between opposite charges). In effect, the actor must offer her- or himself as a conductor between the opposing poles of discipline and spontaneity, to permit the current to flow. Grotowski:

> The tropistic tension between the inner process and the form strengthens both. The form is like a baited trap, to which the spiritual process responds spontaneously and against which it struggles. [73/17]

In addition to the application of the principle of *conjunctio oppositorum* in the work on the construction of a performance, there were other key phrases Grotowski used which related to particular aspects of the process: body-memory; body-life; association; impulse; partner/screen. Actors in creative research, Grotowski says, must search within their 'body-memory' and 'body-life' for the inner response to the external stimuli or confrontation (i.e. the text, or the actor-colleagues present). As we saw when examining the concept of body-memory in relation to the actor training exercises, Grotowski underlined the corporal aspect of the process, in line with much contemporary thought in psychiatric practice. Stanislavsky, for example, through his application of 'emotional memory', founded much of his work on the belief that true emotional experience is dependent upon will. Grotowski, at least during the theatrical phase of his researches, insisted that this was patently untrue: 'These recollections (from the past and from the future) are recognized or discovered through what is carnal in nature ... in other words body-life'. [94/117] If we give ourselves freely to this process, said Grotowski, there is released from within the being an impulse, which is concretized as an association, or a physical action. This process, he continually stressed, can only happen in a living relationship to something else:

> Each physical action is preceded by an inner movement, which flows from the interior of the body, unknown but concrete. The impulse does not exist without a partner. Not in the sense of a partner in acting, but in the sense of another human being. Or simply – another being. [94/117]

Therefore, Grotowski elaborated, the association is an action which is simultaneously a response to memory and imagination (i.e. body-memory – what has been or what may be) projected onto one's partner as onto a screen, and at the same time an impulse incarnated *in this moment* as a response to one's partner (i.e. body-life).

These 'studies' or 'sketches' as Grotowski has called them, form the base material for what will eventually become the 'acting score'. This is the concrete and disciplined structure, akin to Stanislavsky's 'prepared line of action', which Grotowski insisted is indispensable to a work of theatrical art:

> Finally, creativity in theatre does not exist if there is no score, a line of fixed elements ... What is an acting score? That is the essential question. The acting score is the elements of contact. To take and to give the reactions and impulses of contact. If you fix these, then you will have fixed all the contexts of your associations. Without a fixed score a work of mature art cannot exist. That's why

a search for discipline and structure is as inevitable as a search for spontaneity. Searching for spontaneity without order always leads to chaos, a lost confession, because an inarticulate voice cannot confess. [42/45]

The actual phase of constructing the score is a long process of work undertaken by Grotowski and the actor.

To begin with there exists that score of living impulses which can then be articulated into a system of signs. . . . When such a sketch is already living there are sought in it the essential points, the impulses, which can be recorded, obviously not in writing, but in the body. When it is recorded the actor can repeat it many times, eliminating everything that is not essential; and so there remains the conditioned reflex, based on 'recorded' points, and such a sketch becomes a small fragment of the work. As a rule that is so much more interesting than structures contrived by the director. [46/72]

In a chapter of her book dedicated to Grotowski, the American critic Margaret Croyden has condensed the whole process described above into her own words, and it is quoted here as a recapitulation:

During rehearsal, the actor's physical actions arising from impulses are scored and fixed; that is, a physical action becomes a 'sign'. A 'sign' is an outward response to a pure impulse that precedes that response, action or sound. The finished performance is composed of such signs, and scored like music by the director. . . . The score is a complete cycle of physical actions attached to impulses, which are linked up moment to moment so that the performance is tightly knit. Supposedly these signs, when added up, are easily discernible by the spectators. [213/167]

In Grotowski's theatre the director is an essential and creative part of this process: there is no room here for Meyerhold's dual actor/observer, described by Meyerhold as embodying 'both the organizer and that which is organized'. (The precise formula was expressed as follows: '$N = A_1 + A_2$ where $N =$ the actor, A_1 the artist who conceives the idea and issues the instructions necessary for its execution, $A_2 =$ the executant who executes the conception of A_1'. [171/198]) For Grotowski, the realization of the fertile conditions for productive creative work is dependent not on the conceptual organizational ability of his actors, but on the nature of the working relationship between actor and director:

There is something incomparably intimate and productive in the work with the actor entrusted to me. He must be attentive and confident and free, for our labour is to explore his possibilities to the utmost. [73/25]

Within this relationship it is the director in the final analysis who is able to encourage the journey to and beyond the actor's psychical barriers, to select from this process the points of truth in the actor's work and, most importantly, to manipulate and utilize the precise sketches arrived at to build up a creatively cohesive score – the 'system of signs'. Grotowski himself has described this process in the following very simplistic terms:

> Working as a director I can say to the actor: 'I believe' or 'I understand'. In the phase of researching the live impulses, that line, that flowing out from oneself, I use 'I believe' or 'I do not believe'. Next, when there is the question of structuralisation in daily work, I use rather 'I understand' or 'I do not understand'. When I say 'I understand' or 'I do not understand' it concerns significantly the non-abstract aspect of a sign. 'I do not understand' – in other words that may exist, but only for you. If it also exists for others, it has meaning, and you unintentionally created a sign. Next, if I say 'I believe', this signifies that you maintained that life-line, that line of living impulses. [46/72]

What Grotowski was emphasizing again is that this process, for the actor, is essentially not intellectual in nature and that over-conceptualization or verbalization would impede the process.

> In rehearsals I did not look for this in words, in some terminology. Between the actor and myself there took place a kind of intimate drama. We looked for sincerity and revelation, not needing words. In fact this is only possible in relation to someone else. For me this became possible in relation to the actor, as a being. I looked for the conditions in which that could be possible for the actor in relation to me. [94/116]

Another light on the process has been thrown by the actor Zbigniew Cynkutis, who has attempted in interview to describe what happened from the actor's point of view:

> Grotowski was listening, watching, trying to fix something almost impossible to fix, points that may not have been aesthetically interesting, but were important as part of the process. I remember that he selected from improvisation points that weren't even important for me – but he was using them as reminders, bringing them to my notice. He recalled for me, for instance, certain positions of my body, or the place I was in – not *how* I did something, but *where* I was and *what* I did, without attention to the quality of voice or intensity of action – and when I tried to repeat it, by means of these small details the process returned. And I was able, never to repeat exactly what I had done before, but to improvise again. And the more often we worked that way, the easier and more certain it became that there was a real possibility, to fix something that seems impossible to fix. And something that leads not to repetition, but to re-improvisation, re-creation.

Once the acting score for a production had been crystallized and fixed by this process, there began the long work for the actors of assimilating and absorbing the score, letting it soak into the skin until the actions were both rigidly orchestrated and as fluent as instinct – at the same time working on maintaining the life of the score, of each moment, each minute action and reaction. Bearing in mind the emphasis in this work on the discipline of the structure, and the fact that the Laboratory Theatre's later, more celebrated productions were presented on tour and in Poland over a period of several years (twelve in the case of *Apocalypsis Cum Figuris*), how was continuing vitality assured for the process? In so far as the Laboratory Theatre work *was* a process, this implies the fact that, in attitude, there was no division between periods of preparation of a production, and periods of performance. In this respect the same basic principles applied to the performance work as have been described in relation to the preparation.

On the one hand there was operative, as always, that interdependence of spontaneity and discipline that underlies all Laboratory Theatre practice:

> It consists, for example, in the analysis of a hand's reflex during a psychic process and its successive development through shoulder, elbow, wrist and fingers in order to decide how each phase of this process can be expressed through a sign, an ideogram, which either instantly conveys the hidden motives of the actor or polemicises against them. . . . The more we become absorbed in what is hidden inside us, in the excess, in the exposure, in the self-penetration, the more rigid must be the external discipline; that is to say the form, the artificiality, the ideogram, the sign. Here lies the whole principle of expressiveness. [73/39]

Flaszen has referred in interview to Grotowski's metaphor of the horse's bridle to further illustrate this point. A bridle used on a horse will augment the intensity of its reactions: 'In other words, if you restrain by discipline what is spontaneous, the force of the actor's art increases'.

Allied to this was a principle which Grotowski described in his interview with Richard Schechner in 1967 as 'unity of action'. This is not, however, the classical 'unity of action' of a play:

> The audience knows that they are not seeing the real Hamlet in Denmark. One must always look for the word-for-word truth. The audience can watch the process of the confrontation – the story and its motives meeting the stories and motives in our own lives. If there is this contradictory action, this meeting, if the audience sees all these small details which lift the confrontation into flight, if they, as spectators, become part of this confrontation, we have the essential unity of action. [42/45]

This technique could be called an evolution, within a performance principle, beyond Grotowski's own concept of 'body-memory' – applied in the training techniques and in the preparation of a production – towards a total awareness of the present (body-life). Grotowski believed it possible for the actor, at every stage in the performance process, to test each aspect and action of role-life against personal experience in the moment. The reaction, which may be sympathetic, negative, reinforced, or any one of various shades of response, will give organic life and meaning to the action in that moment. As Grotowski says above, the constructed sign either 'conveys the hidden motivations of the actor or polemicises against them', but it will be rooted in and organic to the carnal being of the actor at that moment.

Grotowski is suggesting that it is possible for the actor to find a certain quality of attention, or consciousness, characterized by a full presence in, and recognition of, the moment. Stanislavsky certainly grasped the nature of this quality of consciousness, the 'special condition' which he termed the 'creative mood'. He went part of the way towards understanding it in his awareness that it arose when the actor's attention was on the perception and states of the body: 'I perceived that creativeness is first of all the complete concentration of the entire nature of the actor'. [400/465] But Stanislavsky limited himself to training in physical concentration. Grotowski has expanded this and proposes, in effect, a transcendental state of being, the nearest parallels to which are mystical and transpersonal states of consciousness and experience. He has described Ryszard Ciéslak's realization of the Constant Prince as a 'psycho-physical peak like ecstasy'. [42/43]

David Feldshuh has explored these parallels (without reference to Grotowski) in his article entitled 'Zen and the Actor'. He describes the inner condition known as 'Zen Mind' as a 'mental "potent state"', an optimum inner condition for creative functioning', which is an 'emancipation into full participation in the present moment':

> This quality of consciousness resembles an animal state in its reliance on the wisdom of the total organism. In this state thinking becomes an instantaneous, non-deliberative reaction. The mind is not confined, the attention is not limited to any single aspect. Self-consciousness disappears because there is no split in awareness. . . . Even though the actor has rehearsed a movement or line again and again, each creation is new, coming alive and dying every moment in front of the audience. [244/86]

Feldshuh in fact quotes scientific data (using Electro-encephalogram and Galvanic Skin Response readings) that support the seemingly paradoxical co-relationship of the 'non-deliberative' and the conscious in Zen meditation states, and indicates the relevance of the results to performing artists and particularly actors. The paradox of the relationship is one that Grotowski has fully grasped:

> Spontaneity to be truly spontaneous is to allow full rein to the profound flux which rises from my own experience, even physical, but related to my consciousness, for how could I cut myself off from my consciousness even in order to rediscover my spontaneity? I am as I am, as far away from mechanics as from chaos: between the two shores of my precision, I allow the river, which comes out of the authenticity of my experience, to advance, slowly or rapidly. [47/174]

Grotowski himself never made any direct reference during the phase of his theatrical research to what could be termed the more esoteric aspects of the creative process, although recent texts dealing with the post-theatrical work have been more explicit. It is, however, something that other actors or directors have attempted to clarify verbally, as in this passage from Joseph Chaikin's book:

The basic starting point for the actor is that his body is sensitive to the immediate landscape where he is performing. The full attention of the mind and body should be awake in that very space and in that very time (not an idea of time) and with the very people who are also in that time and space. . . .

We are trained and conditioned to be 'present' only in relation to the goal. . . . This teaches us to live in absent time. . . . The first step in preparation for an actor, and very often the longest step, is for the actor to find in himself one clear place. Quite often the actor mistakenly assumes that his preparation should consist of filling himself with broad emotional experiences. Instead, the actor must find an empty place where the living current moves through him un-informed. [206/65–66]

Obviously these processes cannot be quantified, compared or assessed in any objective manner. The only question of any value is: what is at stake? In a conventional approach to acting, whatever emotions are called forth are required to be truly felt, but on a proxy basis. The actor, the individual, takes ultimately no responsibility for these emotions. Stanislavsky, for example, clearly says: 'In his own person he would never dare to speak as he does in the character of this other personality, for whose words he does not feel himself responsible'. [401/30] But the Laboratory Theatre actor must, or should take the spiritual responsibility for emotions felt and displayed before witnesses – and thus pay the penalty as a human being. This is the aspect of Grotowski's acting ethic against which Helmut Kajzar rebelled so fiercely – the 'frontier between pretence and possession' that he likened to 'corporally portraying the stigmata'. [290/10]

In his chapter on Artaud in *Towards a Poor Theatre* Grotowski quotes Artaud's phrase, which he says 'holds the very foundation of the actor's art of extreme and ultimate action' – 'Actors should be like martyrs burnt alive, still signalling to us from their stakes'. [73/93] Similarly, David Feldshuh refers to the Zen precept: 'When you do something, you should burn yourself completely, like a good bonfire, leaving no trace of yourself'. [244/88] He further clarifies this by reference to the ancient Japanese art of swordsmanship – Kendo. This, in common with the sister arts of Aikido and Karate, demands 'full presence . . . and the experience of acting from a region beyond conscious control' but with one important difference – 'the undeniable possibility of death':

Faced with the possibility of death, the swordsman is freed from consideration of life. He need not *pretend* to live in the moment for he knows that the moment is all he may have to live. Paradoxically, the awareness of death enables full presence in life. . . . The swordsman's lesson is straightforward: the performing artist must be capable of risking all of himself. He must be willing and able to dissolve himself into the process of acting, to surrender: to 'die' each moment and to be born fully each moment. The swordsman knows he must risk all. The actor must convince himself. [244/88–89]

It is at this point precisely that there appears that fusion of technique and ethic that is manifest in Laboratory Theatre productions in the pervasive Romantic theme of the sacrificial act: the individual action, founded on what is common and permanent in humanity, made on behalf of human society, involving suffering and ultimately salvation. This theme, which is at the root of the entire Polish Romantic movement, has appeared in almost all of Grotowski's productions. In the earlier productions Grotowski took a highly individual, intellectualized stance in relation to the theme, employing his 'dialectic of apotheosis and derision' in an attempt to break the outer mould of habitual thinking, and penetrate the familiar mythic fantasy.

In *Dziady*, the main character, Konrad, was seen as Christ making the Stations of the Cross, weighted down by a prosaic broom, to demonstrate the 'naivety of the individual who believes himself to be a Saviour'. A similar position is adopted in *Kordian*, in which the main character, who has pledged to sacrifice himself for his country, is seen as a lunatic having hallucinations in an asylum. Grotowski explained:

> After a few minutes the audience understood that this was not a joke: the greatest myths of Poland were analysed as the myths of the insane ... Kordian gave his blood for others – literally – but his death is completely solitary, without collective backing. A cynic would say in such a situation: 'This must undoubtedly be a madman'. [42/40]

And in the final scene from *Akropolis*, in which a resurrected Christ/Apollo figure led a procession of hope and progress for Poland and European civilization, the participants were in fact inmates of a concentration camp who had, in their hysteria, mistaken a corpse for the Christ/Apollo – 'He' led them, singing a familiar Polish anthem, to the crematorium. Grotowski:

> What is Auschwitz? Is it something we could organise today? A world which functions inside us. Thus there were no SS men, only prisoners who organised space so that they must oppress each other to survive. [42/42]

In all of these productions and images, Grotowski was confronting, on an intellectual level, the myths of sacrifice inherent in his national Romantic literature.

In *Dr. Faustus*, however, although the original ethics were inverted, the principle of sacrifice was already being seen as a sanctifying, as opposed to a demeaning and pitiable experience. Significantly, this change of emphasis took place at the same time as the recognition and emergence of an artistic ethic that could itself be recognized as 'sacrificial' – the 'total act' of an actor before an audience. The relevance of the actor's individuality and humanity was being brought to bear in the realization of the stage role:

> The confession was authentic because the actor really mobilized all the associations of his life. At the same time he made Faustus' confession with the text, he accomplished his own very drastic but disciplined confession. [42/41]

But it was in Grotowski's final two productions that both the inner and outer aspects of the sacrificial theme were explored most fully, and the transgression and giving of self was seen as an illuminating, apotheosizing experience. In *The Constant Prince*, Cieślak was Christ suffering at the hands of the brutal, the blind, the power-mad and the insensitive, and through his suffering and sacrifice attempting in accordance with the Christian myth to bring salvation to his persecutors. Of the 'total act' aimed for in this production, Jan Błoński has said: 'As the Constant Prince saves values by means of passive sacrifice, so the actor redeems the theatre ... by the intense humility with which he offers himself to the public'. [161/147] And it is in *Apocalypsis Cum Figuris* most discernibly that the preoccupations of the two conventionally isolated fields – those of dramatic idea and reason, and of artistic technique – begin uniquely to move together and merge. Sacrifice is taken to a level of personal response and responsibility; the potentialities of the situation are demoted from myth and legend and are recognized as being inherent in our day to day experience. Jan Kott, with reference to *Apocalypsis*, has echoed Błoński's words, above: 'The only ritual which can be repeated in the theatre without blasphemy is the ritual of sacrifice in which the actor is simultaneously the executioner and the martyr. Grotowski demanded such a sacrifice from his actors. . . .'. [323/31]

It was in this act of sacrifice itself that Grotowski felt the Laboratory Theatre research had unconsciously rediscovered ritual, after abandoning the earlier con-

60 *The Constant Prince*
– Laboratory Theatre Company.

scious search for it. Again (as in the case of improvisation) he questioned the terminology of 'ritual in theatre' which he said was associated with certain stereotypes, such as that of 'a literal participation ... The stereotype of a chaotic spontaneity, the stereotype of a myth reproduced and not a myth reincarnated'. [46/73] And he also referred to Brecht's qualification that although theatre begins from ritual, it only comes about when it ceases to be ritual. Nevertheless, Grotowski believed that the actor's gift of self-sacrifice had the potential to realize some of the fundamental aspects of ritual, for which he was searching in the theatrical experience: i.e. an act of revelation and communion between those present which would consequently permit deeper knowledge and experience of self and others (and hence change). The following chapter (and the final chapter dealing with Grotowski's theatrical work) will concentrate on this proposition and consider why Grotowski finally rejected a theatrical path in pursuit of these ideals.

CHAPTER EIGHT
Transition

In December 1970, just over ten years after Grotowski received his diploma from the Cracow Theatre School and the professional title of a qualified theatre director, he announced his departure (and that of his theatre group) from the professional field of theatrical activity. At that point he defined the Laboratory Theatre search as:

> The quest for what is most essential in life ... something like a second birth, real, overt, not furtive, not complacent about one's seclusion. Together with someone, with a few, in a group – the discovering, the revealing of yourself and him. [64/117–119]

As was suggested at the end of Chapter Five (dealing with Grotowski's final theatrical production, *Apocalypsis Cum Figuris*) the abandonment of theatre as a field of activity did not in any way alter the essence of what Grotowski had been searching for in all his years of exploration – the potential for an authentic and revelatory encounter between individuals. Grotowski and his followers were to emphasize this in their statements for many years to come. It was simply that the structure initially chosen for the search (i.e. theatre) was seen in time to be ineffective and inappropriate for fundamental reasons, and was hampering rather than carrying forward the research.

For many it was obvious that Grotowski was abandoning not only theatrical structure but artistic criteria as well, which implied that it was the artistic convention which was no longer appropriate to Grotowski's search – and perhaps never had been. Others maintained (Laboratory Theatre members amongst them) that Grotowski never abandoned theatre or art, but simply chose to invent a new label and new rules. Obviously, these categorizations are in any case a question of convention and as such depend on a consensus for their definition. At that stage in the early seventies, Grotowski obviously felt – and the decade proved him right – that he had an adequate consensus for the establishment of a new framework for the Laboratory Theatre activities, one that would be structured specifically to their requirements. The activity that encapsulated their search (from 1970–1978) became known in time as paratheatre: formally, this related to an activity that had its roots in drama, but specifically did not result in a theatrical presentation before an audience. The terms 'spectator' and 'actor' lost their divisive significance, and both the action and the creation became the collective responsibility.

To understand more fully the transition – which some have seen as a consciously provocative change in direction, but which Richard Mennen (in *The Drama Review*) described more accurately as having 'inexorable logic' [346/60] – it will be helpful to retrace the objectives and resulting work of the Laboratory Theatre over the preceding eleven years. This recapitulation will hopefully demonstrate the precise aspects of theatrical convention and artistic criteria that became an impediment to Grotowski's progress and resulted in the new developments in his work. In broad terms, the origins of the transition from theatre to paratheatre can be seen to lie in two particular areas of preoccupation from Grotowski's early theatrical theory: (i) the actor/audience relationship and (ii) the manipulative actor/director relationship. Both of these, although bound in their theatrical practice by the unyielding conventions of artistic form, proved ultimately to be the basis for the later, individually more fertile activities. What remained from the body of Laboratory Theatre theory – the concept of 'poor' theatre, the experiments in architectural scenic arrangements, the development of the training of the actor's voice and body – belongs in the history of theatre research. In 1971 Grotowski described *Towards a Poor Theatre* as 'only a travel diary, which – telling about the experience of past years – describes my searches. But they are past travels.' [64/129]

The first factor that we should examine, then, which influenced Grotowski's decision to abandon theatrical form, was his experimental approach to the actor/ spectator relationship. In formulating his theory of 'poor theatre', Grotowski eventually arrived at this definition of theatre as 'what takes place between spectator and actor'. [73/32] He acknowledged that since he could not systematically educate the former, his preoccupation had to be 'the personal and scenic technique of the actor'. [73/15] This he elevated to the level of 'secular holiness': [73/34]

> One must give oneself totally, in one's deepest intimacy, in confidence, as when one gives oneself in love. Here lies the key. Self-penetration, trance, excess, the formal discipline itself ... [73/38]

But this process was never intended to be a closed experience, for the sole satisfaction and benefit of the actor: it was intended to facilitate contact in some form with the audience, and consequently affect their experience.

Hence Grotowski was never content in his theatrical experiments to renounce fully an investigation into the psychic presence of the audience. For him, this was full of possibilities not only for the internal processes of the actor and the 'unities' of the production, but also for the spectators themselves: 'The performance engages a sort of psychic conflict with the spectator. It is a challenge and an excess'. [73/47] As a consequence, Grotowski was specific and demanding concerning the kind of spectator his theatre was intended for, and the essential attitude:

> Personally, I am awaiting a spectator who would really like to see himself, see the true aspect of his hidden nature. A spectator willing to be shocked into casting off the mask of life, a spectator ready to accept the attack, the transgression of

common norms and representations, and who – thus denuded, thus disarmed, and moved by a sincerity bordering on the excessive – consents to contemplate his own personality. [24/22]

This preoccupation with the quality of contact between the actor and spectator is what conditioned Grotowski's constant exploration of spatial concepts and relationships. For each production, he claimed, 'the essential concern is finding the proper spectator/actor relationship for each type of performance and embodying the decision in physical arrangements'. [1/20] The spatial arrangements and the experiments in role-designation undertaken for each production have been documented in detail in Chapters Two and Four. After his first, still basically conventional stagings (*Orpheus*, *Cain*, *Shakuntala* and *Mystery-Bouffe*) he attempted, in *Dziady*, to create the possibilities for direct audience participation:

> I am trying to create a theatre of participation, to re-discover factors which characterise the origins of the theatre. Place actors and spectators close together, in a new scenic space which embraces the entire room, and you may create a living collaboration. Thanks to physical contact, the spark can cross between them. [332/10]

This experiment did not prove successful, and direct audience participation was not fully returned to as a viable proposition in a theatrical context, Grotowski thereafter maintaining the impossibility of such a relationship 'in an age when neither a communal faith exists, nor any liturgy rooted in the collective psyche as an axis for ritual'. [47/177]

In its place, Grotowski experimented with what he called 'the unities of place, time and action' [42/41] in his attempt to forge a meaningful link between actor and spectator. These were, not the classical unities relating to the structure of a written drama and its realization on stage but, for Grotowski, another way to underline the authenticity of the experience for the members of the audience. And so in *Kordian*, for example, he transferred the action of the play to a mental hospital, in which the actors portrayed doctors and patients, with some spectators also being designated as inmates. The experiences of the main character, thereby, became hallucinations witnessed by the audience as taking place in present time. Grotowski explained: 'The action of the production takes place at the same time as that of the performance. The theatre is literally where it happens'. [42/39]

But this, in turn, was rejected, Grotowski concluding that the unities were imposed 'while ignoring the fact that the spectators were playing the role of spectators. They were able to play the roles of insane people, but their reactions were not natural'. [42/41] Grotowski finally achieved an acceptable compromise in his subsequent productions: in *Akropolis* the spectators became the living, who were witnessing the ghost/dream lives of the Auschwitz dead; in *Dr. Faustus* they were invited guests at Faustus' confession and the dramatic re-enactment of his path to damnation; and in both *The Constant Prince* and *Apocalypsis Cum Figuris* they were simply witnesses:

We found a direct word-for-word situation. The dramatic function of the spectators and the function of spectator as spectator were the same. For the first time we saw authentic spontaneity. . . . If the contact between the spectator and the actor is very close and direct, a strong psychic curtain falls between them. It's the opposite of what one might expect. But if the spectators play the role of spectators and that role has a function within the production, the psychic curtain vanishes. [42/41, 43]

Grotowski admitted that he was impotent to influence directly the spectator's spiritual and psychic responses to the acts witnessed. Nevertheless, he suggested that it was possible for there to be a direct relationship between the inner processes of the actor (realized through long improvisational work and reactivated in performance) and the processes set in motion within the individual members of the audience. Grotowski continually used the terms 'provocation' and 'challenge' of the relationship between the actor and the spectator, believing that

If the actor, by setting himself a challenge publicly challenges others, and through excess, profanation and outrageous sacrilege reveals himself by casting off his everyday mask, he makes it possible for the spectator to undertake a similar process of self-penetration. [73/74]

As was outlined in the preceding two chapters, the idea was that these collective processes would in some way function in place of the missing 'liturgy rooted in the collective psyche' and become the 'axis for ritual', permitting a healing communion to take place between those present.

What Grotowski was aiming for, at this stage, was also a form of self-analysis. Eugenio Barba:

The actor neither lives his part nor portrays it from the outside. He uses the character as the means to grapple with his own self, the tool to reach secret layers of his personality and strip himself of what hurts most and lies deepest in his secret heart. . . . The actor deliberately breaks the shell of his social identity. This destruction of the stereo-type is a sacrifice, a renunciation, and an act of humility. . . . Through the attack on the most sensitive spots of his psyche, through the humble acceptance of this sacrifice, the actor, and the spectator whom he tries to subjugate, go beyond their alienation and their personal limitations; they reach a climax, a summit of purification, and accept their true selves. [116/173]

In interview with Grotowski, Eugenio Barba further described the process of analysis as 'a sort of disintegration of the psychic structure' [73/45] and questioned the inherent dangers of experimenting in this area. In reply Grotowski claimed that, for the actor, the process is only 'psychically painful' if it is not engaged in fully and unreservedly. The same applies, he stated, for the spectator – resistance to the process will bring confusion, although even this confusion may be regarded as beneficial, as 'a form of social psychotherapy'. [73/46]

But it is patently misleading to regard the processes activated in both the spectator and the actor as analogous in any real sense. Not only, as Grotowski readily admits, is there the factor of the intense preparation of the actor, but Grotowski is constantly at pains to emphasize that the engagement of the actor's being in the processes must be 'total', i.e. whole, organic, involving both body and spirit. This carnality, fundamental to the 'total act' of the Laboratory Theatre actor, and the resultant 'wholeness' which is one of the essential aims of the process, is, through the conventions of theatre, denied the spectator. It follows that the resulting psychic dichotomy, which is in itself contrary to the values expressed in the Laboratory Theatre work, will only further be accentuated the more intense the actor's performance.

As Richard Mennen pointed out in his article in *The Drama Review*, at the point of relative perfection in the process of elimination that was the basic principle of the Laboratory Theatre's technique

> an implicit contradiction became evident. The actors had worked to remove masks, disguises, defences, roles etc., that had divided them from each other, but relationship to the audience was that of a role – an actor. The honesty and brilliance that their craft exposed hid the fact that the actor/witness relationship reinforced a basic division between people. . . . If they were to follow their quest to its logical (and psychological) conclusion, they would have to eliminate the last division. [346/60]

This 'last division' separating the actor from authentic communion with the audience was the very concept of performance itself, which contains the fundamental criterion of artistic form.

Mennen further noted that 'the company could "not-perform" during rehearsal, but not, in a radically existential sense, "not perform" during performance'. [346/60] A consequence of this was that the steps taken towards eradicating the barriers between *actor* and *actor* during their 'not-performing' rehearsal work could, in fact, even further reinforce the conventional distance between *actor* and *spectator*, already accentuated by the extremity of the actor's performance.

It is evident from what documentation exists that there was a wide variety of response to the spectator experience in Laboratory Theatre performances, and much confusion. Neither is the response necessarily consistent with the intellectual judgement of the critic or reviewer. We saw from Alan Seymour's response to *Dr. Faustus* (see page 71) that he was much impressed with Grotowski's construction of the performance, and admitted to 'actions and images that seared and troubled beyond the grasp of words': [387/13] nevertheless he finally claimed to have been alienated by the intensity of the acting. Similarly Irving Wardle, whilst admiring the 'sculptural beauty' of Grotowski's theatre and admitting that Cieślak's performance in *The Constant Prince* 'exceeds anything I have seen in extreme human exposure', found that this discouraged, rather than permitted, identification:

> I did not learn anything about my own response to suffering through watching

Cieślak suffer. One reason, perhaps, is the huge gap between these productions and any common experience. They start on a note of intensity and ascend from there with no relief. [427]

Similarly, in a series of critiques in *The Drama Review* in 1970, Peter Feldman confirmed the negative and divisive aspects of the extreme performance experience, referred to by Richard Mennen above (Feldman is describing his reactions to Cieślak's Constant Prince):

> Grotowski pulls us in because our envy of Cieślak's intensity and freedom forces us to look at ourselves, our limitations, those exterior forces that shape our internal lives ... (but) eventually you may come to resent those who make you feel inferior. ... This resentment can become a block to one's receptivity to the event, to one's search within. [243/195]

And in a programme broadcast on Radio 3 on 11 March 1977 the speaker described *Apocalypsis Cum Figuris* as a 'self-deception performed by the Laboratory Theatre of Poland'. The audience, according to his judgement, were left 'untouched. ... It didn't seem to be done for us, we felt like intruders', and he experienced an acute sense of the exclusivity of the inter-personal relationships of the members of the acting team. Their dialogue, he said, seemed like 'another language, their own private language based on a knowledge of one another outside the characters they were playing, which was foreign to us.'

But both Józef Kelera and Jan Kreczmar have stated that their direct experience of a Laboratory Theatre performance (again, *The Constant Prince*) was something in the way of a revelation. It caused them to affirm unreservedly certain theoretical statements concerning the actor and spectator processes that they had previously hesitated in accepting intellectually. And finally Eric Bentley, in a detailed (and in places damning) critique in the *New York Times* during the group's 1969 New York tour, suggested that it was the potential for revelation in the 'peculiar intimacy' of Grotowski's theatre that was its redemption:

> During this show, *Apocalypsis*, something happened to me. I put it this personally because it was something very personal that happened. About half-way through the play I had a quite specific illumination. A message came to me – from nowhere as they say – about my private life and self. This message must stay private, to be true to itself, but the fact that it arrived has public relevance I think, and I should publicly add that I don't recall this sort of thing happening to me in the theater before. ... [157/7]

It was in *Apocalypsis*, in some ways, that Grotowski took the element of human confrontation between actor and spectator to an extreme. In the years following the premiere of *The Constant Prince* a change of emphasis had become apparent in Grotowski's approach to the actor/spectator relationship. In an interview given in Montreal in 1967, Grotowski stated: 'The core of the theatre is an encounter.' [73/56] But what he was here referring to, as he explained at length, was essentially the encounter between the actor and the text, the actor and the director, and the actor with the actor's self. The spectator, at that stage, was not referred to at all. And it was apparent from *Apocalypsis*, the final production, that Grotowski was prepared at last to abandon the earlier charades, in which he had pursued the ideal of a reciprocally satisfying actor/spectator relationship, and confront the audience with the reality of their conventionalized positions, unrelieved by any artificially imposed roles. It was the furthest Grotowski could proceed in his obsessive manipulation of that elusive relationship and still remain within the bounds of theatre.

In *Apocalypsis Cum Figuris* the scenic space was created entirely by the actions of the actors and the constantly shifting relative positions of actor/actor/spectator. When at one point the central persecuted character encircled the tight-knit group of the other actors, who were placed in the centre of the room, he was not only excluded from their group consciousness – but also trapped in the narrow channel between their active rejection, and the passive refusal of the surrounding witnesses to intervene. By their own awareness of the roles that they had accepted for the duration of an hour, and their inability to cast off these roles, all present permitted the cycle of events to reach its pre-ordained conclusion.

Just as there was no previously constructed scenic arrangement, so for this final production the audience were not able to retreat into a specified role. They were witnesses – but it was not possible to seek security in that fact. As the main character, nearing the end of his torment, raised himself slowly to his knees from where he had been slumped in exhaustion, and searched the faces of those spectators sitting only inches from him, the implication was that it was they who chose their position and response, as did the other spectators all around the room who witnessed this silent conversation. Of course, the choice was unfairly balanced, since the weight of convention always rests on the side of the *status quo*. And in this case it was the weight of artistic convention that was delimiting the situation and apparently inhibiting all efforts towards authentic response.

And so it was by means of his final production that Grotowski succeeded in isolating the actor/spectator relationship as one of the central problems impeding his search for authenticity within the theatrical process. Through his work and research he had transformed the art of acting into a vehicle for self-exploration and self-development. He had also tried incessantly – through the experiments with the actor/spectator relationship and the architectural arrangements, and through refining and intensifying the actor's process – to make it possible for the spectator to respond with an equal degree of authenticity. But the full engagement of the actor within the creative process that Grotowski insisted upon was denied the spectator through the artistic convention of passivity. To follow this reasoning to its conclusion, Grotowski had to take the final step of restructuring their work and finding a form (paratheatre) that would accommodate those spectators willing to abandon their conventional passivity.

But the actor/spectator relationship was not the only factor influential in the transition from theatre to paratheatre. Another element in the dynamics of the situation was Grotowski himself, for he was also instrumental in his relationship with the actor. An understanding of the implications of this relationship is essential in order to grasp the fundamental paradoxes at the root of his theatrical credo. Grotowski came to prominence in Polish theatre following an era of directorial supremacy. Although coinciding with a similar period in British theatre also labelled 'director's theatre', the emphases in the two countries were different. In Poland the director was the supreme artist in a period of total artistic liberation, in which design, costume, mechanical and technical media and the actors all became plastic elements in a visual and aural display. In this context Grotowski's theories constituted a strong re-affirmation of the art of the actor.

In Laboratory Theatre practice, the full realization of this scenic technique of the actor was absolutely dependent upon the quality of the actor/director relationship. Grotowski has described, in *Towards A Poor Theatre*, some of the implications of this relationship:

> This is not instruction of a pupil but utter opening to another person, in which the phenomenon of 'shared or double birth' becomes possible. The actor is reborn – not only as an actor but as a man – and with him I am reborn. [73/25]

Grotowski believed that the results obtained through this relationship were deeper and more meaningful than those obtained during rehearsal in a 'normal' theatre. In his interview with Marc Fumaroli published in 1969, Grotowski distinguished three basic alternatives possible in the attitude of the director towards actors. The first is a position of false fraternization without personal commitment, an aspect of 'improvisation' he constantly attacked. At the other extreme, there is an exaggeration of private authority, the 'director as tamer' who wishes

> to extract all the creative elements by force from the actors; he does not respect germination, it is he who always knows in advance what to do. There are actors who love this kind of director; he frees them from the responsibility of creating. [47/175]

(As we saw in earlier chapters, Grotowski himself was not entirely innocent of this in the early stages of his work.) Finally, there is the position that Grotowski himself claimed to adopt. This kind of director

> appeals to them ... defies them ... bestows on them a quality of attention which is like a luminous and pure consciousness, a consciousness that identifies itself with presence, *a consciousness devoid of all calculation*, but at the same time attentive and generous. [47/175] (my emphasis)

The 'opening' Grotowski describes, based on trust, is not however something unique to the Laboratory Theatre rehearsal process, but is a fundamental aspect of any good actor/director relationship. In a study of the Royal Shakespeare Company, David Addenbrooke has described, for example, Peter Hall's attitude:

> For this process to succeed, it is necessary for the actor to leave his ego outside

the rehearsal room – and thus free himself to experiment in any way at all. Hall considers that one of the most difficult problems of directing is the breaking down of an actor's automatic defence barrier; he feels that his actors should be able to make utter fools of themselves within rehearsal, and in doing so, reveal to themselves (*and the director*) exactly what they can and cannot achieve. [148/98] (my emphasis)

But whereas Peter Hall was quite prepared to admit to the limitations imposed by the relationship, Grotowski seemed to be aiming for a purity that went beyond those limitations:

> The producer can help the actor in this complex and agonising process only if he is just as emotionally and warmly open to the actor as the actor is in regard to him. I do not believe in the possibility of achieving effects by means of cold calculation. [73/47]

In his theatrical work Grotowski never seemed to face the fact that within this 'open' relationship the director must retain an element of both the observer and the manipulator, since actor and director are subject to the demands of art and the need for form and structure: these qualities must obviously, in some degree, affect the relationship. In fact in a review in 1960 of one of the earliest productions, the critic Jan Pawel Gawlik remarked that, as a man of theatre obsessed with form, Grotowski was very successful, but questioned whether the preoccupation with form was not in fact detrimental to his success as a director in relation to the actors. [256] This issue was also raised by Jan Błoński some years later. Grotowski was of course not completely blind to these characteristics, which 'follow the producer like his own shadow even in the poor theatre'. [73/48] But he did not seem prepared to admit them openly into his idealized actor/director relationship, in the same way that he seemed reluctant to face the limitations of the actor/spectator relationship. It was not until much later, in retrospective statements, that there was to appear some recognition of these paradoxes. In a statement given at a meeting in Moscow in 1976, and published in Poland in 1979, Grotowski said:

> As I said, our questioning at that time was about the presence of the actor: what did his skill depend on, does there exist a system of signs for the actor? We asked questions above all about signs. We attempted in practice to define the elements of expression: movement, impulse, sound, intonation.... I must say, however, that in his experiments on the sign the actor could not be himself, he could not reveal himself as an individual. Someone apart from himself built the structure of signs. This someone was the director. That's precisely what I call intrusion. [85/139]

There was, however, another more personal aspect of the director's work – beyond that of the encouragement of the actor's development and the construction of scenic form – which Grotowski seemed to move closer towards in the last few years of his theatrical work. Just as Grotowski visualized an analogous internal response from the spectator to the inner processes activated in the performer, so he was also concerned with the internal rewards for himself as director in his work with the actor:

> I am interested in the actor because he is a human being. This involves ... my meeting with another person, the contact, the mutual feeling of comprehension and the impression created by the fact that we open ourselves to another being, that we try to understand him: in short, the surmounting of our solitude. [73/98]

This inclination towards a less remote involvement on the part of the director was something that became more pronounced in his later work, specifically, in *The Constant Prince* and *Apocalypsis Cum Figuris*. Flaszen has recalled:

> Working with Grotowski, I understood several things: for example, how, when starting with manipulation (an idea indispensable to theatre) one reaches a point where it all falls away and what remains is something else. The usual professional relationship between master and disciple falls away. What remains can be witnessed by no-one. It happened, for example, in Grotowski's work with Cieślak on *The Constant Prince*. Somehow, Grotowski and Cieślak transcended the director-actor relationship ... This was a departure from manipulation. It was a human relation transcending the professional relation. [143/303]

Nevertheless, whatever Grotowski and his actors were able to achieve in authentic inter-human experience in their non-performance work, the director (as, in some ways, the spectator) was finally excluded from the actor's experience of the creative process on stage. Flaszen poignantly says:

> The director, like Moses, never enters, only leads to the Promised Land. The others reach it, but he dies. Perhaps this connection with the martyr explains the eminence of the director in Poland. He disappears when the actors act: he dies. [143/318]

But ultimately, despite other aspects of the relationship, the ability of the director to retain objectivity, in order to be able to assess the actor's work in terms of its potential in a creative score, was over-riding in the process of role-realization aimed for in the Laboratory Theatre. Flaszen says:

> Art is not pure experience, it is also technique.... Therefore a certain margin of conscious manipulation is involved. This is art — a game between the conscious and the unconscious, between what is carried by the waves and what makes the wave. And all this requires technique. It's a play between manipulation and inspiration. [143/320]

In fact, both the director and the spectator, because of the conventions of their respective positions, crucially affected the validity of the 'total act' of Grotowski's actor, postulated as a possibility in both preparation and performance. For the actor was not performing in a vacuum but in front of the director and before an audience.

And if the one was judging the 'total acts' and using them to construct an artistic framework, and the other was inhibited by that framework and incapable of response – what then became of the giving, the gift? It seemed that the only way in which the spectator, the actor and the director could be liberated from their restrictive roles was to lift the weight of theatrical convention – which is what the Laboratory Theatre finally decided to do when they abandoned 'theatrical' – in favour of 'paratheatrical' – activity. Richard Mennen quotes Grotowski:

> We noted that when we eliminated certain blocks and obstacles what remains is what is most elementary and most simple – what exists between human beings when they have a certain confidence between each other and when they look for an understanding that goes beyond the understanding of words. . . . Precisely at that point one does not perform any more. . . . One day we found it necessary to eliminate the notion of theatre (an actor in front of a spectator) and what remained was a notion of meeting – not a daily meeting and not a meeting that took place by chance. . . . This kind of meeting cannot be realised in one evening. [346/60]

The very concept of the roles of actor, spectator and director, however, only have meaning within the conventions of art. The abandonment of these roles in the transition to paratheatre therefore undermined the relevance of art itself to the Laboratory Theatre activities. Finally, it had to be accepted that the formal criteria belonging to artistic convention were no longer appropriate. This served to change only the context, not the essence, of Grotowski's stated aim: 'To cross our frontiers, exceed our limitations, fill our emptiness – fulfil ourselves'. [73/121] One aspect of art is its power to awaken knowledge by presenting shadows of reality that the spectator may never normally come face to face with, or may shun. Flaszen, for example, has said:

> Each work of art is a remoteness, a medium which is not life, but the shade, or image, of life. It is something which lies *between* us; we're not together. It needs gates, mediation. [143/327]

In this lie both its potential strength and weakness. Its strength lies in its capacity to mobilize forces through reaction that could lead to positive action and change. It could be the start of an organic process. It could change people:

> The decisive factor in this process is the actor's technique of psychic penetration. He must learn to use his role as if it were a surgeon's scalpel to dissect himself . . ., the spectator understands, consciously or unconsciously, that such an act is an invitation to him to do the same thing, and this often arouses opposition or indignation, because our daily efforts are intended to hide the truth about ourselves, not only from the world, but also from ourselves. . . . We are afraid of being changed into pillars of salt if we turn around, like Lot's wife. [73/37]

But within the delicate balance of formalized reality lies the potential also for safe and easy evasion. Art may be apprehended increasingly as a formal structure, in which the system of signs and symbols exclusively are credited with intrinsic value. We relate cerebrally and aesthetically to the structure, robbing the underlying reality of its penetrating potential for change. The skull loses its death message and becomes an insignia – we too easily achieve a state of illusory cognizance with the world. As Peter Brook says: 'The audience follows down those dark alleys, calm and confident. Culture is a talisman protecting them from anything that could nastily swing back into their lives.' [180/11]

The spectator wards off the experience of reality itself by means of the cathartic properties of the artistic ethos, and in a sense *catharsis* could be seen to be the crucial factor. The concept of *catharsis* arose in conjunction with written classical drama at a time, in terms of the evolution of civilization, when Apollonian order was imposing itself upon Dionysian chaos. Connected with the Dionysian (feminine) principle were rites and rituals, celebrations of community, corporality and related-ness, movement and change. In contrast the Apollonian (masculine) principle represented order and construction, reason, intellect and language, stability and the status quo. The arrival of written drama represented an intellectual construction or representation of reality. The tragic form, especially, investigated the ebb and flow of chaos and order, in which chaos threatened (evoking terror and pity) but was ultimately punished and order reestablished. George Steiner:

> The tragic theatre is an expression of the pre-rational phase in history; it is founded on the assumption that there are in nature and in the psyche occult, uncontrollable forces able to madden or destroy the mind. [403/342]

Another way of interpreting the sensitive interplay of structure and spontaneity in art, in terms of the experience of the individual, is in the Jungian analysis of the harmonious reconciliation of the conscious and the unconscious. The unconscious throws up symbols and collective images which are numinous (i.e. carrying their own dynamic capacity for change and influence). It is the conscious that receives these, sorts them out, validates them. But if we deny the power and autonomy of the unconscious in the process, giving credence only to the conscious intellect, there is a resultant disharmony and the symbolizing function is rendered impotent, i.e. it can effect no change.

Grotowski has always insisted that the way towards progress and evolution is through work towards indivisibility, towards being whole and not divided into body/mind, intellect/sex etc. In this respect he is working within the context both of the great Eastern philosophies and religions and of contemporary psychological and sociological thought. To evolve, humanity must learn an internal harmony where the Apollonian and Dionysian principles work in union within their appro-priate fields, without conflict. In this context he formulated his fundamental artistic principle of *conjunctio oppositorum*, the balance of structure and spontaneity. But whether he made allowances for it or not in his formulations, the weight of convention of the past many centuries, artistically and sociologically, has been on the side of the Apollonian principle. Therefore, when Grotowski talked about needing to confront in his audience 'the participation of the common mask' it is this 'Apollonian' mask that he needed to crack. For despite his *conjunctio oppositorum* there was in his theatrical work an unconventional emphasis on the Dionysian principle. Its appeal was primarily to the unconscious, using spontaneous, non-verbal, corporeal means. And in both his theory and his actual construction of the theatrical experience the major emphasis was on the *relatedness* and *community* of theatre. In his 1967 talk in Paris entitled 'After the Avant-Garde', Flaszen said:

> Grotowski's productions aim to bring back a utopia of those elementary experiences provoked by collective ritual, in which the community dreamed ecstatically of its own essence, of its place in a total, undifferentiated reality, where Beauty did not differ from Truth, emotion from intellect, spirit from body, joy from pain; where the individual seemed to feel a connection with the Whole of Being. [135/114]

In these terms Grotowski's use of literature was particularly significant. He often deliberately destroyed the formal structure of written drama and used the word not as a carrier of intellectual meaning but as pure sound – incantation, songs and shouts, whispers and ululations in which the words lost their conceptual significance. This use of language (the sword of the intellect) in a non-intellectual way became one of Grotowski's most incisive tools in his aim of 'breaking the mask', and indeed caused a strong sense of affront in many intellectually-orientated critics.

Finally, however, Grotowski abandoned his efforts to discover within the formal structures of theatre and art the authenticity he was looking for. And it is questionable whether the *degree* of authenticity he was committed to was ever a realizable proposition in theatre, bearing in mind Brecht's caution that theatre only begins where ritual leaves off. If Grotowski was really searching for the same level of authenticity as could be experienced in archaic pre-theatrical forms, then perhaps the search within theatre and art was self-defeating – since in one sense it could be said that they evolved as a talisman against that very authenticity. Such conjecture, as may be imagined, provided rich material for debate following on from Grotowski's 'abdication' from theatre. But Grotowski is nothing if not pragmatic, and for him the only valid way such propositions could really be tested was in practice. From 1970, the beginning of the new decade, Grotowski himself rejected the role of 'artist' and began the Laboratory Theatre's new experiments in paratheatre. For his group the issues involved in the abandonment of art could be expressed very simply. In reply to an enquiry from a Soviet literary journal concerning the paratheatrical activities, they issued the following statement:

> Examining the nature of theatre, its unique substance, and what makes it different from other artistic domains, we came to the conclusion that its essence lies in direct contact between people. This in mind, we have decided to get beyond art to reality, since it is in real life rather than on the artistic plane that such contacts are possible. [315/24]

SECTION III
Post-Theatre

By the beginning of the seventies in Poland, despite the continuing lack of available academic material concerning the Laboratory Theatre, and despite its critics' 'resistance against fascination', it seemed that Grotowski was finally being recognized as, at the very least, a major force in contemporary theatre. *Apocalypsis Cum Figuris* was almost unanimously acclaimed by all who had seen it, and in September and October of 1971 Grotowski and his team visited Warsaw for a season of performances and conferences. It was only their second visit to the capital, and the first in over ten years.

Journalists made much of the fact that Warsaw was at last being privileged to experience the same degree of hysteria and sensationalism as had greeted Grotowski's appearances in other capitals. And there were still highly sceptical voices to be heard. Asked at one of his press conferences for his response to the more aggressive of these attacks, Grotowski replied:

> Such a ghost, such a fellow-traveller has accompanied us in the twelve years of our work. This ghost-companion is the laughter of others, their conviction that what we do is ridiculous. I have come across this from the very beginning. At that time I received a letter from the Byrskis (I didn't yet know them personally) and they wrote: 'don't be afraid, don't over-react, they will mock you. If you do something real, others burst out laughing'. That's a very significant observation. . . .
>
> I sometimes wonder why this happens to me, and whether it is something typically Polish, but then I realized that there is probably nothing strange about it, because they say the same about Bergman in Sweden and Brook in England – and sometimes even worse has been said of them. And so perhaps it's normal. Now, of course, I can hear voices indignantly asking what right I have to compare myself to 'such people'. My apologies, but since 'such people' compare themselves to me, maybe I too have the right? [57/34]

There was, however, also much enthusiasm, both from the professional theatrical world and, significantly, from a non-professional public of predominantly young people. Sixteen performances of *Apocalypsis Cum Figuris* were given, eight in the original version, and eight (without benches) for a younger audience. Apart from press conferences there were also public discussions, well attended. All in all the 1971 Warsaw visit may have had the appearance of a reconciliation between

Grotowski and his reluctantly yielding Polish critics. But no sooner had they begun to acknowledge the Western assessment of Grotowski's stature, then he was ready to revoke his newly accredited position. He confirmed his announcement of the previous December in New York: that he and his team would no longer be conducting theatrical experiments; that the familiar acting theory propounded in *Towards a Poor Theatre* belonged in the past; and that they were now conducting experiments in new forms of activity not connected with the conventional theatrical concepts of 'performance' and 'spectator':

> Is the current trend in theatre close to my heart? No. And also, is theatre as an art close to my heart? I should formulate my answer in the positive. But is it essential, basic? No.... I could say that what we are searching for is a certain kind of domain, different from theatre.... The search itself could become a realm. [57/33–34]

Since Grotowski neither clarified at this stage how this 'realm of search' was to be actualized, nor presented the immediate possibility for experience of the proposed area of work, it is perhaps understandable that there was again a certain amount of cynicism in the face of what appeared to be a wilful reversal of role. There was also a great deal of wild speculation in journalistic coverage in the years 1971 to 1975. In the event, it was not until after what was called the *University of Research* in Wrocław in 1975 – when the parathetical activities were finally made accessible – that there was a re-opening of the debate, expanded and given meaning this time by accounts from participants and subsequent critical reaction. These activities, and the issues raised in response to them, will be examined in this final section of the book.

Despite the perspective of more than a decade, the post-theatrical work of the Laboratory Theatre is by no means yet fully delineated, or the area in which it was operating categorically identified. It involved activities bordering on many tangential disciplines (as will become obvious) and a distinctive vocabulary has still not evolved to chart it. Although, after 1975, the practice of commentary by participants was not discouraged, there was never any particular commitment from the Laboratory Theatre itself to a verbal analysis of the work. A healthy emphasis on action was still predominant, characteristic also of the earlier theatrical work. On this theme, Grotowski said at a meeting with students in Wrocław in 1971:

> One must know which area one is entering, but one must not try to contain this 'knowledge' in a formula, or give it a closed definition. The moment one gives it a name, the moment one defines it, one kills something vital in oneself. One must take the risk that certain things will not have a single name or that they will be left in the air. Something will be left suspended, like living matter, not yet set, but fluid and quivering with life. One must not attempt to kill it through premature structuralization. [64/128]

The closest the Laboratory Theatre came to a definition of its post-theatrical activities could be seen on posters dating from the late seventies. The familiar

'Actors' Institute' was replaced by the following vague slogan: 'The Laboratory Theatre is an institute involved in a cultural investigation of the peripheral areas of art, and in particular of theatre'. In documenting those investigations my main aim, apart from completing the history of the Laboratory Theatre in its final phase of work, will be to describe the post-theatrical activities themselves, using where possible accounts from participants. I will be also looking at some of the consequences of working in these 'peripheral areas of art'.

CHAPTER NINE
Paratheatrical Research 1970–1975

The presentation of the *University of Research* in Wrocław in June 1975 was the public culmination of a process that had its beginnings in the Laboratory Theatre's final production, *Apocalypsis Cum Figuris*. That performance, standing as it did at the very outer limits defined by theatrical art, presented in its achievement a challenge to Grotowski and his actors. Tadeusz Burzyński (one of the few Polish journalists familiar with, and sympathetic to the paratheatrical ideals) defined this challenge in his own terms:

> If he is to remain faithful to his principles (which exclude the repetition, recreation and the duplication even of his own achievements and which set out

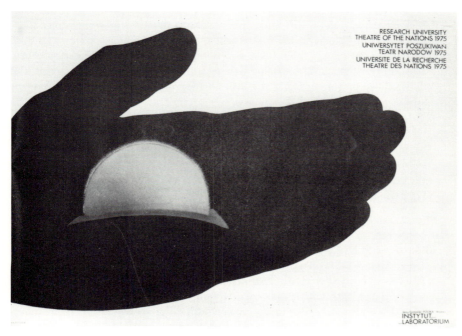

RESEARCH UNIVERSITY
THEATRE OF THE NATIONS 1975
UNIWERSYTET POSZUKIWAN
TEATR NARODOW 1975
UNIVERSITE DE LA RECHERCHE
THEATRE DES NATIONS 1975

INSTYTUT
LABORATORIUM

61 Poster for the University of Research 1975.

that every new undertaking must enlarge the scope of experience, raise new questions and seek new answers) then Grotowski cannot, after the *Apocalypsis Cum Figuris*, produce anything that could possibly remain within the bounds of what is broadly understood as a theatre performance. A step beyond the experience contained in the *Apocalypsis* signifies an ultimate departure from the theatre into the unknown which, if it still lies within the realm of art, will probably become an entirely new form of it. [190/15]

As we saw in Chapter Five, Grotowski and his actors did not therefore cease to experiment within the framework of *Apocalypsis Cum Figuris*. But they came in time to accept that it would be necessary to bring to life a completely new framework, which could encompass the still unexplored area beyond theatrical frontiers. The crucial factor was the eradication of a 'product', which is what essentially divides the 'creator' from the 'observer'. What they were searching for now was a 'process' that could unite these two in a new relationship. But Grotowski was not proposing the eradication of the 'artistic product' merely to substitute for it an 'artistic process' which would fulfil the same function in cultural terms – i.e. something with an external value to be observed more or less passively. *The paratheatrical work was intended not to be observed but to be directly experienced in a participatory way.* In this respect it was the quality of authentic reciprocity between all participating that distanced it from theatre. Jan Błoński summarized the development in the following terms:

> Throughout his theatre work Grotowski maintained a profound conviction: of the need to transform the spectator, by offering him the actor's human truth (and indirectly his own). However, in order genuinely to transform the spectator, one had to persuade him to repeat the gesture of giving or sacrifice; otherwise he would be only a voyeur. The consummation of communication is impossible without visible, enacted reciprocity.
>
> In short, only two people can meet. 'There is a point', says Grotowski, 'at which one discovers that it is possible to reduce oneself to the man as he is; not to his mask, not to the role he plays, not to his game, not to his evasions, not to his image of himself, not to his clothing – only to himself. This reduction to the essential man is possible only in relation to an existence other than himself'. [163/68–69]

The essential problem confronting Grotowski's company at the point of transition from theatre to paratheatre, therefore, was how to involve the members of the public directly in this process. As a group of individuals the Laboratory Theatre actors had many years of experience and preparation in terms of their work on their own selves. This was work directed primarily towards the possibility of authentic spontaneity, and the release of a creative flow of energy: in other words it was a form of de-conditioning. But they were now proposing to involve directly members of the public. They needed to research and discover ways of presenting the work without invoking performance principles and artistic criteria in the response. At a deeper level they also needed to discover a structure which would permit the spectator-become-participant to reach quickly to a similar level of de-conditioning to their own.

Between 1970 and 1973 the team sought the answers to these problems amongst themselves, within closed work. Looking back, the transformative developments that took place in these years have acquired a logical, inevitable, almost effortless appearance. But this masks the reality of another period of uncertainty within the Laboratory Theatre group. Ludwik Flaszen recalled:

> In general, in that period, the question of whether we'd manage to survive, or whether we'd continue our lives as grand and meritorious corpses, was a big problem.... There comes a moment when one must renounce one's previous achievement in order to start again at the 'zero point'. It was, for us, a matter of life and death, and I mean it. [143/323]

Grotowski himself has said of this stage of his work from the end of the sixties and the beginning of the seventies:

> ... it was a time when inertia (natural and innate to man), fear of the unknown, the feeling that leaving the confines of a classically recognized discipline was madness and bound to come to ill – all this meant that whilst being unable to continue with something I considered a beautiful but closed chapter, I hadn't sufficient strength and courage to open another. [169/38]

And in a monograph published in Warsaw in 1979, Tadeusz Burzyński described Grotowski at that time as warning his colleagues that 'what he was aiming at was vague, and that it was not certain to what degree it was real. Everyone ought to ponder well over the dimensions of his own risk, and carefully decide whether to depart or remain in the group'. [360/107] In his public meetings and debates Grotowski was seen to be groping towards the formulation of what appeared to many to be intangible questions and anxieties of a metaphysical and philosophical nature. The *Holiday* text published in *The Drama Review* in June 1973 (which is the most comprehensive statement to date of his paratheatrical work) was composed entirely of transcripts of public meetings from this period. Leszek Kolankiewicz, in an internal Laboratory Theatre document called *On the Road to Active Culture* (which catalogues the paratheatrical work 1970–1977), has said of these texts: 'His pronouncements in that period were based on the logic of paradox. But in their, so to speak, practical premises they were rooted in the realities of life'. [316/12]

Grotowski's statements were certainly paradoxical, if only for the reason that while they appeared to many to be vague, meaningless, mystical nonsense, they seemed to appeal to an equal number as being concrete propositions for existence, and for action. They were also, unmistakably, sincere and personal. The following is a long extract from one of Grotowski's original *Holiday* statements, given at New York University on 13 December 1970:

> In the fear, which is connected with the lack of meaning, we give up living

and begin diligently to die. Routine takes the place of life, and the senses –
resigned – get accustomed to nullity.... This shell, this sheath under which we
fossilise, becomes our very existence – we set and become hardened, and we
begin to hate everyone in whom a little spark of life is still flickering. This is
not a spiritual matter: it envelops all our tissues, and the fear of someone's touch,
or of exposing oneself, is ever greater....

And what remains, what lives? We had a saying in Poland: *We were not there
– the forest was there; we shan't be there – the forest will be there.* And so, how
to be, how to live, how to give birth as the forest does? I can also say to myself:
I am water, pure, which flows, living water: and then the source is *he*, *she*, not
I: he whom I am going forward to meet, before whom I do not defend myself.
Only if *he* is the source, *I* can be the living water....

When someone looks at the world in order to see (and many look in order not
to see), he will notice what is weak and unsure, what is pulsating towards its birth.
It is something new between people – as yet hardly existing, but already to be
felt, a half-impulse, half-need. That thing – I am deliberately using a term which
is, by its nature, cold – is a different sensibility....

Together with someone, with a few, in a group – the discovering of yourself
and him. There is in it also something like cleansing of our life. And it even makes
me think very literally, tangibly, as an action: *cleansing.* There is no other way
out here, but one must talk by association: for some it will seem abstract, even
embarrassing or ridiculous, for others it will be as concrete as it is for me. This,
too, is something we can recognise one another by. And so, I am taking that risk
and will tell you about associations. Here they are, only some of them, they are
very many:

games, frolics, life, our kind, ducking, flight; man–bird, man–colt, man–wind,
man–sun, man–brother.

And here is the most essential, central: brother. This contains 'the likeness
of God', giving and man; but also the brother of earth, the brother of senses,
the brother of sun, the brother of touch, the brother of Milky Way, the brother
of grass, the brother of river. Man as he is, whole, so that he would not hide
himself; and who *lives* and that means – *not everyone.* Body and blood this is
brother, that's where 'God' is, it is the bare foot and the naked skin, in which
there is brother. This, too, is a holiday, to be in the holiday, to be the holiday.
All this is inseparable from meeting: the real one, full, in which man does not
lie to himself, and is in it whole. Where there is none of that fear, none of that
shame of oneself which gives birth to the lie and the hiding, and is its own
grandfather because it is itself born of a lie and hiding. In this meeting, man does
not refuse himself and does not impose himself. He lets himself be touched and
does not push with his presence. He comes forward and is not afraid of somebody's eyes, whole. It is as if one spoke with one's self: you are, so I am. And
also: I am being born so that you are born, so that you become. And also: do
not be afraid, I am going with you. [64/115, 119]

Leszek Kolankiewicz, in *On the Road to Active Culture*, has made a summary in his own words of the preoccupations that Grotowski was expressing during this early phase of the paratheatrical research. The summary may serve at this stage as an introduction to the themes of the work:

> Grotowski formulated it thus, for example: If someone is convinced that the world's life can be changed but lives until that change in a haphazard way, then his behaviour creates a situation in which he produces work calling others to improve the world and life, while he himself derives advantages from it as it exists. If, on the other hand, someone comes to the conclusion that the change begins with the attention to his own life, sooner or later he is confronted by the question: can he change himself without ties with others? Because it is not possible to have meaningful contacts with everybody, one ought to look for such people who are, to start with, akin; that is to say feel a similar dominant need which surfaces in different ways.
>
> Such a contact – if it is to be something vital cannot, of course, be realised in a situation where the particular social roles dominate communication but can only be realised in a situation where unique individuals are able to communicate with one another. A new special situation must be created which would not hamper such a contact, and which would facilitate and strengthen it through the establishment of a 'rhythm of space, time and freedom'.
>
> Such a situation, in order to be complete, should embrace not only people, but also the tangible world. It would then enable man to find himself in the situation where existence itself would look at him; where his senses would not be walled up; where he would be immersed in existence. Where – as Grotowski puts it – he would enter the world as a bird enters the air. Such a situation would enable man to take from the world its repose and the stability proper to inanimate objects. [316/12–13]

These, then, broadly speaking, were the themes of the proposed work in the early seventies. And despite the uncertainties of the period, Grotowski found collaborators, both within his established group and from his predominantly youthful public following, willing to join him in his proposed explorations. In November 1970, there took place in the theatre building in Wrocław a meeting with 70 volunteers from about 300 who had initially responded to Grotowski's 'Proposal for Collaboration' (see page 100). This meeting was of an entirely improvised nature and lasted four days and four nights. It resulted in a reduced group of ten people who, during the following year, worked first with Grotowski and then with Zbigniew (Teo) Spychalski (who had joined the Laboratory Theatre in November 1967). By the end of this period there were only four people, who were joined in time by three others.

Up until this point the group of newcomers, and the established group of Laboratory Theatre actors had worked apart. But on 15 November 1972 they joined into a 14-strong team – the above mentioned seven, plus Albahaca, Cieślak, Grotowski, Jahołkowski, Molik, Spychalski and Andrzej Paluchiewicz from the old team (the last mentioned had joined the company in the 1966/67 season and performed in the fifth version of *Akropolis*). The whole ensemble came together for the purpose of renovating some old farm buildings on a plot of land at Brzezinka, near Oleśnica (40 km from Wrocław) which had been allocated to the Institute by the Wrocław authorities earlier in March. Between November 1972 and June 1973 work was carried on alternately in the theatre buildings in Wrocław and at Brzezinka:

> They began to work here and even to live; but by no means permanently; periods of several days spent in the forest were accompanied by days of break for repose, during which each returned to the town, towards his own private life, family and personal affairs. Life in the forest had some features of a community life, but with observance of strict 'rules of the game': the principle of personal ownership was observed, and there was nothing of what could be called a family-erotic commune.... Retreating into the forest (which is not a return to nature) permitted the creation of another rhythm of work than the more restricting life in town. [70/48]

The buildings at Brzezinka, and the surrounding countryside, in becoming the main physical point of orientation for the research, introduced into the work the element – new to the Laboratory Theatre but familiar to Stanislavsky and Copeau amongst others – of an ecological interrelationship, which was in time to become an important structural element in the paratheatrical activities. Leszek Kolankiewicz has defined this relationship as 'the confrontation of a man or a group of people with the open or circumscribed space where their contacts with others and with the phenomena of the perceptible world becomes the "work" itself'. [315/24] Within this framework, then, the newer members, in bringing to the original team the impulses springing from a new generation's consciousness, stood before the former actors in a similar role to that of the participants they were hoping in future to recruit from amongst their ever-growing audiences. This is not, however, to suggest that the new members of the Laboratory Theatre group were being used as 'guinea pigs' in their experiments. Both subsequent developments, and statements from individuals made it clear that the work from this period entailed a completely new perspective on the nature and organization of the Institute. Flaszen has said:

> In the past, when young actors joined us, they were considered as 'apprentices' without rights, passing through an actor's purgatory. But the new young ones in 1970–1971 were given full rights from the beginning. Amongst the rest of us, the previous hierarchy was destroyed and everybody had to begin anew.... A young, unknown man, with no professional past (no one knew him) was now equal to Cieślak or Rena. As it turned out, he was leading the more important experiences. He was the most advanced of us all. I think this gave us new life and a new impulse. [143/323–324]

Finally, in June 1973, there took place at Brzezinka the first paratheatrical meeting

62 Brzezinka – Zygmunt Molik and
Jerzy Grotowski.

63 Jacek Zmysłowski.

64 Brzezinka – Włodzimierz Staniewski and Jerzy Grotowski.

with the participation of selected guests from outside the Laboratory Theatre group. The meeting lasted three days and three nights, and although initially called *Holiday*, in line with Grotowski's earlier texts and statements on the theme of this work, it was later given the official title of *Special Project*. Thus, after nearly three years of very hard work – of meeting and selecting new candidates for this intensely exploratory phase of the Institute's research, of seeing many people arrive expectantly and almost as many people leave again – the Laboratory Theatre group stood ready in the summer of 1973 to leave the secluded security of their new 'laboratory' at Brzezinka, and bring the work into confrontation with new and foreign groups of participants. The 'paratheatrical generation' of the Laboratory Theatre at this stage numbered six: Irena Rycyk, Zbigniew Kozłowski, Aleksander Lidtke, Teresa Nawrot, Włodzimierz Staniewski, and Jacek Zmysłowski (the last having been invited to remain with the group after participating in the June 1973 *Special Project*).

The opening of the paratheatrical work to participation from the outside demanded a new perspective, amongst other things, on the method of entry into the work. This was necessary to replace what Kolankiewicz called 'the criteria of ticket purchase', which he described as an 'imperfect and anachronistic purchase of participation in culture'. [315/24] Since the work was not, at this stage, opened up unconditionally for participation, what was implied, and required, was a selection process. Grotowski, in forceful terms, described the chosen participants as 'our kind...', those who breathe the same air and – one might say – share our senses'. [64/114] Kolankiewicz calls this the 'principle of mutual recognition' but elaborates upon the requirements demanded of participants: a basic desire for a meeting with others 'above the maze of more or less conflicting social roles'; [315/25] the courage to search for the 'sources of life'; and the acceptance of certain pragmatic assumptions in order to avoid chaos. [316/16] Ryszard Cieślak has also described the selection process as 'mutual', but in simpler terms:

> The participants are selected on the same basis as people are attracted to each other, that is on the basis of similar needs, aspirations and desires.... Anyone can apply, tell us what he's looking for and what he expects to find. The decision after that depends on many factors, namely whether our needs and desires are congruent, whether we are looking for the same thing, whether our mutual understanding is on the same 'wavelength' and many many other things. [140/6]

The implied elitism of the selection process for the participants was not unique to paratheatre but had also been an aspect of Grotowski's theatrical credo. Grotowski was proposing a theatre for an elite at a time when much of Western theatre was striving for an ideal of 'public theatre' – in the form of the Living Theatre's public events, the Happenings, street theatre, or Peter Brook's 'new Elizabethan relationship.... a crowd on stage and a crowd watching.' [73/12] In contrast, Grotowski stated: 'We are not concerned with just any audience, but with a special one'. Grotowski's ideal spectator was one

65 *top left* Jacek Zmysłowski.

66 *top centre*
Andrzej Paluchiewicz.

67 *top right* Irena Rycyk.

68 *left* Teresa Nawrot.

69 *right* Teo Spychalski.

who has genuine spiritual needs and who really wishes, through confrontation with the performance, to analyse himself..., who undergoes an endless process of self-development, whose unrest is not general but directed towards a search for the truth about himself and his mission in life. [73/40]

Although the form and conventions of Grotowski's work changed in the early seventies therefore, these requirements did not: the continuation was emphasized by the way that, in the early paratheatrical work, *Apocalypsis Cum Figuris* was used to recruit participants. The Laboratory Theatre team simply invited interested members of the audience to remain behind directly after a performance, to meet them and discuss the possibilities for work. This meeting was in some ways a response on the part of the spectator to the acts that had just been witnessed. Thus the dialogue, commenced in theatre, led the way through to the less familiar context of the paratheatrical work.

In the summer months of 1973 Grotowski travelled extensively – to the United States, New Zealand, Canada, Australia and Japan. Although he occasionally gave public talks, his major purpose was to negotiate a series of foreign tours that the Laboratory Theatre were to undertake in the 1973/74 season, in which the para-theatrical projects were to be presented. The first of these tours took place in the United States in September and October 1973. It began with 14 performances of *Apocalypsis Cum Figuris* in a cathedral in Philadelphia and then, with participants selected mainly from amongst the student population of Philadelphia and Pennsylvania, an 8-day *Special Project* was conducted in a rural locality. The tour had been well-prepared. In the previous June *The Drama Review* had published four of Grotowski's texts dealing with the new work under the collective title of *Holiday*, and there had been preparatory visits by Grotowski in February and July.

According to Richard Mennen, in one of the first extensive articles by a participant in the paratheatrical work to appear in the West, Grotowski sought in the organization of this *Special Project* to duplicate as stringently as possible the conditions that had evolved in seclusion in Poland. Mennen described the involved preparatory procedures: after extensive search a suitable rural retreat was located, the need for isolation being considered so important that the only inhabited building in view was screened from the sight of the participants. Work was conducted in the main buildings atop a hill: these were even internally architecturally altered to resemble more closely the buildings in Poland, and sealed to ensure that total black-out was possible, as was the case in both the performance room of the Wrocław theatre and in the barn at Brzezinka. The interior of the buildings was cleared of anything that could prove a dangerous obstacle to those working in the dark; electric lights were removed, and secure positions arranged for candles. Any neighbours in the remote area were forewarned not to be alarmed by loud or unusual noise.

Domestic activities – food preparation etc. – took place in buildings set apart. Those concerned with these practical organizational activities (Mennen called them 'support personnel'), as opposed to those participating, were not allowed to intrude into the work areas once the paratheatrical activities had commenced. The selected participants were told to bring sleeping bags, old clothes and musical instruments – but were forbidden the use of cars, mechanical equipment, and any form of stimulant. These, then, were the basic practical conditions for the paratheatrical work – conditions that, in all but detail, changed little in the subsequent few years.

The overall title of the large-scale project of this period started in the States was *Complex Research Programme*. In Philadelphia, apart from the performances of *Apocalypsis Cum Figuris* and the paratheatrical *Special Project*, there had been separate, 'theatrical' workshops conducted at Pittsburgh University by Zbigniew Cynkutis, Rena Mirecka and Ludwik Flaszen. The format of the event was repeated on subsequent occasions in the 1973/74 season, each time involving an evolution on the organizational level. In France (in November for the Festival d'Automne) and more particularly in Australia (where the Laboratory Theatre worked, at the invitation of the Australian Arts Council, from March until June 1974) the basis of the work began to broaden and outside participants were admitted in larger numbers – although these still did not include journalists or critics. According to a newspaper interview with Flaszen in Australia at that time, there were in all more than 1,500 applications to participate, or as Flaszen put it, 'to prolong the mutual encounters beyond *Apocalypsis*'. [137] In particular there evolved already two subdivisions of the paratheatrical work. These were called (rather comically and clumsily): (i) *Large Special Project* – directed towards group work and (ii) *Narrow Special Project* – devoted to the individual work of the participants (in which Grotowski himself took particular interest). Kolankiewicz has described the latter as 'internal work leading to, in (Grotowski's) words, "experiences of direct perception, with the whole self, literally"'. [316/30]

During the 1974/75 season, which the Laboratory Theatre spent at home in Wrocław, there were further developments. There was, principally, an intensification of the work, with the paratheatrical *Special Project* being undertaken on a more regular basis, and with the involvement of an increasing number of participants. These included for the first time journalists, although as Kolankiewicz pointed out, only those 'who demonstrated (along with other candidates) a human non-professional readiness to take part'. [316/17] This development introduced a new element. Since a condition of entry was a commitment to participation, and since there was no 'product' which could be assessed according to artistic criteria, the critic or journalist found his conventional position put in question. Tadeusz Burzyński was one of the first journalists to be invited, in the early spring of 1975, to participate in a *Special Project*. He has written of the particular problems for a writer attempting to describe the activities, and of the imperative of suspending the professional habit of observation:

> The personal experience I carried out of the event seems to me unmarred by professional bias. And in this and only in this respect, it does not differ from the experience of other participants. It must differ, however, in quality, but this is a very individual matter and I imagine that everyone brings with him and

carries out of there something that is uniquely his own. Although many observations would be the same for all of us, yet each of us, I imagine, would give a completely different account. It is questionable whether a comprehensive account is at all possible. [194/11]

Nevertheless, numerous accounts of paratheatrical work have been written since the opening of the work in the 1974/75 season, in a variety of styles and from a multiplicity of viewpoints, and published both in Poland and abroad. And it is from these participatory accounts that many people have had the opportunity to become familiar with concrete elements and aspects of the work. The following extract is from an account by Leszek Kolankiewicz of the very first *Special Project* undertaken in Poland in the 74/75 season. It was in two stages: the first, longer stage was undertaken by a small group of individuals under the leadership of Ryszard Cieślak. It was part of their work to prepare the environment and a skeleton of a structure for the second stage of the project, when they would welcome a larger, incoming group for a period of about 48 hours:

> For the first few days we do household work. We do not talk about what is to happen here. Habits brought from the city slowly die out: the defensive attitude (necessary there), the dullness of the senses, and indifference.... Gradually we become sensitive to one another, we feel our constant, tangible, warm presence. We grow into one, moving, many-peopled body. The work here is hard: we dig a deep pit, grub up stumps of trees, chop wood, carry coal and stones....
>
> Our collective body touches the ground more strongly, as it were, and – because it is collective – nestles in it more closely. We learn to inhabit it. We build a large shed which will be our Home. We bring from the woods, and take from the river, trunks of trees and bring armfuls of branches. The work goes on all day and long into the night.... On another day we disperse in the forest.
>
> I stand face to face with a tree. It is strong – I can climb it, support myself delicately on its branches. On its crown, a strong wind blows on us both, on the tree and myself. With my whole body I feel the movements of branches, the circulation of fluids, I hear the inner murmurs. I nestle into the tree....
>
> On some nights we go, several of us, to the woods. We walk without any light. We communicate in whispers. With my whole skin – particularly against my back – I feel the quiet breath of trees. We are gathered in by the thick of the woods opening to receive us. The forest plunged in darkness lives in a different way than in daytime....
>
> That unceasing presence of nature has its meaning. It sharpens the senses, as if it were giving birth to them anew, it confirms that we are embodied creatures....
>
> In the forelair (a small room where one sits on the floor among candles) we make music together.... The rhythm grows and ebbs away quietly, in turn. After many hours in the night I am giving myself totally to the waves of rhythm. I do not feel the pain of my fingers, the fatigue of my muscles. A song is born –

without words at first, then comes its text. It speaks about what is simplest, closest: about tree, earth, water, fire. About the white horse and the seagull, about a child being born. It speaks about a man who is near. This is our Song – it will never be repeated anywhere. . . .

What is most important takes place in the lair, in the coach house, in the mill, in the river, in the muddy pit, on the meadows, by the fire, in the pillar of fire, in the shed, in the woods. The lair is a large room without windows, with a smooth floor, and a hearth. Huge barrels with water heated by stones are standing here. There is a lot of grain in sacks and a heap of leaves, there are coniferous branches. Over the canal we hung a big fisherman's net. . . .

We are digging in the earth like boars, we throw ourselves on it all together. We climb a huge tree, we swing on a rope. We walk in a line, one behind the other, with our eyes closed. We sing. We give one another apples on the moss, we dig ourselves in a heap of leaves, we wash ourselves with grain. We run, the whole bunch of us, in the river, we fall into the net and immerse in the water, we jump headlong into the muddy pit, we dance in the barrels with hot water. We wipe ourselves with conifer needles. We roast meat, keep watch by our fires, we dance frantically on the flaming earth, we fly into the pillar of fire. Motionless in the forest clearing we take leave of the departing sun; in the morning we welcome it murmuring, standing closely in a circle. [316/21–25]

To complement this account there follows a skeletal form of inventory concerning environment, properties and a basic scheme of events. It is based upon reports of *Special Projects* that took place at Brzezinka in the spring and summer of 1975.

Each selected individual was given detailed instructions of what should be taken – e.g. several changes of clothes, specifically clothes which could be dirtied, soaked, or even destroyed; a good pair of walking shoes or knee-high rubber boots; a sum of money for food; a favourite musical instrument; enough cigarettes or tobacco for two to three days if required; sweaters, personal belongings as necessary. When the participants congregated in Wrocław, money was collected and communal food bought, and they were transported into the countryside to Brzezinka. On arrival luggage was checked to make sure that participants had all the essentials, and superfluous items (in particular watches) were temporarily taken away. The participants were briefly introduced to the geographical lay-out of buildings and surrounding countryside, but not given any unnecessary information about the forthcoming project. The building in which the indoor activities took place was a converted barn – there were several rooms used for work and given familiarizing names such as *Matecznik* (the Lair). The surrounding countryside, in which the outdoor work took place in both daylight and by night, consisted of fields, densely wooded areas, streams and a lake, and was uninhabited and unfrequented. The arriving group was put to work on some form of physical labour.

After several hours, usually late at night, they gathered around a fire for food and drink followed by improvised music and dancing. The group might then move outside into the countryside. The subsequent 48 hours were spent in more or less continuous activity, which alternated between one or other of the inside rooms and the surrounding countryside. Outside, the participants were encouraged to run for long periods to the point of exhaustion; swim in the lake or stream; climb trees or perform other minor feats demanding a degree of agility normally lost after childhood; and play and improvise with fire, earth, stones and a variety of natural objects. There were activities that encouraged specifically communal experiences, and those in which contact on a one-to-one basis was more natural. In addition there was a period (usually at night) when the group dispersed into the forest for each member to spend some time in isolation.

Inside, the activities were naturally of a more confined, intense nature, often involving improvised music, drumming and dancing. There were occasionally a variety of properties brought in from outside – straw, sand, earth, water in barrels. But there were also possibilities for tranquil periods: resting, eating, sleeping. Participants were not given in verbal form a set of rules or code of behaviour with which to confront the work, nor any information in advance as to what to expect. The only occasion on which words were employed by the organizers apart from practical usage, was infrequently in the form of brief, poetic and metaphoric injunctions, used as a spur to action. And it would seem that verbal communication, consciously rejected as a matter of principle by the organizers, soon became redundant to participants also. Burzyński again:

> I cannot stop wondering to this day that after a while we stopped talking. . . . Having arrived at other, simpler and less artificial modes of communication, we became distrustful of words. . . . There are, now I know there are, other ways of communicating oneself and one's emotions to others, other ways of sharing joy. [194/17]

This synthesized account of a *Special Project* can be concluded with a longer extract from the Polish journalist Tadeusz Burzyński, written after his first experience of paratheatrical participation in April 1975.

> Our activity – which was not an ordinary, everyday experience – was not especially extraordinary when viewed in terms of individual actions. Some of these are experienced by us in our daily life with greater or lesser intensity. They are incipient in our ordinary actions, adventures and games. In the *Special Project*, these situations were simply condensed in time and put in a certain order. For although spontaneous reaction imparts a human content and impact to these situations yet they involve some planning, namely the direction, and certain points which the actions were expected to reach. There was no plan of the road, the variety of options, roads and paths was practically unlimited. Thus what we had was a skeleton of experience (in order to avoid chaos) which was clothed during the various activities with the living tissue of impulse, reaction and emotion contributed by the participants, exchanged between them and mutually inspired. The skeleton was neither immutable nor imposed. [194/16]

Apart from the intensification of the participatory work in the *Special Projects* (under the leadership of Ryszard Cieślak and with the collaboration principally of Elizabeth Albahaca, Antoni Jahołkowski and Zygmunt Molik from the 'old team') there were, during 1974 and 1975, developments in aspects of theatrical and paratheatrical work involving other members of the Laboratory Theatre acting team. In time a pattern of subsidiary projects evolved from the central *Special Project* (which incorporated, in perhaps the purest form, the principles of *Holiday* propounded by Grotowski in 1970). The form of these projects was fluid: it is not really feasible to select any one individual and delineate in any permanent sense the form their project may have taken. But each individual's work had certain characteristics recognizable from their theatrical past which helped to mould the structure of their project (such as Ludwik Flaszen's natural preoccupation with the word, or Zygmunt Molik's awesome experience with vocal blockages).

The following is a brief description of the form these projects took during 1975 (but it should not be taken as an indication of work conducted at the Laboratory Theatre at any other time). The accounts of the workshops are based on those given by Grotowski in two articles published during 1975, and in the internal booklet on the paratheatrical work compiled by Leszek Kolankiewicz:

I.   *Acting Therapy* – led by Zygmunt Molik (and later also by Antoni Jahołkowski and Rena Mirecka): described as work on the release of the actor's inhibiting organic reactions – of body, voice, breathing, energy. This was extended to include participants from professions other than acting where the voice is important (e.g. teachers).

II. *Meditations Aloud* – conducted by Ludwik Flaszen and evolving from his theoretical workshops: these soon became paratheatrical in nature. They aimed 'through the process of the word to liberate within the participants the ability to recognize their own impulses or motives'.

III. *Event*–led by Zbigniew Cynkutis (in collaboration with Rena Mirecka). This was originally mainly for people still working in theatre (an indication of Cynkutis' own personal inclinations). Involving 'non-technical aspects of the actor's art' it invoked 'an awareness of the personal oscillation between game and play'.

IV. *Workshop Meetings* – led by Stanisław Scierski: an exploration of forms of contact between people using the exercises as a departure point. 'Training was only the springboard, which would catapult the participants in the direction of human meeting beyond exercises and game'.

V.   *International Studio* – led by Teo Spychalski: this in effect was a develoment from the annual practical course for visiting foreign students, which had in more recent years been Spychalski's responsibility. The activities developed from the earlier pedagogic courses in a manner naturally parallel to the basic progress from the theatrical to the paratheatrical and were fluid to the extent that they were formally moulded by the particular energies of each group of students. In 1975 Spychalski's project was called *Song of Myself* and was 'an attempt by each participant to build an individual path through time and space (in the city and the country). It was also a search for the mutual intersection points of those unique paths built by the different people'.

VI. *Special Project* – group work led by Cieślak, Albahaca, Jahołkowski, Kozłowski, Molik, Nawrot, Rycyk, Paluchiewicz and Zmysłowski: 'The aim was Meeting, conceived of as an inter-human encounter, where man would be himself, regain the unity of his being, become creative and spontaneous in relation to others'.

Each of the above individual projects defined fine areas of distinction within the general principles of the paratheatrical activities, and the pattern of these projects was finally unveiled in Wrocław in June 1975, for the *University of Research* of the Theatre of Nations festival.

The re-establishment of the Theatre of Nations festival, after several years of eclipse, was a proposition placed before the International Theatre Institute Congress in Moscow by the Polish delegation in 1973, and was realized in Warsaw from 8–28 June 1975. It was the largest theatrical event that the country had experienced, comprising fifty performances of productions from sixteen different countries, in addition to twenty productions from Polish companies. In conjunction with these events, and under the official auspices of the Theatre of Nations festival, Jerzy Grotowski – in collaboration with his former student, Eugenio Barba – presented a *University of Research* in Wrocław from 14 June to 7 July.

70 Eugenio Barba and Jerzy Grotowski.

71 Jerzy Grotowski and Jean-Louis Barrault.

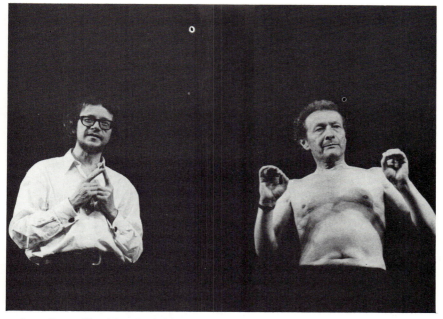

72 Jerzy Grotowski and Jean-Louis Barrault.

The range of activities encompassed by the *University of Research* was super-ficially quite broad. There were presentations of performances by the Laboratory Theatre, Barba's Odin Teatret and other companies; public meetings and work-shops with Peter Brook, Eugenio Barba, Joseph Chaikin, André Gregory, Jean-Louis Barrault and Luca Ronconi; films of present and past work from those theatres and directors already mentioned, as well as films on Balinese theatre and trance techniques, and a season of films by a Swedish director, Marianne Ahrne; workshops and training demonstrations from the Odin theatre and the Daidalos group from Malmö; daily consultative workshops presented by Stanisław Scierski, Ludwik Flaszen and Zygmunt Molik; and consultations directed by medical and psychiatric specialists.

Over five thousand people attended the public meetings and conferences at the *University of Research*, and according to Kolankiewicz there were at least another 4,500 'active members' of the *University* (i.e. those who actively participated in the various paratheatrical activities conducted during the *University*). There were the official guests – foreign journalists, friends of the Laboratory Theatre such as Raymonde Temkine and Ninon Tallon Karlweiss, and of course those invited professionals who were collaborating in the project and in some cases running their own workshops (as did André Gregory and Peter Brook). But information had been circulated world-wide to universities and student centres, and by far the greater number of those attending were young people, who arrived daily from as far apart as Canada, Greece and Australia (Tadeusz Burzyński, in an article from the period in a local Wrocław newspaper, mentions 26 countries of origin). [189] All those arriving were issued with a 'membership card', either green or yellow. Journalists, or anyone else in an observational capacity, received the green card, which per-mitted entrance to discussions, performances, films and demonstrations, but not to participatory work sessions. The yellow card, on the other hand, was inscribed *Karta Robocza Uczestnika* (Work Participation Card): a holder of this card was accorded entry into any of the activities organized, with the proviso that possession of the card signified a commitment to total participation in the work.

The participatory work organized by the Laboratory Theatre took two basic forms: the first of these came under the heading of *General Laboratory*. This, as well as encompassing the daily consultative workshops already mentioned by Scierski, Flaszen and Molik (on exercises, meditative conversation and acting therapy respectively), also took the form of nightly paratheatrical work sessions which were given the name of *Ul* (Beehive). These were openly accessible to all those who were willing to participate (rather than observe) and the numbers attending ranged from only three on one occasion to over 220. According to Kolankiewicz's documentation, there were in total 21 'Beehives' attended by 1,842 people. The second category of participatory work comprised the specialized workshops enumerated earlier – each project led by an individual actor with the assistance of others of their colleagues or a smaller group of young Poles enlisted temporarily to help in the organization. These workshops generally lasted not more than 48 hours, and were conducted in specific isolated locations – either at

73 Participants of the University of Research 1975.

Brzezinka, or in the countryside surrounding Wrocław, or in sealed-off rooms within the actual theatre complex. The number of outside participants at any one of these self-contained, intensive work sessions was usually less than twenty, and participation was not a consequence of holding a yellow card (as with the daily consultations and the 'Beehives') but resulted from direct consultation with Grotowski.

The combined force of all the activities enumerated above, in fact served to centre attention on precisely the area that, after a long journey of sixteen years, was immediately confronting the Laboratory Theatre: that is, the as yet ill-defined borderland where, in the face of the more immediate and effectual, the transcribed reality of theatre and the performing arts loses validity. Grotowski was the only one of the assembled company who had taken the step of categorically abandoning theatrical convention, but each of the others contributed something of their own personal, relevant researches. Both Chaikin and Gregory spoke of their anxiety concerning the current theatrical experimentation in the United States and their gradual loss of faith in theatre as a valid art form. Chaikin had disbanded the Open Theatre and Gregory had come to Poland to look for a group of non-professional young people with whom to work. In interview with the Polish writer Andrzej Bonarski, Gregory said:

It is not important that one creates art, which is then presented to people but it *is* important that people – individuals who are relevant in life and in work – are involved in the creative process.... Here and now – in what is happening

74 André Gregory and Jerzy Grotowski.

here – the barriers are simply disappearing between those who are the audience and those who are the artists. That's a development of something we've been working at for the last seven years. [169/47–48]

Both Peter Brook and Eugenio Barba, as well as leading workshops, showed films documenting the experiments in cultural interchange undertaken when their companies went amongst people unfamiliar with performing techniques (Brook in Africa and Barba in Southern Italy). At his public conference, Peter Brook said of his work in Africa:

The trip to Africa was a challenge for us. To play for people with whom one not only does not have a common language, but with whom it is not even possible to communicate through a common culture.... What mattered was that one always had to begin from scratch and create, because of that, the rules of the game gradually, together with the people assembled around us. The basic lesson was to be the live experience, in conditions of something like a public performance; the experience of a chance to achieve a genuine interhuman exchange. It is

75 Jerzy Grotowski and Peter Brook.

pointless to ask about the content of that exchange: the exchange itself is the content. [316/33]

This summary of the *University of Research* (which was, in its time, a highly innovative and ambitious undertaking) cannot convey the underlying sense – very strong at that point in the Laboratory Theatre's work – of the possibility at last of effecting real changes in the relationship between a Western society and its culture, and the significance of the artist within society. Allied to this was the extent to which the creative work was being opened out, in an unprecedented fashion, to the experience of interested members of a wider public. And these were, after all, developments that Grotowski had by implication been working towards throughout his theatrical career. But for Grotowski himself, with his restless desire for exploration, the achievement of the *University of Research* – and its successful opening of the paratheatrical work to a wider public – signalled already the beginning of a new phase of work. In an interview published in the following year he said:

> The *University* was the end of one stage of research, which we have been involved in ever since the presentation of *Apocalypsis Cum Figuris*. It was also the opening of the next phase.... It was the first, very important step for us in making accessible what in the preliminary period had had to be very restricted. [81]

CHAPTER TEN
Mountain Project 1975–1978

The few years which followed the Wrocław *University of Research*, up to and including the realization of the *Mountain Project*, can already be seen retrospectively as the second phase of the Laboratory Theatre's post-theatrical activity. The work itself, in its basic elements, was no longer either a novelty or a completely unknown quantity. It was evident from the participatory work that had already taken place that an appropriate form had been discovered. And it was also evident from the sheer numbers of those wanting to participate – and from their response – that the direction the Laboratory Theatre was taking was in sympathy with the needs experienced and expressed by their followers in Poland and the other countries they visited. With the security of this knowledge behind them the Laboratory Theatre team – and particularly some members of the 'paratheatrical generation' – were ready to take the work in new directions. This phase of research was to culminate in the *Mountain Project*.

The venture which had initially been undertaken during the Theatre of Nations festival in Poland in the summer of 1975 – of making a variety of paratheatrical work accessible to the public within the framework of an organized event – had an even wider public trial during La Biennale festival in Venice, from 22 September to 22 November 1975. On this occasion, as in both earlier and later sessions of paratheatrical work, *Apocalypsis Cum Figuris* was used as bridge for the transformation of the spectator into the participant. After each presentation of the performance, interested members of the audience were given the opportunity for direct contact with members of the Laboratory Theatre, with the aim of reaching a mutual decision as to which workshop, if any, they should join.

The Laboratory Theatre was allocated four separate locations for their work. Three of them (the Villa Communale at Mirano, the Biennale Pavilion in the Gardens of Venice and the Castello di Montegalda at Vicenza) were used for the six subdivisions of paratheatrical work (led by Cieślak, Cynkutis, Flaszen, Molik, Scierski and Spychalski). The fourth location – the tiny, spectacular island of San Giacomo in Palude, lying between Murano and Burano – was used for the *Apocalypsis* presentations. The performances alternated in three or four day cycles with a project run by Włodzimierz Staniewski (with occasional assistance from Grotowski and other members of the Institute) in which predominantly experimental Italian theatre groups were invited to the island for an exchange of work.

The activities of the Venice Biennale, which had attracted large numbers of participants, also naturally attracted a great deal of critical attention. For many international critics it was their first acquaintance with not only the organization and realization of the events, but with the very concept of paratheatre, and there was much speculation. Consequently Grotowski organized a separate conference – which he termed wryly a *Scientific Session* – in the small town of Mirano on 23 and 24 November 1975. There were public debates, presentations of Laboratory Theatre film, and meetings between Grotowski, Luca Ronconi and Peter Brook. All those interested – including journalists and members of the public – were invited, and it was hoped that a frank exposition and discussion of the paratheatrical activities would be possible. Nevertheless, there were constant accusations, directed towards Grotowski, of secrecy and evasion. In response – on the final evening – Grotowski asked several participants from the paratheatrical events to recount their experiences and to answer questions.

It was precisely during this period of the Laboratory Theatre's stay in Venice that the journalistic repercussions of the Wrocław *University of Research* were being fully felt in Poland. There were virulent debates in the major cultural periodicals between participants and non-participants of the paratheatrical work, devoted enthusiasts and entrenched opponents. For many conventional critics who had only just, by the beginning of the seventies, reached an uneasy acceptance of Grotowski's theatrical work, the demands made upon their tolerance and understanding by this new work were too much (particularly in the face of the explicit personal statements contained in some of Grotowski's texts). The debate surrounding the work of the Laboratory Theatre (never entirely dormant once again descended to the level of invective, and Grotowski's personality, motives and sincerity were held up to question (all of this, as Osiński has pointed out, in a tone completely opposed to the principles contained in the paratheatrical work itself).

Where any valid theoretical discussion was entered into, the main preoccupation seemed to be a searching for definitions, boundaries, labels, parameters. Was Grotowski a theatre director, prophet, guru, magician or charlatan? Were the practitioners of paratheatre actors, disciples, puppets, retarded delinquents or indulged elitists? Were the paratheatrical activities theatre, therapy, escapism, insanity or reality? Grotowski himself took the position he has always adopted in such debates. Whilst freely and almost carelessly inventing new dimensions for his work and new labels where appropriate (Holiday, paratheatre, active culture) he has only concerned himself with designating them in practice and has been indifferent to the theoretical necessity of constructing the conceptual map necessary for an intellectual understanding of the new territories – to show their borders and relationships to territory already charted. In the December 1975 issue of a Russian literary magazine there appeared a joint statement from Grotowski and Flaszen, which contained the following:

The real challenge is life. That challenge is always difficult, as is the reply, and the reply is nothing other than the creative process. The impulses which come from art are merely one of the many kinds of impulse in which life abounds.... In our practical researches we create our own language. But the question of which art this belongs to is not our business, but that of the critics and theorists'. [361/160]

Despite the happy disregard of the creators of paratheatre for the necessity of definitions, the issues raised by the journalistic debate did help to clarify (albeit only conceptually) some aspects of the post-theatrical work and the consequences of the abandonment of artistic form. In many cases it usefully prompted hitherto silent participants to publish factual descriptions of the events, to give personal testimonies of their experiences, and to state their own analyses of what the work was about. What seemed to confront and confound commentators most (including both opponents and admirers) was in fact a very simple proposition: Grotowski's continuing and increasing emphasis on authenticity. It is difficult not to conclude that the unwillingness or apparent inability of many to abandon artistic criteria for paratheatre justified one of its basic underlying propositions – that in contemporary culture artistic form is used to ward off, rather than promote, direct experience.

One example can be seen in the account by the American critic Margaret Croyden, who took part in a *Special Project* during the *University of Research*. Writing from an impersonal position of aesthetic judgement she considered the experience to be 'pure, ritualistic, sacred theater'. Grotowski, in stepping outside the confines of theatre had taken the accessories of art with him – the magnificent sets (the mountain, the forest) and the most dramatic of props (candle-flame, fire, water, stone and earth):

> During the course of the night, it became clear that a metaphysical system, *theatrically translated into stunning visual configuration* was at work. Its leading theme was the human drama..., the series of events were designed like a long poem with *material symbols actually there*, not imagined.... Each was 'staged' against a simple but deliberately chosen background – a lagoon, a tree, a windmill.... Fire was perhaps the most impressive image – fascinating in its flickering self and *symbolising* as it does enlightenment, *warmth* and life.... (my emphases) [214/198]

This form of intellectual evasion is an extreme consequence of the misapplication of artistic criteria, and one that Grotowski had already foreseen. In his original *Holiday* statement in December 1970 he had said:

> Perhaps, everything I am talking about just now, you take to be metaphors. They are not metaphors. This is tangible and practical. It is not a philosophy but something one does; and if someone thinks that this is a way of formulating thoughts, he is mistaken; this has to be taken literally, this is experience. [64/117]

What became evident in the response from non-participatory commentators to the accounts of participants was that the role of theatrical critic in paratheatre was redundant (which did not, of course, stop most critics from trying). They were able to examine the activities and the objectives from an ethical viewpoint: and could justifiably question, for example, the validity of Grotowski's position as 'prophet', the ethical nature of the selection process, or the abdication of political and social action that the activities possibly implied. In this the critic could react in a philosophical, sociological or political, but not *artistic* capacity. Within their capacity *as* critics, it was not to Grotowski or the members of the Laboratory Theatre as 'creators' of the events that the commentators had to address themselves, nor to the participants of those events as 'co–creators – and not even to Grotowski's statements as an artistic doctrine – but to those participants who chose in some way to relate the events and activities.

For what many commentators consistently refused to recognize was that the activities themselves did not represent a *transcription* of experience, and thus could not be criticized according to formal criteria. It was the participants who chose to write about their experiences who stood in the same relation to those experiences as the Laboratory Theatre actors did to their internal and creative processes in a theatrical context – or as any artist does in relation to her or his internal creative processes – that is as transcribers of their own reality. And the critic only has a validity in response to the transcription, not to the reality. In the context of the paratheatrical events the critic (or even the observer) was as completely inappropriate as in relation, for example, to a religious or mystical experience, or to the act of love. At a talk given in New York in 1978 Grotowski said:

> When we are dealing with a product – for example a production – we can describe it from the outside. We may write that such and such a thing happens, that things turn out in such and such a way. But when there is no division between actor and spectator, when every participant of the process is a person who is doing, then a description ostensibly from the outside, that is one that tries to grasp what is happening and why, such a description can only lead to misunderstandings. Why? Because it is made from the standpoint of observer, whereas the process may only be experienced by a person who is doing. Only a description 'from within' is possible here. [84/96]

Indifferent on the whole to this debate (which was to last throughout the seventies) the Laboratory Theatre continued their paratheatrical research undeterred. At this stage, despite controversy, Grotowski was far too established a figure on both a national and international level for the security of his work and institution to be seriously threatened by the aggressive and defensive response of his critics (as opposed to the earlier years in Opole). From the beginning of 1976 the para-theatrical work began to diversify even further. There were experiments in a form of activity called *Otwarcia* (Openings) – for the first time freely accessible and without limits as to the numbers participating. These took place mainly in the theatre buildings in Wrocław, but with occasional excursions into public surround-ings (for example the Wrocław Railway Station). They were led in spring 1976 by Scierski, Cieślak and Spychalski, together with some of the younger members of the group.

From May until July 1976 the Laboratory Theatre were in France at the invitation of the French Secretary of State for Culture, Michel Guy. There they conducted another large-scale project at La Terraille Abbey near Saintes in south-west France. It was the first time that the Institute presented their new work abroad without performances of *Apocalypsis Cum Figuris*. There were two directions: in both cases the work was organized as a series of 2-week workshops, in order to accommodate the maximum number of participants. The first of these projects was the more professionally-orientated *Acting Therapy*, which, without being directed towards performance, maintained concrete links with the Institute's past theatrical research. In an interview published in *Le Monde* in March 1976, notifying potential participants of the forthcoming events, Grotowski spoke in more detail of the *Acting Therapy* workshop, emphasizing to begin with that the work had nothing to do with medical therapy:

> If we have chosen this terminology, it is in order to stress two points: first of all that aesthetic considerations are not taken into account. We are concerned with all those who, more or less professionally, use their bodies, their voice. Actors, but also for example teachers. Secondly, we are not setting up a technical school, or an experimental centre. We are content just to transmit knowledge acquired through fifteen years of work at the Institute. In particular, we know how to determine the origin of certain vocal and respiratory blockages, blockages of muscular response, and we can pinpoint the cause of particular trauma. We make no claims to being relevant for everyone. At times the blockages require medical help, or psychiatry or else it would take too long to counteract. In that case, we say clearly that we can do nothing. [79]

The second aspect of the work undertaken in France in 1976 was a paratheatrical project under the general title of *Vers un Mont Parallèle*. This poetic phrase really only achieves any meaning in the context of the planned *Mountain Project*, an idea first referred to by Grotowski before even the *University of Research* was under-taken in the summer of 1975. In that year he had described the notion of work around the theme of a Mountain, in both its metaphorical and literal senses, and the guardianship of a flame upon the Mountain (again, literal and metaphorical). Grotowski wrote:

> The Mountain is something we aim towards, something which demands effort and determination. It is a kind of knot, or central point, a point of concentration – but focal, not divergent. If there are places on earth where something beats like a pulse, or a heart, then one of these terrestrial pulse-spots would be the Mountain. The Mountain contains a sense of distance, but from which you return. The Mountain is a kind of test.
>
> You must remember in all this that we have in mind a real, existing Mountain and not some kind of image. [75/23]

In the event the *Mountain Project*, which covered in its entirety a period of activity in and around Wrocław from Autumn 1976 to the end of July 1977, was probably the largest of the paratheatrical projects to be realized, both in its practical scope and in the breadth and depth of its conception.

Shortly after the theatre's return from France there appeared in the press announcements regarding the forthcoming realization of the project and the appointment of Jacek Zmysłowski as its director. At that time Jacek was only 22 and was still technically a student of Polish studies at Wrocław University (although since 1973 he had been concurrently participating in the Laboratory Theatre paratheatrical experiments). He had, however, never been involved in any theatrical enterprise, and Leszek Kolankiewicz has described him as 'one of those whose coming to the group was naturally connected with seeking new ways and discovering new areas'. [315/24] Jacek had been involved in the paratheatrical work in France, and in an interview published in November 1978 he described how, in experimental work undertaken there in a small, international group of non-professional young people, there had been an unexpected and unplanned breakthrough in the work: 'We discovered our own flow of work, going beyond any previous experience'. [141] As a consequence of this work the nucleus of a small group was set up. It was to this group, under Jacek's leadership, that Grotowski entrusted the full realization of the Mountain Project (although he maintained a perspective on the work, and participated himself in the final phase).

Later in 1976 Grotowski gave an interview, published in the Polish Party newspaper *Trybuna Ludu*, in which he described the three distinct stages of the ambitious *Mountain Project*: *Nocne Czuwanie* (Night Vigil), *Droga* (The Way) and *Góra Płomienia* (Mountain of Flame). [81] The first of these – *Night Vigil* – was an open session of work lasting several hours and conducted regularly during 1976 and 1977, in work rooms inside the theatre buildings in Wrocław. The number of participants in a *Night Vigil* varied from a few to several dozen, the majority of whom had responded to the press announcements and an invitation printed on posters. Besides having intrinsic value as a paratheatrical experience for those taking part, *Night Vigil* also served pragmatically as a means of assessing the participants' readiness to proceed to later stages of the project (a process that ideally operated mutually). The first *Night Vigil* took place during the night of 27/28 September 1976. Leszek Kolankiewicz, who was one of the participants on this occasion, later published a lengthy and detailed description: the following is a brief extract relating, in a subjective style, some moments of intense activity:

> Someone suddenly gets up, and so do I. Someone else is still beating the rhythm, but more and more of us are now upright. Nobody speeds up. The beats stop, but the rhythm continues just the same. We help ourselves, marking with our feet the fragment of movement, but after a while that too is superfluous. There is the almost soundless, perpetual movement of nine shadows. At a certain point this begins to feel weird. I sense how the waves of rhythm, consisting of breathing and the rustle of bare feet, gradually sift up to the ceiling....
>
> All at once I leap into a rhythm of raised knees, arched back, fluttering hands, shaking head. With my feet bouncing off the floor, I mark a circle around Jacek's

76 Poster for *Night Vigil*.

flickering movements.... It is as if I were a shadow thrown by his movements onto the surrounding air, a trail after the flight of his body. As if he were tracing on shifting sands the marks of a field I have trodden, the centre of my movement. [314]

The next stage – *The Way* – took place in the summer months of 1977, and constituted in fact the journey to the *Mountain of Flame*. The participants (who had been selected either subsequent to participation in *Night Vigil* or on the basis of previous work with the Laboratory Theatre) departed from the theatre buildings in Wrocław in small groups of about eight, at regular daily intervals and under the guidance of two experienced 'leaders'. They had spent a few hours in preparation of a strictly practical nature, advising what should be taken and supplying basic necessities. The group was transported into the countryside by van, and left to find their way on foot. At this stage no–one knew how long the journey would take, or had certain prior knowledge of what to expect ahead. In the event *The Way* involved one or two nights in the forest regardless of weather and was physically demanding. The following is another extract from a longer account which I wrote for one of the Dartington Papers published in 1978:

> *The Way*, at first indifferent, has become hostile. Water scornfully invades and takes possession of every part of the body. The thread of human forms, like a lurching, drunken centipede, makes a hesitant path through the forest growth. From any and every angle it looks pathetic and uncomfortable and insignificant. From inside an individual body it is a massive experience. Robbed externally of all vision, the alternative perception is not completely reliable. The blackness pressing against the face and body has sharp edges and extrusions; skin-ripping electric neck-snapping sensations of pain which catapult without warning against the flesh. There is no way of preparing the organism against these assaults. To withdraw, to close up, to clench the muscles ever so slightly, detracts from the priority occupation: maintaining contact with the organism ahead. It is this which demands meditational concentration from every cell in the body. [331]

The final stage of the work – the *Mountain of Flame* – is actually located in a gently hilly area north-west of Wrocław. Its sides are deeply wooded and it is surmounted by an ancient castle, part in ruins. A national and historic monument, and naturally the property of the State, it was placed at the disposal of the Laboratory Theatre during this period for their paratheatrical projects. Most remained out of use but a section of the interior was extensively repaired and modernized, with wooden floors laid, massive log fires put back into service, and toilet and kitchen facilities added. All rooms were completely bare and cut off from the outside.

There were two main work areas in the castle, with rough stone walls and wooden floors. The upper room, massive and lofty, led through an archway into a smaller annexe used exclusively as a domestic area, where a log fire burned constantly. All 'domestic activities', such as eating and sleeping, were dictated by the random pattern of the work periods: these were not controlled in any way by the organizing

77 Poster for *The Way*.

group, but commenced spontaneously in the main room. There was always the possibility for any participant to inaugurate, join or leave a session. In the work room there was absolute vocal silence. All impulse – for expression, contact, physical endeavour, disarmament, exposure – was channelled into dynamic physical action, according to the needs of those taking part.

In addition it was possible for a group to leave the castle temporarily and work in the surrounding Polish countryside for several hours. This presented the framework for a very different state from that of the castle workshops – where the containment had created a density of awareness and experience. Similarly, on the return, the perception of the almost claustrophobic environment of the Mountain was heightened. There was no predetermined period of time for an individual's sojourn upon the Mountain – it was decided for each by the leader, Jacek Zmysłowski. As the cycle of work came to a close, the participant was led with others to retrace their journey out of the castle and down the Mountain, until they were picked up and transported back to Wrocław. To conclude the account of the *Mountain Project*, the following is an extract from a text by the Canadian anthropologist Professor Ronald L. Grimes: it was written in response to Grotowski's own words concerning the Mountain, at a meeting during a festival in Ontario in 1976:

> One cannot with fidelity merely speak of Grotowski; one must speak with him. Merely repeating the words of his five hours of lecture and discussion is as inconsistent with his message as gymnastically repeating his exercises, so I have chosen to write a meditation rather than a report. Grotowski is in process, and his words, like his exercises, flow. Hence, to be faithful to him is not to imitate him but to transform him. His words are performative utterances – not things, but actions. Either we let an action die or we respond to it without repeating it; we 'tell it forward', in other words.
>
> The 'other word' I would use is 'pilgrimage'. In 'pilgrimage' Grotowski and I have a meeting of words. Pilgrimage is a process of taking leave of a bounded space, searching and researching for a way, ascending a mountain of first-seeing, and then making one's way home. A pilgrim is a person in motion, a person whose action originates in the deep roots of his own physical, cultural and spiritual home; who then proceeds to a far away place (often a mountain) in search of shared adventure; and who descends finally to a new or renewed home-space. In short, he is en route to his roots.
>
> A pilgrim is an ordinary person – student, actor, professor, sales-person. As pilgrims we are incidentally, not primarily, our roles. Grotowski as pilgrim is, incidentally, a director. His home-space is Polish and theatrical. Pilgrims leave home when the doors of perception no longer swing in and out, but rust shut, turning home space into prison space. If one would be fully at home, one must sometimes move. Grotowski is on the move to a mountain, literally and metaphorically: Fire Mountain, June 1977. [263]

There was clear evidence within the *Mountain Project* that the paratheatrical work had developed beyond the earliest *Special Projects*, and the workshops and

Uls that took place during the *University of Research* in 1975. In a report of the Laboratory Theatre's activities published early in 1978, Tadeusz Burzyński considered those developments, and the particular characteristics of the new phase of work:

> Were we to look for comparisons with the earlier *Uls*. . . . or with the outdoor *Special Project*, we might say that the present project has evolved towards a purification of the location, and the circumstances of these encounters, of everything that could be a relic, symbol or stimulus of the theatre. The situations were reduced to the simplest terms in order to add depth to them. In the *Uls* 'props' were sometimes used. They prompted a series of associations and gave direction to the reactions of the participants. But in the *Night Vigil* there was only the empty hall and the people, largely a haphazard collection. In *The Way* the area is as it is, without any planned 'surprises' adapted to the specific nature of the place, as in the case of the Special Project. One might say that this raises difficulties because there are no catalysts. Everything boils down to the simplest elements: you, others and some kind of space. The rest remains to be found: in yourself, in others, in the space. Not as an intellectual exercise, but as an active search with the whole self. [196/19]

Thus it would seem that paratheatre, in its turn, was eventually subjected to the same process at the hands of the Laboratory Theatre team as the discipline of theatre – a process of refinement, and a stripping down to the basic elements required for the release of the creative process. Jacek Zmysłowski described the transformation that had taken place in France in the year preceding the Mountain Project:

> We led highly intensive open-air work which lasted several days and consisted – to put it simply – of movement, of the perception of space through movement, being in space in continual movement. The environment and the exceptionally well-chosen group of people resulted in that being one of the fullest experiences in which I have participated. It suddenly became clear that the only essential thing is the special preparation of a place – and that 'props' directing or inspiring action are meaningless: there were too many objects and too much calculation. What is left is only what is essential, but literally, essential to life. It became possible to eliminate everything artificial and leave the most simple of relationships: an individual/space – in fact an individual in space and us in the face of ourselves. [141]

As we have seen from the descriptions so far, the aspect of location, or environment, was always of paramount concern in the organization of the paratheatrical work. On a practical level this was due in part to the need for security – that is, the creation of an environment into which no spectator could intrude and where each individual had the possibility of being a participant.

Maybe one must begin with some particular places, yes, I think that there is an urgent need to have a place where we do not hide ourselves and simply are, as we are, in all possible senses of the word. [64/118]

But there was also in evidence the desire to find a meaningful space, almost magical, and certainly untouched by the patterns and rituals of daily life. As Ronald Grimes said: 'Though a pilgrim is an ordinary person, he is proceeding through extra-ordinary space – in-between space, "liminal" (threshold) space, boundary-crossings, he is in para-ordinary space.' [263] Occasionally this was fulfilled in a spectacular manner, as when the company conducted its project on an uninhabited island in the Adriatic, or indeed in a castle on top of a mountain in Poland. But more often it was in a less spectacular but equally secure and secluded spot such as an isolated farm, and it may even have been in rooms within an ordinary building in town, sealed off for the duration of the project.

Apart from the practical consideration of isolation, there was of course a quite logical development from Grotowski's earlier experiments in 'enviromental theatre' (although strictly speaking it would be more accurate to call the process a 'reversal', considering the pre-theatrical origins of the environmental tradition). Grotowski's environmental experiments in a theatrical context were all basically motivated by his desire to establish the most effective conditions for an authentic contact between actor and audience. In the same way it could be said that the aspect of environment in paratheatre was influential in the releasing and encouraging of the spontaneous reactions which were being sought. There was a precedent here in the utopian experiments of Stanislavsky. He dreamt of creating a 'spiritual order of actors' who would take their living from the land and give their performance on an Estate far from the city:

.... if besides meeting on the stage, they met in nature, in common work on the soil, in fresh air, in the light of the sun, their souls would open, their physical labour would aid in the creation of unison among them. [400/537]

Accounts by participants have also tended to underline this aspect of the para-theatrical work. Richard Mennen, for example, described the projects that took place in the country as being 'concerned with man acting as a wild animal' and at the conclusion of his work with Cieślak said: 'By the end, I felt a profound connection with the natural world, and that I had begun to search in a very physical way for roots and sources' [346/69]. Conversely, the obvious elements of naturism and even animism have also evoked much criticism, from both participants and non-participants alike. Maciej Karpiński, describing an account by one participant in which the experience in the forest is referred to as 'a meeting such as man would have had with the forest at the time of his initial contact', called the premise 'absurd', claiming that in such conditions an individual would be concerned exclusively with self-survival [293]. Similarly Zygmunt Rymuza, who had parti-cipated in a *Special Project* himself, attacked any attempt to construct an idealized relationship with nature. Our relationship with nature is still based broadly on survival, he claimed: in artificially manufacturing the circumstances whereby a relationship may be established that does not take this into account, the activities of the paratheatrical projects reminded him of 'games of the eighteenth-century aristocrats. In those days they used to build Arcadias and Utopias, the only purpose of which was to play.' [375/1]

Such a judgement is perhaps conditioned by a misconstruction of some of the basic premises of the post-theatrical work. Grotowski has stated clearly: 'It is not really critical, if this takes place outside the urban environment or not. What is important, however, is what is happening to the participant'. [84/86] And what it was hoped was happening to the participant was not an artificial recreation of innocent primitive experience, but a form of 'de-conditioning' of the individual's response – to the environment, and to the other participants. To have a deconditioned response means to react to something in a manner not conditioned by past experience or future conjecture – in other words to be fully in the present and fully spontaneous. This is the true meaning of 'meeting with a forest as if for the first time', as Grotowski clarified in a later text:

> In fact I am talking rather of an original state. And this, the original state, is something that it is dangerous to speak of: it goes beyond conditioning, it appears inhuman. It is like arriving at a self-evidence of being which is close to that of the forces of nature, of original powers, one of the powers of the original world. One appears to act in self-evidence and without premeditation, as if it were inevitable.... Talking about such things we often think of children.... It is exactly this that touches us in a child. That it lives in the beginnings. That for the child everything happens for the first time. The forest it enters is its first forest. It is never the same forest. And we – we are already so taught and so tamed, our intellectual computer is already so programmed that every forest – even the one we see for the first time – is the same and we say the same to ourselves: 'this is a forest'. Despite the fact that even the same forest is different each day. [96/12–13]

The de-conditioned attitude Grotowski was proposing can be equated with the notion of 'disarmament', which he had postulated as a prerequisite for the paratheatrical experience in his *Holiday* texts. Flaszen has said of this concept:

> In *Holiday* there is a sphere where man disarms himself, and is himself; and another sphere, where he's armed and must act and play along. In the latter there are so many obligations that we don't confront our own feelings.... We pretend, when confronted with others. Thus our group is tempted by the possibility of creating conditions where it is possible to avoid the second alternative: that is, to drop the 'arms'. This kind of activity may be a necessity for some. For others, it may be a kind of violence. And so, it's very important that those who disarm themselves do so only where the environment allows it. Where a struggle and 'armament' is needed, they must be armed to be able to fight. One must develop the ability to live in the two spheres, passing from one to the other....
>
> Not all disarmament is real of course.... But in what I'm calling 'disarma-

ment', the idea is not to be 'good' but to have the courage to be one's self, without hiding, and not intruding or imposing on the others. Now, how do I go about 'being myself'?.... Certainly, there is no technical solution here. Rather, we begin with anything – an activity, an action – and either it works or does not. There is no recipe or trick, although the preliminary conditions can be fixed by us. What we're looking for can't be defined. If we have an image of the result, then we have lost the way. We must avoid expectation. This is like the Sufis or Zen. But we are not in those traditions; they're in their own religious traditions. We have no traditions to rely on. [143/312–313]

There were many discernible elements characteristic of most of the paratheatrical work which, seen in this light, could be considered as the 'preliminary conditions' established by the Laboratory Theatre team in the process towards disarmament. There were the factors of unfamiliar surroundings, and even contrived spatial disorientation: on some projects the participants, transported by van, were completely unaware of geographical location. Unfamiliar rooms were almost invariably dimly lit, or even in total darkness. And during projects taking place in the countryside, there were occasions when participants were required to run, in blackness, through forest or over awkward terrain. Allied to these factors was the consequent experience of danger and fear of the unknown. Richard Mennen summarized this in a retrospective reaction to the work: 'Also suddenly had these irrational fears and feelings of panic about what I had just been through. Got scared about it'. At a later date, he rationalized these reactions:

> The semi-conscious fears were simply a recapitulation of the crises or disintegration I had weathered. Under the force of the circumstances I had not allowed the fears to take control, but they surfaced at the point I gave in to exhaustion. [346/69]

Overcoming these fears, Tadeusz Burzyński believed, was a crucial factor in the process:

> The first step towards disarmament, in my opinion, is the loss of fear of others. This cannot be programmed, one cannot talk or force oneself into it. It may or may not materialize in certain circumstances. And when it does materialize it's as if the filter that regulates and blocks the light had been removed. One can actually see in a different way, in a deeper and truer light. To 'see' means to feel, react, act and stop being afraid (afraid of people, of inexplicable situations, afraid to be laughed at etc.) and that became a natural state during the Special Project – one began to realize a new potential. [194/17]

Although the Laboratory Theatre 'leaders' of the paratheatrical work were able to research and set up the circumstances and conditions for this process to take place – in terms, for example, of environment, properties, sequences of events – the actual step towards 'disarmament' was the sole responsibility of the individual participant. It was their free choice and could not be enforced externally (by the leaders of the events or other participants) or internally (by feelings of submitting to the pressure of the group, or through mental command). In this respect there can be seen a clear parallel with aspects of the earlier theatrical training, most specifically perhaps in Grotowski's application of the principle of 'via negativa', and the use of the physically demanding *exercises corporels* as a platform for transcendence of self (see pages 122–123). The participants of parateatre had to 'let go' of their fears and resistances to the process in the same way that the actor had to 'submit' to the challenge of the physical training.

In an interview conducted after the successful completion of the *Mountain Project*, Jacek Zymsłowski demonstrated how the same process applied in his group's refined version of the parateatrical activities. He is describing the beginning of a *Vigil* (which was openly accessible work taking place in the theatre building in Wrocław):

> There's a poorly-lit room, some figures sitting in silence on the floor. You don't know how to behave, so you wait for the first sign. You sit stiff and tense and sink into yourself, shut off from others and ill at ease: you lower your eyes or glance furtively. The period in which nothing is happening – at least visually – is particularly difficult: both for the leaders and the participants. It's time for overcoming doubts, a gradual revelation through mistrust in oneself and others, and then slowly an entering into the action which by degrees embraces everybody. There is movement, voices, sound, sometimes even an instrument. And a totally empty room. It sometimes happens that we pass the point at which what is planned, learnt, foreseen comes to an end. And we then touch upon the unknown, upon what is both self-evident and natural. . . . It is as if an individual suddenly discovered that movement exists, and discovered their body in movement . . . and that there is the kind of energy in the body that you don't come across everyday; for some people such an experience is completely unknown. The most immediate reaction is a joy at discovering unknown resources, then a searching through movement for others, a reaching towards them, co-action, improvisation. Afterwards comes the revelation that touch, sight, hearing – in fact all the senses – have been made more acute, they have been restored to their full sensitivity. . . . Sometimes there is an eruption of joy, a vibrating 'mad' joy. It happens in different ways – each individual is different, and so are groups.
> [141]

The processes described above – leading to disarmament, or a de-conditioned response – are clearly related to a spontaneity in action, which Grotowski was continually searching for in his theatrical equation of 'spontaneity and discipline'. At that time he insisted on a dialectical approach, a *conjunctio oppositorum*, although (as was suggested on page 156) the emphasis was always on the Dionysian element of spontaneity. Within these terms the paratheatrical work can be seen as a further abdication of the strictly dialectical approach. Conceptualizing existence as a struggle between the 'field of battle' (involving social roles) and the 'field of disarmament', Grotowski was setting up the circumstances (artificial in the sense of consciously contrived) for a privileged abdication of one 'pole' of life in favour of complete disarmament. But, according to the terms of the *conjunctio oppositorum*, it might be supposed that the increased emphasis on disarmament and spontaneity would lead, with the absence of formal discipline, to the chaos Grotowski was always at such pains to avoid.

In reality this rarely happened. In recounting his experience of the completely unstructured form of the *Night Vigil* Leszek Kolankiewicz noted: 'There is an acute awareness which helps to avoid collision. There is violent freedom and uncanny precision' [316/110]. Similarly, in an account of a *Night Vigil* undertaken by a professional psychologist she comments: 'I find it difficult to comprehend what kind of experience the "guides" of the *Night Vigil* have behind them, to ensure that this meeting, balanced as it is at the limits of self-control, does not turn into a brawl, orgy or stupor' [229]. This phenomenon was also evident in the work on the Mountain. Considering the lack at any stage of a guiding code of behaviour, combined with the anarchy of a completely unstructured form, there was at all times in the work rooms a remarkable cohesion of consciousness and awareness, which appeared to preclude intrusive action or discordant response. This was not necessarily merely conformity. Ideally, it was a search, in the void, for the most truly individual response, stripped – by disposition, effort, and the prevailing conditions – of the many social and personality levels, of what Grotowski, in a theatrical context, has called the 'life-mask'. What is remarkable in the process is that alevel of non-individual consciousness seems invariably to be reached. The effect is of a vital and spontaneous cohesion within what is superficially a very narrow band of undisciplined human behaviour – namely the basic physical activities of running, jumping, dancing, fighting, simply moving in space.

The completion of the *Mountain Project* marked the end of both the 1976/77 season of activity at the Laboratory Theatre and the second phase of the para-theatrical work. The preceding period had been characterized predominantly by the emergence of some of the younger members of the Institute to positions of maturity, and the refining, or stripping down of the paratheatrical work which resulted through their influence. There also developed clearer demarcations within areas of the post-theatrical work, and the first indications of real divisions into different streams of interest at the theatre. These in fact had been implicit ever since the official transition from theatrical to paratheatrical work in 1970 (in that they were related to fundamental differences of attitude at the Institute to the work Grotowski was pursuing) and within the subsequent few years these divergences were to become gradually more evident.

CHAPTER ELEVEN
Dissolution 1978–1984

This final period of the Laboratory Theatre work and activity was a time of continual movement and change. There were, apparently, many initiatives for new work, led by separate individuals or in groups. And there seemed to be less of a conscious effort, on the part of those overseeing the general direction of the work, to present the image of a cohesive and communal search. In 1975, at a time when the experimental post-theatrical work was being initially opened up for the public, there had been a deliberate emphasis on the unified nature of the direction of the work, despite the variety of separate workshops being offered under the label of paratheatre. Grotowski said in an article at that time:

> This Group is not a portion of land to be divided out, each individual having their own part. It is basically a communal affair and consists of one common impulse, from what has already been experienced towards what awaits us. And it is only this impulse, this *élan*, which gives those belonging to the group the strength and right to undertake research, together with others from the outside. [75/27]

In an interview conducted three years later, after the completion of the *Mountain Project*, Jacek Zmysłowski was still stressing the communal direction of the researches being undertaken at the Institute, but this time with a more natural emphasis on the inherently different approaches used:

> 'At the moment, when the Laboratory is concurrently realizing a whole series of different projects and programmes, it is natural that a different path is taken in the experiences with our older colleagues (sometimes referring to a technique and method worked out earlier in theatre) and a different one in ours. But there exist nevertheless convergent points, which we are all approaching by our different routes. You can take as a starting point acting exercises, or actions not invoking such associations, and in both cases reach what – in simple terms – could be called an 'opening', an unblocking, through energy, of the processes. [141]

In an article published in the same year, 1978, constituting a public statement of the Laboratory Theatre's programme and plans, Zbigniew Cynkutis (at that time Vice-Director of the Theatre and in charge administratively) was even more explicit

78 Poster on the occasion of the Laboratory Theatre's 20th Anniversary.

concerning the individuality of the researches, listing the contributing members of the Institute by name:

> I mention these individuals, because in the following information I consider it essential to emphasize the phenomenon of the various specializations which are attached to each of these names.... Each of these experiences is connected in a precise way with a specific individual or group of individuals from the Institute team, and being characterized by the individuality of the leader – crystallized in the course of many years of communal research (already nearly 20) – it possesses its own character and relevance for the different interests, needs and expectations of those wanting active participation in the creative act. [142/83]

What Cynkutis was officially announcing in this document was the completion of the cycle of research undertaken at the Laboratory Theatre from 1970–1977 and known as parateatre. Although brought to a close by the *Mountain Project*, the paratheatrical work nevertheless still formed the foundation for the Institute's current and future activities which at that point were being called 'cultural activities'. The impulse for this direction, as Cynkutis explained in the article, was the notion of 'active culture' which he called the 'principal concept ... instilled in the programme of the Institute's activities'. Grotowski had already identified this, in an interview conducted for *Trybuna Ludu* in 1976, as being the aspect of the Institute's work with the greatest social significance, and at that time he elaborated at some length:

> I think that the most direct (social) connection is with the attempt to depart from the classic division into active and passive culture. Action in terms of active culture – which gives a sense of fulfilment in life, an extending of its dimensions, is needed by many, and yet remains the domain of very few. The writer, for example, is engaged in active culture when writing a book. We were engaged in it when preparing performances. Passive culture – which is certainly highly significant and rich in ways it would be difficult to discuss here in depth – is the relationship to a product of active culture, such as reading, watching a performance, a film, listening to music. In an appropriate – let's call it laboratory – dimension, we are working upon an extension of the sphere of active culture. What is the privilege of a few, may therefore be shared by others. I am not talking about some mass production of works of art, but a certain kind of individual, creative experience – of significance in the life of an individual, and in their life with others. Working in theatre, doing performances over many years, step by step we came closer to this concept of an active individual (the actor) for whom the idea was not to represent someone else, but to be oneself, to be with someone, to be in contact, as Stanislavsky called it. One step further and our adventure with active culture began. Its elements may be reduced to what is most simple: action, reaction, spontaneity, impulse, song, compatability, music-making, rhythm, improvisation, sound, movement, truth and the dignity of the body. And also: one individual in relation to another, in the tangible world. That

sounds somewhat over-sentimental, and maybe it's better not to formulate it in this way ...? Besides, the simplest and most elementary things are the most difficult to achieve, demanding continual discipline, great effort, and attention, particularly so that it is not done at the expense of others. I think that active culture (most commonly called creativity), and above all the concomitant perception and experience, do not have to be the privilege of small groups of professionals or unique individuals, although it is they who create and will continue to create plays and performances. [81]

The concept of active culture can, from the present perspective, be identified as one of the two main streams of work to develop from the history of the Laboratory Theatre researches, both theatrical and paratheatrical. In so far as all of Grotowski's work was concerned with contact, and specifically what may be called a spontaneous, de-conditioned contact, then this is the form of the work that evolved from Grotowski's preoccupation with the quality of contact between the actor and the audience, between one individual and another, in a group context. It can be generalized as a centrifugal movement, an evolution of the work outwards, into making the work and the experiences more accessible on a wider scale. This movement was realized on a practical level in the coming years through a deliberate policy of both intensive touring of the participatory work in Poland and abroad, and a systematic lifting of restrictions to participation in the work, making it in fact (and not just in theory) fully accessible.

But there was another trend, or direction, evolving from the Laboratory Theatre work and strictly speaking it was to this that Grotowski gave his fullest personal commitment. It was still connected with the concept of active culture, in that its aim was to make more accessible, in an active, experiential sense, what had formerly been considered a privileged process for a few. But this work was more personal and concerned with the processes within an individual. It could in some ways be said to have evolved from Grotowski's preoccupation with the relationship between actor and director, in which all the circumstances are conditioned by the demands of the individual's internal processes. And the division between this stream of work and the active culture described above was implicit, for example, in the early paratheatrical *Special Projects*, and the separation between the 'Large Special Project' (led by Cieślak and involving group work) and the 'Narrow Special Project' (concerned with the individual and in which Grotowski took a particular interest). In very broad terms this movement could be described as centripetal, in that the focus of the work was centred upon the inner processes of the individual and it came in time increasingly to resemble individualized 'spiritual' training from different cultures (and indeed called in practice increasingly upon them). In these latter researches, preparatory work for which was being undertaken less than a year after the end of the *Mountain Project*, there was no pretence at a movement towards making the work publicly accessible. In the initial period, as with paratheatre, there was intensive closed research with selected individuals, and when the work was finally 'opened', it was again for people who had been carefully selected.

In the autumn of 1977 (directly after the *Mountain Project*) work was recommenced by the Institute. Jacek Zmysłowski's international group began the new season with a series of openly accessible participatory work sessions, called *Czuwania* (Vigils). Comprising Poles and non-Poles (including Zbigniew Kozłowski, Irena Rycyk and Małgorzata Świątek from the Laboratory Theatre company) their work was carried on continually until the late spring of 1978. Jacek had in mind at that time a sequel to the *Mountain Project*. Called *Earth Project* it was similarly in three parts: *Czuwania*; *Czynienie* (Doing) and *Wioska* (Village). During the winter and spring of 1977/78 Jacek's group was already looking throughout the surrounding Polish countryside for a rural base which could be used for *Wioska*.

In the meantime the actors were continuing with their individual workshops, and in May 1978 there was a one-month tour by the Institute in the northern port of Gdańsk. The tour commenced with sessions of *Czuwania* undertaken by Jacek's group, and subsequently participatory workshops given by the actors. This tour was an important development for the company. It was the first time that the post-theatrical work had been taken on tour within Poland and the move – to spread the work to new environments and new people – was indicative of an increasing commitment from the Institute to reach areas and communities not accustomed by convention to cultural participation. After the work in Gdańsk there was a temporary halt to the development of the *Earth Project*, as members of Jacek's group became involved in other developments. On 5 June 1978 there was an International Theatre Institute symposium held in Warsaw, on the occasion of the first International Theatre Meeting. The chosen theme of the conference was 'The Art of the Beginner' and Grotowski gave a talk which was later published under the title of 'Wandering towards a Theatre of Sources'. This was Grotowski's first mention of the *Theatre of Sources* – a project conceived on a vast scale which was to consume his interest over the coming few years. Grotowski issued a press statement at the ITI conference concerning the *Theatre of Sources*:

> The participants of the *Theatre of Sources* are people from different continents, cultures and traditions. The *Theatre of Sources* is devoted to those activities which lead us back to the sources of life, to direct, primary perception, to an organic, spring-like experiencing of life, of existence, of presence. Primary, that is a radical, dramatic, phenomenon – it is an initial, codified theme. The *Theatre of Sources* is planned between the years 1978 and 1980 with intense activity in the summer periods and with a final realization in 1980. [96/19]

At about the same time as this announcement, work began in Brzezinka and other locations which the Laboratory Theatre had used for their paratheatrical research. It was intensely experimental closed work conducted by Grotowski and Teo Spychalski, and involved Jacek Zmysłowski, Irena Rycyk and Zbigniew Kozłowski, as well as other invited participants from Poland and abroad.

In autumn 1978 work resumed amongst members of Jacek's group, with presentations of *Czuwania* in the theatre buildings in Wrocław. But this was undertaken in the context of a growing need for the development of some new work, involving the actors, which would carry into practice the principles of 'active culture'. The decision was also made at this point to extend the theatre's new policy of taking their participatory work to other communities within Poland. In the late autumn there was a tour to the small Polish town of Tarnobrzeg – again, with presentations of *Czuwania*, and participatory workshops directed by the actors. During the subsequent winter, work was once more halted for Jacek's group: some members joined Grotowski's exploratory work, others joined together with some of the actors in developing and preparing a new form of participatory work, called *Drzewo Ludzi* (Tree of People).

The preparation of this new project had already been announced the previous November by Cynkutis in his article in *Odra*. He had called the *Tree of People* the first step towards a concrete realization of active culture, being fully accessible to all those wanting to take part (up to 400 people at a time) and in which it was envisaged that the group would abandon even the division into leaders and participants still a feature of the paratheatrical work. Cynkutis called this development a 'work-flow'. This was a term being used at that time by Grotowski to signify an attitude to work in which there was no division, strictly speaking, between purely 'work' periods, and periods of 'domestic activity' (like eating and sleeping) such as had been the case in the earlier paratheatrical work. All aspects of life during the time spent in the project were now to be 'in the process'. The *Tree of People*, Cynkutis also announced, would become the main piece of work for the Laboratory Theatre team, being presented on a continuous basis wherever the group happened to be. It was envisaged that it would, in time, fulfil the same function as *Apocalypsis Cum Figuris* – as a focal point for the group and for members of the public wishing to make contact.

On 5 January 1979 the first presentation of the *Tree of People* took place in the theatre building in Wrocław, with about sixty participants invited from Poland and abroad, and most members of the Laboratory Theatre team, including Grotowski and Flaszen. The action, which lasted seven days and nights, was conducted on all four floors of the theatre building, with the *Apocalypsis* performance space on the third floor as the main work area. Arriving participants were guided around the building and shown the areas allocated for work, eating and sleeping, and then left, for most of the time, to follow their own direction. An American participant, Robert Findlay, afterwards described aspects of the events that took place in the work room:

> The activities occuring in this space were collective and improvisational, usually involving as few as twenty and as many as sixty people. It was not against the rules to sit and watch for a time. Grotowski, for example, watched frequently from as unobtrusive a position as possible. Early on in our stay, the members of the Laboratorium functioned most clearly as guides or leaders in this room, creating physical images and vocalized sounds that the rest of us would follow. But as the days and nights progressed and further silent agreements arose within

79 Poster for *Tree of People*.

the entire group, the Laboratorium members retreated from these roles of leadership, seemingly encouraging them to be handled by those of us from the outside. As most came to see eventually, however, one functions best both as leader *and* follower simultaneously if the group itself is really functioning creatively together. One may initiate an action, movement, chant or melody, and it will be either accepted or rejected by the group. It is accepted if others build upon it; it is rejected if it is ignored. One comes to choose what one does individually within the parameters of what others have chosen. Despite the fact that many of the participants were not performers, not theatre people *per se*, the general creative and intuitive level was high: most found it fairly easy to connect spontaneously a new action, movement, chant or melody to what had been established. I was reminded frequently of the manner in which a jazz ensemble improvises spontaneously, listening to one another, and playing off one another. When the work on the third floor was really operating well, there was an unmistakable group sense of flow and spontaneity.

It is, of course, difficult to describe these collective creations in much detail and perhaps not even at this point legitimate to evaluate them. Each lasted for a period of approximately an hour or two and seemed to have a clear beginning, extended middle, and definite end. That is not to say that there was necessarily any traditional linear progression or story line. Rather their form, again using the analogy of the jazz ensemble, was more like improvised music created not only acoustically in time but kinetically in space. And just as jazz musicians are capable of following one another through a progression of chords, so too did we

80 Elizabeth Albahaca.

BENEFIT

HUNTER COLLEGE & DEPT. OF THEATRE & FILM
& JERZY GROTOWSKI
present the work of JACEK ZMYSLOWSKI
leading member of THE POLISH LABORATORY THEATRE
in the documentary presentation "VIGIL"

Personal appearance & commentary by JERZY GROTOWSKI

Hunter College Playhouse
East 68th Street between Park and Lexington
Wednesday, May 20, 1981 8:30 pm
Tickets $25 Patrons $50 Tax deductible
Please make checks payable to
Atlas Theatre Company, Inc.
P.O. Box 523 Ansonia Station
New York, New York 10023
For information call (212) 869-3530
The benefit will help pay for medical treatment of Jacek Zmyslowski
at Sloan Kettering Hospital

81 Poster by Krzysztof Bednarski.

seem capable of following one another not only melodically and contrapuntally but also through a progression of kinetic images. [248/352]

Throughout 1979 there were presentations of the *Tree of People, Apocalypsis Cum Figuris* and the actors' workshops, whilst in the summer months Grotowski again conducted closed work at Brzezinka towards his *Theatre of Sources*. In the autumn and winter, work started in earnest towards the 'opening' of the *Theatre of Sources* to outside participants planned for the following summer. Invitations were sent out world–wide and Grotowski himself travelled with his group – to Haiti, India and Mexico amongst other places – to meet future participants and collaborators. The opening was conducted finally during the summer months at Brzezinka (under Grotowski's direction) and another base, Ostrowina (under the direction of Teo Spychalski). During this time both *Apocalypsis* and the *Tree of People* were being presented in Wrocław to incoming visitors by the rest of the Laboratory Theatre team – and it was in this period that *Apocalypsis Cum Figuris*, with no public announcement, received its final performance.

In the autumn of 1980 Grotowski temporarily disbanded his international group of collaborators for *Theatre of Sources* and departed himself on solitary travels. Teo Spychalski and Elizabeth Albahaca went to Venezuela (Elizabeth's home country) to undertake their own work. Jacek Zmysłowski (who had gone to America in late spring for medical treatment) was in Poland during the summer and was present at the *Theatre of Sources*: but at its conclusion he also departed, for further treatment in New York, where he was later joined by his family.

At this point there was what seemed to many a completely unexpected development amongst those of the Laboratory Theatre remaining in Wrocław – the preparation of something in the nature of a 'theatrical' presentation. Its working title was 'À la Dostoyevsky', and during the winter months of 1980 it was prepared as a collective piece of work by six members of the company, under the direction of Ryszard Cieślak. The 'performers' consisted of three of the original acting team (Antoni Jahołkowski, Rena Mirecka and Stanisław Scierski) and three younger members (Irena Rycyk, Teresa Nawrot and Zbigniew Kozłowski). It was first

82 Rehearsal for *Thanatos Polski* – Stanisław Scierski, Teresa Nawrot, Zbigniew Kozłowski, Irena Rycyk and Rena Mirecka.

presented publicly in Wrocław in February 1981 under the title of *Thanatos Polski* (*Polish Thanatos*), and the programme prepared for the event bore the following disclaimer:

> *Thanatos Polski* is not conceived of as a theatrical performance, although there is a fixed structure and programmed regions of association (the 'theme').
>
> It is possible for those present – without constraint – to enter the action.
>
> Your participation in the particular life of this group may be active, vocal, or simply by being with us. [144]

The structure for *Polish Thanatos* was far less precise than, say, for *Apocalypsis Cum Figuris*, and was very obviously conditioned by the presence and participation of the three 'paratheatrical' members of the company. The whole was composed in a similar way to music, with each interlude having its own energy, internal rhythm

INSTYTUT AKTORA – TEATR LABORATORIUM
Kier. GROTOWSKI – FLASZEN
WROCŁAW 1981

THANATOS POLSKI
INKANTACJE

z udziałem: Antoniego Jahołkowskiego, Zbigniewa Kozłowskiego,
Reny Mireckiej, Teresy Nawrot, Ireny Rycyk, Stanisława Scierskiego.

cytaty: Mickiewicz, Miłosz, Wojaczek

Praca zbiorowa pod kierunkiem Ryszarda Cieślaka.

INSTYTUT AKTORA · TEATR LABORATORIUM
27 Rynek Ratusz, 50–101 Wrocław, tel. 340-67

83 Poster for *Thanatos Polski*.

and an associated quality of emotion. There were contrasting movements of playfulness, sadness, and instances of totally unexpected dramatic action. At one moment, for example, Rena Mirecka held up a white cloth stained dramatically with red paint: in response Antoni Jahołkowski plunged a knife into the cloth, cutting it up into six portions which were distributed to the other participants. There was very little text – all of it poetry – and almost all of the vocal work consisted of singing, chanting or just humming. There was a poem by a young Wrocław poet which was sung about halfway through the action and then again as the final song. It had a nostalgic, melodic refrain which was often taken up by members of the public and sung together with the participants of the action:

'We are waiting by the shores
of the vast waters of our weariness
for a sign to lighten our eyes
with joy – and humility'.

There was also a fragment of a poem by the Romantic poet Adam Mickiewicz, which was chanted by Antoni Jahołkowski, still holding the knife after the division of the white cloth:

'Hands that fight for the people shall by them be cut off
Names beloved of the people shall by them be forgot
All shall pass – after the turmoil, the clamour, the strife
The simple, muted, little people shall take their inheritance'.

The final piece of text was spoken in darkness by Stanisław Scierski: it was a poem called *Naród* (*Nation*) by Czesław Miłosz, a contemporary Polish poet acknowledged in both Poland and the West:

'The purest of the nations of the earth judged by the flare of the thunderbolt,
Unthinking yet cunning in the toil of a working day.

No pity for widows and orphans, no pity for the old,
Stealing a crust of bread from out of the mouth of a child.

Gives its life in sacrifice, to call down upon the foe heavenly wrath
Paralyzes the enemy with the weeping of orphans and women.

Gives sway to those with the eyes of gold-merchants,
Lets rise those with the conscience of brothel-keepers.

The best of its sons remain unknown
Appearing but once to die on the barricades.

This people's bitter tears break in upon their songs
And at the fading of the songs are bandied loud jokes.

Great nation, unconquered nation, nation of irony,
Can recognize the truth yet holding it in silence.

84 *Thanatos Polski.*

85 *Thanatos Polski.*

Camping on marketplaces, communicating in jests,
Bartering in old rubbish filched from ruins.

A nation in crumpled caps, its belongings on its back,
Wanders seeking abodes to the south and west.

One man from this nation pausing at his son's cradle
Repeats words of hope until now always futile.'

Directly after this Stanisław Scierski sang, in a barely audible tone which petered out into the darkness, the first two lines of the Polish national anthem:

'Poland is not yet lost
While we are still living
. . . we are still living. . . .'

During the spring and summer months of 1981, *Thanatos Polski* was presented, together with the *Tree of People* and the workshops, in Wrocław, on tour in Poland, and in Sicily in March and April. But this was within the context of the political events of 1981 – the increase of open support for Solidarity and the free trade union movement, liberalization on the street and in the media, and the crippling strikes, shortages and rationing. The atmosphere within Poland during that period was one of extreme tension – between on the one hand an almost frenetic hope, and on the other the draining experience of domestic shortages and administrative chaos. In the summer months there was another 'opening' of the *Theatre of Sources* by Grotowski – but this time much smaller and mainly for Polish people. There were already severe problems of organization and food supplies due to the rationing.

The events that took place in the autumn and winter of 1981/82 were decisive for the future of the Laboratory Theatre. In September Antoni Jahołkowski died after a long, and at times painful illness. He had been with Grotowski for 22 years, since the establishment of the Theatre of Thirteen Rows in Opole in 1959, and he worked with his colleagues at the theatre until shortly before his death. On 13 December 1981 Martial Law was declared in Poland: there was a curfew; intensified food rationing; theatres and cinemas were closed; and people were forbidden to gather in large groups or leave town without permission. The only work that took place was private, closed work within the theatre buildings in Wrocław.

In January 1982 Grotowski left Poland for Denmark – from there he went on further personal travels in connection with his own work for *Theatre of Sources*. On 4 February 1982 Jacek Zmysłowski died in New York, also after a long illness. He was at the time of his death only 28 years old. In the autumn of 1982 Grotowski went to the United States, where he has remained until the present, carrying on his own work. In July 1983 Stanisław Scierski died suddenly, in his home town in Poland.

Finally, on 28 January 1984, the local Wrocław newspaper, *Gazeta Robotnicza*, carried the following article, entitled 'It has lasted 25 years . . .':

86 Poster for Sicily Tour 1981.

Yesterday, we received a report from the Wrocław Laboratory Theatre. We quote it in full:

'For some time our group has in practical terms ceased to act as a creative ensemble. It has become a cooperative of individuals conducting a variety of multidirectional work and independent research.

That is in the nature of things. We believe that, as the group of the Laboratory Theatre, we have fulfilled in the course of its existence what we had to fulfil. We ourselves are astonished that we continued as a group for a quarter of a century – in continual change, in mutual inspiration, radiating our common energy towards others.

The creative age of a group and the creative age of an individual are not one and the same thing. Some of us will take the risk of a fully independent artistic life, others will perhaps want to continue their activity together, within some other new institutional framework. Each of us remembers that our origins lie in the common source whose name is Jerzy Grotowski, and in Grotowski's theatre. There is sadness amongst us that in the course of recent years there departed from us in their prime Antoni Jahołkowski, Jacek Zmysłowski and Stanisław Scierski.

87 Entrance to Theatre Offices 1981.

After a 25-year long communal path we feel as close to each other as at the beginning, regardless of where each of us is at present – but we are also changed. From now on, everyone must in their own way accept the challenge presented by their own creativity and the times in which we live.

The group of the Theatre of Thirteen Rows, of the Institute of Actor's Research, of the Institute of the Actor, in other words the group of the Laboratory Theatre, is determined on 31 August 1984, after exactly 25 years, to disband.

We convey our gratitude to everybody who during these years has helped, accompanied and trusted us, in Opole, in Wrocław, in Poland and in the world.

> Founder members:
> Ludwik Flaszen
> Rena Mirecka
> Zygmunt Molik
> Ryszand Cieślak
> and the group.' [145]

CHAPTER TWELVE

Grotowski

The dissolution of the Laboratory Theatre in August 1984 should not be seen from a negative perspective. As its members said in their own testimony – they fulfilled in the course of the Institute's existence what they had to fulfil. Over the years, in common with the theatre's founder Jerzy Grotowski, they demonstrated a continual reluctance to remain in what is familiar territory, to stay with the tried and tested, the known and secure. And the fact that they chose at this stage to dismantle the official and administrative structure surrounding their communal work (and let go of the personal security it ensured) is further evidence of this attitude. Like Grotowski, they also have moved on to individual work and research elsewhere. But their major achievements as a group will remain, and it is these that this book has attempted to isolate and celebrate.

At this stage I do not wish to construct a conventional 'conclusion' to their work. Grotowski said of Stanislavsky that his research never reached a conclusion but continued until his death, which is why it could not really be encapsulated into a Stanislavsky 'Method'. I anticipate the same from Grotowski and his Laboratory Theatre colleagues. Therefore – although it coincides with the end of the institution of the Laboratory Theatre – the conclusion of this study merely marks one chronological point in the process of its members' researches.

The remainder of this chapter consists of extracts from statements by Grotowski in the ten years since 1975. Although most of them have been published in Polish, few are yet accessible in English. They have been chosen for the particularly personal and revelatory nature of the statements, or because they illuminate more recent work undertaken by Grotowski, or because they constitute what is, for Grotowski, a rare summarizing of his work. There are some points that I would first wish to make clear. Almost nothing that has been published in Grotowski's name has been actually written by him – in the sense of a document that is constructed in an intellectually coherent way. Most are the result of improvised speech at public appearances or interviews, and thus have a particular flavour. Tadeusz Burzyński, a Polish journalist familiar with Grotowski's appearances and writings has commented:

> Grotowski has a special way of speaking, very much his own. He always improvises, inspired by questions. His books are simply transcripts of his public appearances. He is precise and logical, complementing his statements with

metaphors, particularly when he wants to name something which defies definitions. Those complementary statements hidden not only in words, but often also in pauses, accents, tones of voice, gestures, enable one to receive a deeper meaning from ordinary, everyday terms. He attributes considerable significance in such attempts at communication to *key-words*. Some grasp them, following the chain of associations, to others they seem abstract, lacking concreteness, maybe even ridiculous. [360/108]

This has caused misunderstandings from those who have looked in Grotowski's published writings for the coherence of a constructed manifesto. It should not be taken as evasion or elitism to say that, in his uncompromising way, it is probably not these people that Grotowski would consider himself to be addressing.

88 Jerzy Grotowski.

89 Jerzy Grotowski.

CONVERSATION WITH GROTOWSKI
Extracts from an interview conducted by Andrzej Bonarski and published in the Polish periodical, *Kultura*, in 1975. (169/19–44)

AB: Much has been written and spoken about you, much is said. At times I find that irritating, at times pleasing. Your reputation has moved people to extreme opinions. But I am interested in what you think about yourself. What is your own picture of yourself? Your self-image?

JG: The trouble is that I can't find a personality model. I couldn't say, like Napoleon (to quote a well-known example) 'I am Alexander'. I can't say 'I am such and such'. There were moments in my life when I tried: there was a time when I wanted to be Stanislavsky. To begin with this naturally took the form of imitation on the professional level. And then, conversely, I became preoccupied with how to maintain respect for the father whilst filling, so to speak, his role. But then that ceased to interest me, together with professionalism in general. Only the respect remained.

In another period of my life, let's call them the October and post-October years, I wanted to be a political saint, one of the foremost. And I was so fascinated by Gandhi that I wanted to be him. I came to the conclusion that not only was this improbable for objective reasons, but incompatible with my nature – although equal to fair play I am incapable of a total and generalized assumption of everyone's good intentions. I have given you examples, one of them perhaps slightly anecdotal. But there was a picture of sorts.... If I were ever to build the self-portrait of my dreams – at the very centre would be a liberated life, the original state, freedom. But not what the westernized idea of a 'Man of the East' would call liberation. The concept of liberation – such as is indeed used by the westernized idea of a 'Man of the East' – assumes that evil is ascribed to our bodily existence and that we must therefore liberate ourselves from bodily existence. I don't feel that. And I would not confuse the word 'freedom' with 'freedom of choice' or a surrender to the whims of fate; so that I want first one thing, and then another. For me, freedom is connected with the supreme temptation.

JG: For me, freedom is connected with the supreme temptation. It exists for the individual, even if unaware of it, but it is there and it is squandered, this way and that, as if it were a heap of rubbish, it is lost, forgotten about. We could call it the supreme desire, what we long for the most and is the most essential. And even if what draws us were apparently commonplace or foolish, yet the individual who follows that single, fundamental, all-consuming thing to its limit will to some extent undergo transcendence, and will surpass what is banal and mundane. And how much more so if the desire is something more than banality. Freedom is associated neither with freedom of choice, nor with sheer voluntarism – but with a wave, with giving oneself up to this huge wave, in accordance with one's desire. And when I speak of desire, it is like water in the desert or a gasp of air to someone drowning.

. . . . .

AB: Fulfilment and self-fulfilment are connected, I believe, with some kind of vision. And so: who would you like to be? I ask you that, but retain the impression that you are domineering, pragmatic and yet at the same time apparently easy, in other words not difficult, accessible. I am not thinking personally here, but of your accessibility in relation to others.

JG: For a long time I suspected myself of non-existence. I suspected that everyone else existed and the world existed, but that I did not really exist. I think that that was to do with reservations about my own nature, in biological terms as well.

Not that I considered raising any major or irrevocable objections against my nature; I was of the opinion that others were superior. I had no confidence in my own endurance. I provoked danger, but in such a blind way – both protecting myself beforehand, and closing my eyes.... That way I could have the feeling of non-existence, whilst seemingly existing. It was all to do with shame.

AB: What were you ashamed of?

JG: Myself.

AB: Your body?

JG: Myself, in every respect.

AB: Soul, expression?

JG: Everything, in totality.

AB: You didn't love yourself in any sense?

JG: I didn't like myself, that's for sure. To exist without liking myself, I had in some way to be superior to others, I had to be a leader for bad or a leader for good. That's why I became domineering, as you put it. But nowadays this is residual, and sometimes a matter of appearance. If I now have to bring myself to be dominating, it calls for bluff or effort. Domination was necessary for me at one time, I had no other way to exist. It was as if I had burnt my boats. There was no way back, it was a one-way journey. That was all quite some time ago. It had many nuances, since my interest in technique, methodology, and art derived from my overwhelming desire to exist – a desire accompanied by domination, dictatorship, severity, consistency. It was not, however, premeditated in the sense that 'I must exist': it was different. It was like suffocating and needing air. It gave a single-minded strength – a strength arising from the lack of any other possibility. But then contact with what was the subject-matter of my profession brought about contact with people. Most likely the central problem of my non-existence was that I felt a lack of relationship with others, because any relationship I had was not completely real. And the more domination there was on my side, the more it had to be unreal.

AB: You were afraid of people?

JG: Yes.

AB: You were afraid of people, you didn't love them or yourself?

JG: I loved them so much it sometimes seemed to me that I would die – from despair. Then again I didn't love them and was afraid. Occasionally, there was aggression: since you don't love me, I will hate you.

I want to stress that this trismus had already passed away before the satiation with public opinion and prestige. I have heard it said that prestige subdued me, and that's an attractive alternative, but it's not the case. Human relations brought about the change. What appeared to be an interest in the art of acting proved to be a search for and discovery of partnership (and the trismus faded when I was able to grasp this) – with Someone, someone else – and someone who, in the moment of action, at the time of work, I defined then in words used to define God. At that time this meant, for me – the son of man. Everything was transformed, became dramatic and painful, and there was still something of a

predatory nature. But it was already something very different. And then there was a fading away. This was connected with the next phase of my life, with wandering – maybe more with the myth of the wanderer? and anonymous freedom? Meeting people without fear – in other words meeting those before whom there was no longer fear or shame. Myth or reality, it still led onwards in the search for people from the High Way (and I mean High Way and not autoroute). And so I set out towards something, which for me lies beyond art.
. . . .

AB: In October 1973 in Wrocław, at one of those terrible press conferences with the participants of the Open Theatre festival, you spoke to several hundred people, who were listening to you intently, about two poles of existence: the pole of disarmament, of trust, of going out to one another, and the second pole – more often to be found on the level of daily life – the pole of conflict, war, armament, deceit, lies, strategy, tactics. If I asked you what you are, I asked that in the context of the existence of both of these poles. I can't make a saint out of you, because that's not what you are. As near to the pole of war and conflict – being a man of action when needed for the benefit of your cause: armed, breathing fury, strong, perhaps cruel through necessity, and through the same necessity cunning – as you are to the pole of disarmament and trust, when you transform yourself from the being who spreads terror into an acquiescing and trustful man. Is that how it is?

JG: I would like it to be so.

AB: Some people say that Grotowski is immoral, because what does Grotowski propose? Grotowski proposes to a limited group of people (a group that is exclusive through a form of selection) experiences that are more or less – but rather more – esoteric; while millions upon millions are born, live and die in the battle of everyday life, which starts with birth in a district hospital, ends in the cemetery, and runs its course in one home after another, each larger in size than the last, and at places of work, in offices and institutions. Grotowski is immoral, because he does not remember, or does not want to remember what everyday life is today, and that the overwhelming majority of humankind lives in a struggle for existence. Although I think that the drama of this struggle is not directly dependent on poverty or wealth. Are you really immoral?

JG: What seems immoral to me is an acquiescence in someone else's hard struggle for existence, and preying on it through creative means, through sharing concern with others, but from the kind of privileged position achieved by the status of an artist.

Either we assume that all efforts are pointless that do not lead directly to the relief of all poverty and misery – the material misery of humanity – in which case one should throw oneself immediately into the turmoil of battle, become a revolutionary (and I mean that literally, like Che Guevara) – or we assume that the evolution of the species is highly complex and thus the needs that emerge do so in phases, so that what still seems exclusive maintains a relationship to, and somehow changes, what we consider universal. If people do not devote themselves immediately to action defined as political, regardless of what field of the humanities they are involved in, they are assuming that there exist other needs apart from the material. Then they must naturally assume that the range of these needs is varied. When it comes to a comparative satisfaction with material goods – I say comparative, thinking not of wealth, but just of a point where there is no longer hunger – at this point there emerge needs in people, which at first go under many different guises – a need for theatre, films, television etc. But from behind these needs arises an elementary and fundamental need for a disinterested relationship. Because a self-interested life is connected with the daily grind, with the struggle for existence.

AB: What you have achieved, you achieved in the class of artist, and it seems apparent to me that you have taken a jump, if not a tectonic leap. Because what does it mean when you say 'what is beyond art'? Does that mean that art is finished for you? That you no longer want to be an artist, but a thinker, a philosopher? Does it mean that you are forsaking your kingdom, throwing off your crown, abdicating....?

JG: I am not so naive as to abdicate – then you have no chances at all.

AB: Wait a minute....

JG: Holding onto the crown, until it's torn from your head.

AB: Now wait! They are already beginning to lose faith in you, they are already beginning to ask, what's going on, what's he up to now?... You need heart and a great soul – and this isn't flattery – having once climbed this great mountain to then deny it, not to remain there and take a firm stand, saying 'This is mine'. Coming down from this mountain is a question either of tiredness, weakness, lack of oxygen, heart failure, or an act of choice, to do with such things (not equivalent in value) as a higher understanding, humility, or the perception of more important issues and higher peaks as yet unseen by anyone else. But remember daily life. Remember that there is the press, the mass media, there is an Institute named after you, there are your followers, I would even call them your artistic disciples. When you announce an intake they come from Iceland, the Honduras and Radom, don't they? And all of a sudden you say: 'Stop my friends – theatre? That's all in the past. Now I have gone beyond art.' And people could ask themselves whether you're following your own tail or have caught sight of something else. I would ask you the same thing.

JG: I understand.

AB: Did you, at a certain moment, feel that theatre has finished for you, and did you also at a certain moment see that there is something more than theatre. That's how I would put the question bluntly.

JG: Magnaminity exists when an individual has a choice. I had no choice. I had no choice on the mountain, because I know that the position there is precarious. If there's someone sitting on the mountain, then all around they are working. There is a forum, below are set up the arc-lamps, they are waiting, all lit up. The person on the top sneezes – and that's it; it's transmitted. Ha, a sneeze! But the mechanism of this transmission works on the principle that it isn't important who is on the mountain, or what is done on the mountain, the only important thing is the fact that – look, we have someone on the mountain. What follows is the creation of an idol and its inevitable downfall. Back in '66, when we were at the Theatre of Nations in Paris, I held a meeting with journalists at which I said: Well, well! Here you are saying these things and asking your questions, but I see what will happen in a few years. In a few years time, here – and this was taking place in the Odéon theatre – someone will come down these steps, someone who has discovered, let's say, a savage theatre. Maybe it's a man from Montreal called Dupré, and maybe he'll be from the Gold Coast and be called Kumba, I don't know. He'll walk down and you'll be standing with your cameras and will say 'It's all over, nothing counts now but savage theatre'. And there, at the bottom of the steps I will be standing, cap in hand, and I'll approach him and say: Give me five francs, Kumba. I too was once famous.

The scale of the mass media means that while you are in the limelight you have possibilities. On condition that the individual is not personally identified with the created figure-head. It's the figure-head which receives the awards, the titles, the honours, is greeted by men of state or received by monarchs. All of that belongs to the figurehead. It's important to know about it, to know that it exists and not to identify with it, because it's a manufactured creature. In the middle ages such creatures were called 'egregors' – their existence was believed in, and I also believe in them. So long as an individual is not identified with the egregor, but it exists, then there are considerable possibilities to have means at one's disposal. For example, we are now conducting experiments in various countries, where we do not have a permanent base, and for that reason they are costly; it's necessary to adapt the entire area, and build a base far from town. Throughout several days we must provide for the participants – people who can't pay for it because they aren't rich. And so if there were no egregor, there would be no money; nobody would give a penny for it, because it's not the value of the thing that they are paying for – if that exists, which I know it does – but they are paying only for the egregor. From this point of view the existence of the egregor is expedient and you must remember that. It gives considerable access to people, it provides a forum. But it is precarious. If you were to sit it out at the top, until you went mad, they would tear the crown from you. I thought that would have happened long ago – it may happen tomorrow, or the day after. The next sensation, the next thing for consumption, is the overthrow of the idol. Ha! there it lies! Trampled upon! It never existed! It's finished with! It's an old corpse! They say that a dancer should stop in good time. Well, I stopped being a director after *Apocalypsis*. I moved on to another domain. Anyone saying I should continue directing implies that I was not a bad director, that I achieved something, that there is sufficient proof that I deserve confidence. Now that I have moved into another domain, into what I call the paratheatrical experience, I need that confidence. I am speaking all the time in the convention of the first person; but I am thinking of our whole group.

. . . .

You have commented that in abandoning theatre – theatre, that is, in its civilized sense: as a place where creative products are manufactured – and in retaining from this period, from this previous classification a hunger for communion, then I must – perforce – tend in the direction of the thinker, the philosopher. I have often encountered this conclusion, but it is mistaken. I make use of the computer that is the mind, but I am certain that it doesn't come from the source. Certainly it can serve me in a particular anticipatory mode, to establish negative probabilities – where there is danger or things may go wrong – but nevertheless I owe no revelations to this computer. And when I say computer I am talking of the mind, the intellect, the programming or indeed what we call knowledge, information, erudition. I never felt and I do not feel that the source lies there. But I do not underestimate the computer. I consult it, I programme it, I use it. It's important that it functions, for otherwise an individual may tumble or slip on a banana skin, on their way to what is essential, to what their true needs dictate – and when I say true needs I am talking of what is necessary to me in my totality, skin and all....

Moving on to what I describe as leaving theatre behind; initially I knew very little; I knew on the one hand that there are no stories, plots, no tales of anything or anyone. Secondly, that the selection of those taking part must be mutual. For the press we can say that it's a workshop demanding appropriate predispositions, and not skills. In addition I knew that only the most simple of things should take place, what is most elementary and trustful between beings; that there would be stages, or levels, but that it could not be a rite – in the sense of a structured ritual – because it must be simpler than a rite. It must be based on such things as the fact of recognizing someone, as sharing matter, sharing the elements – even in the archaic sense but without thinking about it – as space is shared, water is shared, fire is shared, movement is shared, earth is shared, touch is shared. There is such an opening, such a transcendence of the barriers of self-interest and fear; there are meetings involving the wind, the tree, earth, water, fire, grass. And there are meetings with them: with the wind, with the tree, with earth, with water, with fire, with grass – with the Animal. And the experience of flight. The individual abandons all stories concerning themselves or someone else, and abandons all armour – communion is restored. What I am talking about demands very delicate conditions. And yet I believe that that can in some way spread, that it will not remain an experience for so terribly few.

AB: Well then tell me, do you not feel remorse that from amongst all those people who would want to participate because they have the disposition, the specified prerequisite, only so few can permit themselves, because the rest are bogged down in the mud of existence?

JG: That appals me, I regret it deeply, and I hope that despite everything these people will be found. But I don't know whether we will succeed in that, or maybe others.

ACTION IS LITERAL

Extracts from a conference given by Grotowski at the Kościuszko Foundation in New York on 19 April 1978. The text was published in *Dialog* in September 1979 [84/95–101], and Leszek Kolankiewicz, who prepared the text for publication, wrote in an introductory note:

> 'The printed word does not render, in the case of Grotowski's speech, all aspects of his message. In these circumstances, it is important that the reader remember that the author is constantly formulating his message in live speech before the participants of the meeting'.

Usually in theatre we are dealing with an area defined by the set and the props. It may have a literal or associational character, but the final distinction is of little relevance. We are in agreement that what is taking place on the stage is taking place

90 Jerzy Grotowski and Andrzej Bonarski.

in someone's home, for example, or in a meadow, in moonlight, in the universe, in someone's head. But at the same time we know that the house, the meadow, the moon, the universe or the contents of this head are on stage, or – in the case of street theatre – in the street etc. So at the same time we all know, that this is taking place on stage.

Now let us imagine that what is happening is taking place in the place where it is happening. The space does not represent any other space. If something happens in a room, then it happens in a room. If something takes place on the floor, then it takes place on the floor. If it takes place in town, then it takes place in town. And if it's a meadow, it takes place in the meadow. If there's a sun, then it's a real, actual sun. And if it's a tree – then that's a real tree. So then, each thing is what it is. That is the space.

In this space there are people. If there is a tree under which this is happening, then it is simply a tree. A man standing under that tree is simply a man, himself. It's not a matter of him pretending to be something else, only that he should be himself. He is with some other people whom he knows or does not know. If he knows them, he should not pretend that he does not. But at the same time if he does not know them, he should not pretend to be acquainted with them. This seems to be very simple, but it is not so. On stage in a theatre we usually play some role. If I am to play King Lear, the difference between myself and Lear is big enough for me to be aware that I am playing someone else. But if I am to be myself under that tree, a terrifying question arises: which self? The one known to my friends? The one known to my enemies? The one that I would like others to know? The one I dream about? The one I do not like?

The tree is our teacher. It does not ask itself such questions. It is itself. It gives fruit, when the time comes. It does not calculate. For us, this is much more difficult.

Maybe there is no way in which we can answer in words the question – how to be oneself? But without a doubt it can be found in action, if we forget about ourselves. If we forget all these thoughts. Like the tree. But in order that a man may forget about himself, he must be whole, within something. In what he is doing, in what he desires. Or to be whole with someone who is present. In other words, he must stop thinking of himself all the time.

What happens then? Let's imagine we're on a trip. We have to make our way through a certain space, we are going from town towards a mountain, maybe we have a tent with us, we are heading for some rise in the terrain. So we are on our way. But all the time we are incessantly engaged with something. With something that is already behind us, or something that is still before us. This something, that is behind us, it is something that we have left behind, something that has happened to us: have we not forgotten something? Do we have enough food? Is there a hole in my rucksack? Have I lost my money? Do we have enough time for this trip? That something that is before us is what we call our 'goal'. The goal is something we think constantly about, so that we experience nothing. Everything then becomes some kind of bus ride from one stop to another. The city is behind us, we must have somewhere for lunch, somewhere to sleep. 'When will we arrive at our goal?'

And if there is, besides, some other group, which set off at the same time as us, we ask ourselves: is our bus high-speed or not? 'Who will be the first to reach the goal?' Always, in our thoughts, we are at that place to which we have not yet arrived. We can cross ten streams and ten forests, and see nothing, hear nothing, but our own noise. If someone feels that something is really happening, then – so that he may avoid this sensation – he seeks to formulate it in words. For example: 'Oh, look! What a beautiful sunset!' In the moment that he speaks, he is already freed from the 'experience of sunset', because 'sunset' becomes an instrument for the expression of his aesthetic sensibility and a pretext for idle chatter. Not to say anything seems an outrage. If someone is in the forest, he lights his torch. If he hears birds he shrieks, so as not to hear them (or else he says how beautifully they sing). In a word: we are engaged ceaselessly with maintaining our trivial chatter and with reaching our goal. In this case it would appear better to use motorized transport (unless the point is to keep in good condition). In any case, practically any road we are used to following is just so much distance endured. I'm either behind myself, or ahead of myself, but never there, where I am.

So what then takes place between the people? I shall return to a theatrical language. If I know someone, then I have created between us certain playful conventions – for example, either seriously or jokingly, with bombast or irony. The moment we find ourselves in a group, we begin constructing our defence before the others by means of these conventions. We start, through our very own conventions, as in a conspiracy, to defend ourselves before the others with these conventions. If we do not know somebody, we behave in relation to him in a similar way to when, on our journey, we are thinking about it coming to a quick end. We either want it to be over as soon as possible, or we want it to be an immediate friendship, or we decide to remain indifferent to each other. If there's a difference of sex involved, there is the temptation to play on this – there is, for example, coquetry or defence. Each time we 'see' in advance what the end result must be. In a word: we refuse to accept someone else's presence, in the same way that we do not accept the road. We imagine to ourselves the final goal. In this way we experience nothing.

And therefore the first action is non-action. The first thing to be done is what is necessary. We do not have to leave town for this – it can be experienced in a closed room. Let's imagine a closed room, in which there is a certain number of people. These people do not have a goal in view. They begin with what is self-evident. Someone is thirsty and drinks water. There is no goal in this. He drinks water because he's thirsty. This has both purpose and self-evidence. How often does it happen that we drink water because we are thirsty? Rarely. Mostly we drink water because we do not know what to say, we do not know what to do, we are confused, we are looking for a pretext to enter into a conversation. Because we are not able to 'do nothing', so we drink water. But it's not just water. And it's not just that we drink something. We begin for example to eat, not because we're hungry, but because we don't know what to do. He who drinks – or eats – because he's thirsty, or hungry, possesses very beautiful 'expression' – he has self-evidence.

Because he's not searching for expression. Let's say that the work has lasted all day and evening has arrived, so the group is preparing for sleep. Some are sleepy and some are not. One person is not sleepy, and yet he prepares for sleep. Why? Because it's the hour for sleep. That is his goal. 'I must go to bed at 11 o'clock, I've had a full day's work'. He cannot sleep so he takes a pill. But let us imagine that someone falls asleep because he is sleepy. Maybe even in the middle of doing something, and not necessarily at night. When we reach the point where, in a certain space someone is drinking water, because he is thirsty, a second is singing, because he really wants to sing, a third sleeps because he really wants to sleep, a fourth is running, because something drives him to, and a fifth is fooling about, because of an interest in the others – then we are dealing with the phenomenon of the present. There is no being ahead of oneself, or behind oneself. One is where one is. This is only a first step, but it is the first step towards being what one really is.

If someone were to describe this from the outside – well there's nothing unusual about it: someone's drinking water, someone's singing, someone's sleeping, someone's running, someone's playing. Is there anything unusual about this?

We lead different kinds of work, with different people taking part, and the groups are set up in different ways. It all depends on who is leading the experience, and on those who take part. In other words, it depends on the needs. But were I to find one common formulation for any of these very differing types of work, in that moment when they reach a fullness, then I would say that their essence is: to be in the present, to be – where one is, to do – what one does, to meet – whom one meets.

In a theatrical language we may describe this by saying that action is literal – and not symbolic, there is no division between actor and spectator, space is literal – and not symbolic.

. . . .

An experience may last many hours, it may last many days and nights. The most critical moment arrives at that point where those participating cease to hope that something will happen. As long as they still have hope, they still have their notions of what is to happen. They are heading towards the goal, they are not – being. To begin with each participant thinks that he must do something. Something he thinks should be done. For example, someone thinks that he should sing or dance. Someone else that he should have rich inner experiences, so let us say he meditates. Someone else considers that he should be unrestrained, in other words wild, so he shouts a lot. Still someone else thinks that this should be an amicable meeting, so he tries to be warm to those he does not know. It is difficult to understand why one should be warm to someone, if there are no reasons for it. Someone practically fondles someone else. Yet another is searching for contact, so he either touches someone, or stares hard at him. Well, we must be patient. Let each sing his aria. And then find himself at the starting point. He has already played everything – and nothing. He is already even sweating, he is already tired, he has even given up. And it is only then when everything is possible. For suddenly someone sees another. Suddenly someone does something that is self-evident.

. . . .

A man arrives then at the point, which has been called 'humility', at the moment in which he simply is and in which he accepts the self-evidence, and together with the self-evidence – he accepts the present, together with the present – he accepts someone, together with his acceptance of someone – he accepts himself, because he forgets about himself. He forgets thoughts about himself in the moment before and in the moment to follow. When a man arrives at this point it is as though he emerged from an enclosed space, as if he emerged from a dungeon into open space. Outer and inner. And without the differentiation between outer and inner, between the body and the soul, for example. There is simply free, open space. And where am I in this? I don't know. Maybe I do not exist? Maybe I have thrown off this accursed image?

When we reach that point, we touch in this experience something that people sought within the 'dramatic religions' (the Eleusian rites, for example) – something which preceded yoga, something which preceded the Indian forms of shamanism, something which preceded Zen, something which preceded the experience of a poet, who writes without knowing how this is happening to him. But it is very important to make one reservation: we do not arrive at yoga, tantra, zen, shamanism, Eleusis, poetic inspiration – we arrive at something that precedes. For that which precedes is always present. We could say that it is inscribed in our genetic code. The beginning is present.

WANDERING TOWARDS A THEATRE OF SOURCES
Extracts from a talk given at an I T I conference in Warsaw on 5 June 1978 on 'The Art of the Beginner'. The text (again edited by Leszek Kolankiewicz) was published in *Dialog* in November 1979. [87/94–103]

When a Samurai has mastered all the skills and it appears that he has arrived at the optimum of practical – let's say 'technical' – knowledge, he is obliged to let it all go, to discard everything and to behave as a beginner. It is said that if he is unable to discard a warrior's knowledge, if he cannot become as a fool, a madman, a child, as an animal or a force of nature – then he will be killed. To confront the 'opponent' like the unknown, to remember that this battle may be the last, and hence the only, battle: the last, for he may be killed, and this means the only battle. To forget all skill, to be completely without skill, to be almost as in a dream. Only then, when the warrior is able to forget victory, has he a chance.

It is to some extent in this meaning – although neither primarily nor exclusively – that I speak of the 'beginner's art'.
. . . .

In seeking an original state we have two possibilities. The first possibility is by means of a training which will be later abolished. As in the art of the Samurai: there must first take place a conscious mastery, then an almost unconscious mastery, then practically on the principle of a conditioned reflex, and finally a mastery of the warrior's skills. But at the point that he becomes a real warrior, he must forget everything. The second possibility is through untaming. From the moment we are born we are tamed in everything: how to see, how to hear, what is what, how to be, how to eat, how to drink water, what is possible and what impossible.... And so the second possibility is to untame the tamed. This is very difficult work. Untaming demands greater effort and self-discipline than training.

. . . .

When we speak about the art of the beginner, we speak about the beginning, we speak about beginnings. What does it mean, to be in the beginning? Does it mean to look for the historical beginnings of something, to look for something which once was? Can we ask how theatre began, how it originated, how it developed? Yes, we can ask such questions. But I am not talking about that. To be in the beginnings or to be in the beginning – this is something to be done....

To be in the beginning means *hic et nunc*, or rather *hic stans* and *nunc stans*.

Whenever we do something we are always thinking of something that has already happened. Of each tree we encounter we think in terms of a formula concerning trees. Or in terms of memories. We also have in mind some daydreams and foreboding for the future. In this way we find ourselves constantly between the past and the future. To be in the beginning is to renounce absence. All these tricks, in fact, originate in our intellectual computer. The intellectual computer is one of the most fundamental things we have received from nature. The problem is that there is a time when it should work and a time when it should rest. And in any case one must take responsibility for its programming. What is perception? It is experience. It is something incredibly tangible, something organic and primeval – and extremely simple. But our computer is so constructed that we are detached from that most simple of things. So we perceive thoughts, and not facts.

And therefore, because we perceive thoughts and not facts – I prefer to speak of the body rather than the soul. When we speak of 'soul' or 'spirit' it is extremely easy to get caught up in something sublime, pseudo-mystical and, in fact, sentimental. It is very easy to become, in one's own way, falsely poetic. At the same time, in many languages the word 'spirit' is now so much connected with 'intellect' that it denotes just another way of dividing the human being. Therefore I prefer to speak of the body. But when I speak of the body, I speak of the human being.

What are our limits? But what are the Sun's limits? We look – it is a vibrating sphere which emits protuberances, eruptions, solar storms, expansions. And we think that those, more or less, are its limits. But these are not the limits of the solar body. For astronomers speak of the 'solar wind'. What is this wind? It consists of particles of solar matter penetrating far into our planetary system, and forming a kind of membrane which encloses the entire system, protecting it from cosmic rays from outside. So is that where the limits of the Sun are to be found? Perhaps. But if so, then we are in the Sun. The same applies to our body. When I think about myself, is it my circulatory system? Of course it is. But it is also what we call 'inner world'. My body has its fourth dimension. But it is also what we call 'outer world'. In order to discover my body it may well be good to discover your body. But I can't discover your body if in my own way I don't love you. After all, when I discover a body I discover the body of a tree, the body of the sky, the body of the earth, I discover the body of every single thing. This dimension which is not built from my circulatory system ... it's like the dimension in which we find ourselves when we face the astronomers' sky and the stars look down on us.

When I speak of the technique of the beginnings I do not mean being attached to the past, rather I mean a commitment to the beginning. As if in each moment we were served with that very first of sentences: 'In the Beginning'. In the beginning there was the now, every time is in the beginning.

In order to achieve the experience of the beginning one must undergo something that precedes the notion of a group. A group may be something essential, something that supports us, that is true. But if it is to avoid being merely a gathering of individuals who are condemned to be together because of their jobs or a fear of life, if the group is to be a natural and not coincidental meeting, this experience must – in order of importance – precede the group. That 'before the group' must be something individual, a being-to-being experience. Only after this, comes the group as something creative.

There exists – as I have already mentioned – two possibilities for being in the beginning: technique one – through training and its complete abandonment, and technique two – by means of untaming. My preference – and I have also stated this – is for the second possibility. That second possibility is a strategy, it is long term work, it is bashing your head against a wall, obstinacy and persistence, consciousness and oblivion – sharpness of vision, behaviour, expectations ... it is heavy work, please don't forget that. To yield to whatever may be is not this second possibility, it is no possibility at all. ... Why begin with the strategy of untaming today? Because we live in a technical civilization which is developing in an irrevocable manner. But it also has its positive aspects, and in any case we are habituated to it. In this civilization the colonization of the planet's body, of ourselves, of life, of the senses – this colonization that starts with ourselves, with our organism, with the human beings closest to us – has advanced so far that I feel there exists a need to balance it. It may be said that we are in the process of colonizing our own selves, beginning with what is alive in ourselves, beginning – simply – with the body. Many learned words could be used here, such as 'ecology'. ... But let us not forget that the primary natural environment is the body, my senses. It is the first environment given to man. And in this environment, nearby is you. You and I in relation to ... in relation to the Great Environment? The living world? And when the life around succumbs to the same things as does the human body, if it becomes plaster and paste, then if only for this reason we should maybe start from technique two and not technique one. I see a need for a new equilibrium. But if someone begins with technique one, I understand and respect him. Besides, from whichever pole we commence, we must discover the other pole.

THEATRE OF SOURCES
Extracts from a talk given by Grotowski at York University in Toronto in October 1980. The English version was prepared by myself in collaboration with Grotowski.

I began my own research as a young boy, almost alone, and I have continued it meeting along the way different kinds of people – some normal, some bizarre, some mad. I have continued that work through the years with a group but it has remained nevertheless almost private. One day, I found that it could be a public activity as well – not in the sense of making a public show of it – but in the sense of being able to say publicly that there is a kind of research with which I occupy myself. This work I began long before I ever began my formal work in the theatre and this idea of 'making public' one's explorations has had and continues to have an influence on my theatrical research.

I tended to do a lot of group work during my paratheatrical period, work that was detached in many ways from public meetings like this. Now, given circumstances, it seems a natural time in my life not to do anything else but simply to say, 'all right, this is my work'. It was about four years ago that the occasion presented itself. I was given the opportunity both by my own country and by certain international organizations to create an international programme. I said to myself, 'that's the moment' and I found the name *Theatre of Sources*.

I think it would be much better if we forgot the word theatre for now and talked simply of that which refers to the sources. But be careful. I'm not talking about sources of *theatre*. I am speaking of those sources that present themselves as a kind of work on one's self and which developed in different cultures and different traditions, and, naturally, in different ways. There exists now within our *Theatre of Sources* a trans-cultural group. Within that group, there are people who come from very different traditions. Among them are the different European traditions, Asiatic traditions (which are well differentiated as you know), African traditions, traditions related to the North American Indian and so on. The group is a very mixed one. At times, we work together as a group. At other times, only a few of us work together. The rule is that after a certain length of time, we must each return to our own context to re-contact it. In certain particular traditions in the world, it's difficult to know whether we're dealing with cultural or religious traditions. It's impossible often to separate the two. In this Tower of Babel, we are conditioned by very different cultural and religious traditions. And in several cases, two different members don't even have a single language in common.

Perhaps at this moment, it would be appropriate to turn to the subject of what we call the Technique of Sources. It's very difficult to verbalize but in a certain trivial way one can give some examples. For instance, everybody knows that yoga exists. Yoga to some is a technique. In truth, yoga is an enormous bag within which are many techniques, each different from one another. Whatever one describes it as, it is clear that yoga is a technique of sources of India. Many people in the West today are obsessed by some of the Islamic techniques of the Dervishes. When we focus that way, it is more or less clear what exactly we are talking about. What we are saying here is that there are 'source' techniques of Islam known in our part of the world as Dervish techniques. Ethnographers who study the life and practices of North American Indians (and one can add to these those who study the writings of Castenada) and those who study and become excited about aspects of shamanism know that there exists what we can call a technique of sources of the Indians.

We all know that there exists such a thing as a power walk. That's fine. Because thanks to this more or less confused knowledge, everybody knows that a technique of sources can be something in appearance very simple. Like, for instance, just walking. So, to speak again in an extremely trivial way, there are different techniques of sources. Another technique, zen buddhism. There are certain forms of this that are well-known. Some involve simply sitting down. There are also techniques relating to the martial arts, the art of the warrior, connected with zen for centuries. Here it is necessary to underline that the techniques of sources that interest us are not those most closely related to techniques of sitting meditation but those that lead to activity, in action like the martial art techniques derived from zen.

There are, I am saying, many techniques of sources, some very sophisticated, some not. All nevertheless remain – and must remain – extremely precise.

. . . .

Therefore, it should be clear now that it was not a synthesis of techniques of sources that we were after. We searched for those points that preceded the differences. Let us say that there exist techniques of sources. But what we search for are the sources of the techniques of sources, and these sources must be extremely simple. Everything else developed afterwards, and differentiated itself according to social, cultural or religious contexts. But the primary thing should be something extremely simple and it should be something given to the human being. Given by whom? That's the question. The answer depends on your preferences in the area of semantics. If your preferences are theological, you can say it's the seed of light received from God. If, on the other hand, your preferences are scientific, you can say that it's printed on one's genetic code.

. . . .

So this primary thing that should precede the differences of traditions seemed to me like something very simple, which demands extremely palpable and, I would say, exterior actions in order to be touched. For example, we say you must find your inner silence. Of course. But if you cannot find your own inner silence, I don't think anyone else can help you find it. Also, everyone tends to talk at length about how they fight this lack of inner silence. But you can simply apply exterior silence. And if this exterior silence is truly absorbed then the interior silence has at least a chance of existing. So the first thing may be for us not to talk. The same perhaps goes for our movement. Exterior silence means also that our movement must be silent. We must not be agitated in our movements. They must not be too visible, too loud. But without making a demonstration out of this. If you find exterior silence, then the inner silence will take care of itself.

There's a very old expression that one finds in many different traditions: 'movement which is repose'. We can find this in the Gnostic Christian tradition and in the Tibetan tradition. The very same expression. Also in certain yoga approaches in India it is said that in certain states of de-conditioning we can be fully awake, vigilant, but also in repose. As if we were plunged into a sleep without confabulations. That movement which is repose is perhaps the crucial point where different techniques of sources begin. I'm not saying that movement which is repose is the point of beginning but I am saying that the beginning is closely associated with this notion. So we have two aspects: movement and repose. When we are moving, and when we are able to break through the techniques of the body of everyday life, then our movement becomes a movement of perception. One can say that our movement is seeing, hearing, feeling, our movement is perception.

. . . .

All these things are quite simple. And one of the *Theatre of Sources'* simplest actions is just a certain way of walking which, through rhythms different from the rhythms of life, breaks the kind of walk which is directed towards an objective. You are never on the way, there where you are, but if you change the rhythms (this is a very difficult thing to describe but it can be practised) if for instance you change them into an extremely slow rhythm, so slow that you are virtually standing still – and so that somebody watching would have the impression that he doesn't see anyone because you are almost immobile – then in the beginning you are very irritated, but after a few moments, if you are really attentive, something does change. You begin to be where you are. It depends on a man's temperament. Some have too much energy. One must begin with movements to burn off the energy, to set fire to the body energy, a kind of letting-go, but at the same time one must also retain the organic movement. It's as if your animal body becomes master of the situation and starts to move – without prejudice about what is dangerous or not. It may begin perhaps in jumping. Apparently you would never be able to jump that way. But you do it. It happens. And you don't look at the ground. You close your eyes and you run among the trees but you don't run into them. It's nature and your body nature that is burning off. For your body is also nature. But when it's burnt off something happens. You feel as if everything is part of a great current of things and your body begins to feel it and begins to move quietly, serenely, almost floating. As if your body were conducted by the current. At the same time you can feel that it is the current of all things around you that carries you, but at the same time you feel that something is coming out of you too.

. . . .

In the group of the *Theatre of Sources* each participant is allied to a technique of sources close to him, traditional for him. But this is not shared. That's very important. Though a colleague of mine is a Japanese Buddhist priest, he is nevertheless not doing something that is of his religion. He knows that that is not part of the *Theatre of Sources*. He is studying zen buddhism but he knows that he won't be doing sitting meditation with anyone of the others in the group. He has a very full life and also practises the Zen martial arts. He is a very good teacher of this, a specialist, but he never proposed to any of us to work with him on it. We don't 'share' the technique of sources. There is a Latin American Indian who has been with us for a long time. We began working with him long before the name *Theatre of Sources* was used. There is also an Indian Brahmin. He is deeply rooted in his own traditions but is also keenly aware of the contemporary world. The three of them, the Latin American Indian, the Brahmin and the Japanese man work together but they do nothing that belongs to only one tradition. They look for a simple action, evident in its consequences for all three. That means it works for all three without any difference of cultural context.

Each action begins as a childlike action, or from the almost infantile preferences of each one. It's like one wants to climb a tree but doesn't know why. Someone else has a preference for running but really to the point of letting go. Someone else searches only for a way of walking etc. Someone else has really a very particular idea that you can move without seeing. He puts a handkerchief over his eyes and moves. And he says, if the movement can see, then maybe I can see without eyes. The points of departure are mostly personal preferences but not the preferences of a particular tradition. Somebody makes several actions on the lines of his preferences. Then he confronts someone from another tradition – often without even a language in common – and the first test is whether or not this thing works for someone who has been conditioned differently. If it works for the other people, we concentrate on that in our work. But the thing that appears after a long evolution is always something still more simple. One could say that we arrive at something totally primary and simple.

I watched a person once who was searching simply by walking, just walking from one spot to another in space, and within that he began to lose his heaviness. One day, he succeeded. I said to him that he is now doing the same thing as his four year old. You can't say if this experience is true or false: you can say it is primal. In that sense, in many traditions, we can find the notion of the child which is often confused with childishness. Or confused with playing at being child-like. But in fact, what it is all about is simply something very direct and immediate, and that is what is most touching in the child. This immediacy which is at the same time energetic and at the same time carries in itself joy. Perhaps the word joy is too much. Perhaps we should say only lack of anguish, lack of energetic depression. That's what it's all about. It's quite primal.

Sometimes we take people from outside into this work for short periods. Then the process is very different. Then it is necessary to confront that person with many different practices which have already been tested. In order to see if it works for him, he must do it immediately and not analyze it from the point of view of structure, for instance. The only way of doing this is to ask him to imitate. That process is an amusing one in our contemporary world. We all behave in an imitative way. Most of our lives are based only on imitation of other people's lives. That's accepted. But if you ask someone to simply imitate the person who is guiding you in this action – 'Do it!' – there's an enormous shock. That's how animals learn actions. See how birds teach their young. It's really through imitation. By imitating without analyzing, it's easy to find which actions give you this lack of anguish and this lack of energetic depression. Then you can make choices and the problem of imitation doesn't exist anymore. You must really work yourself in order to penetrate that thing.

A TALK ABOUT THEATRE FOR YOUTH IN SCHOOLS
Extracts from a talk broadcast on Polish Radio in October 1979, and intended for secondary schools (14–18 years). It was again edited by Leszek Kolankiewicz and published in *Dialog* in February 1980. [91/132–137]

The fact is that our activity – that of the Laboratory theatre – is to do with a very altered concept of theatre, with the destruction of the boundaries of this concept. Our activity has in this respect become symbolic for many people. The actual processes, however, took place much earlier – the reform had already begun before the First World War. There were many people searching in a parallel manner to us. . . . In some ways of course our process was very radical. But it cannot be said that it was we who brought about this change. It was brought about by many people.
. . . .
Theatre may also be a place where the division into those who only watch and those who only act can begin to disappear.

And the field of radical penetration into other areas, which we to a great extent represent, can only now really be talked about. What is called 'close to theatre', 'paratheatre', 'cultural actions', 'open participation', 'workshops' (this kind of work had different names) – can in fact only now be analyzed in a theatrical language and – as many people in the world are now beginning to do – can be experimented with in relation to a widening of the concept of theatre.

Let us say that there exist actions, led by a group of prepared people, who present a certain situation to people from the outside. The simplest such situation may for example be whatever is obvious in a given moment: do not dance, unless that really takes you, don't pretend what you don't feel. In this case we have a situation in which one is not looking for how to play, but only for how not to play.
. . . .
And in certain activities it is possible to start *not* from the question of how to play. This means not only not aiming to become a professional actor, but even aiming to become less of an 'actor' than you are an 'actor' in life. That's a remarkable situation. There emerge then the simplest of things, which can be half lighthearted, half deadly serious, as for example when an individual runs through tall grass. Such a simple thing can be something great, if it is linked to a certain kind of non-acting. . . .

And there may be – but this is only the simplest of examples – very complex activities, from which emerges the problem of a natural contact between people – one not built upon an acting situation. In these the elements of conventional contact disappear, for example: 'I am playing someone who is picking up a girl', or 'I am

playing a girl who is being picked up'. And if I do not act? There then takes place
something which is simultaneously mature and childlike. Between wisdom and
childishness – something very particular. It cannot then be said that those who
initiate this are actors in the classical meaning of the word. But they are the initiators
of certain activities, they are active, drawing others after themselves. And drawing
others after them they become actors in the meaning in which this was used, for
example, in the 18th Century. 'Actor' then meant 'an active individual'. That is
the etymology of the word. In this sense there exists the 'actor' – the active person
(like 'actor of one's fate', 'actor of a certain event', 'actor of a certain battle' etc.).
An individual more active than others, drawing them into participation, into action
– but through an attempt at not-acting, a resignation from acting, also a resignation
from daily social roles.

Next: if something happens in a theatre – as one imagines it in its usual sense
– and it is said that it happens in the forest, then scenery is built, real trees cut
down from the forest may be erected (which is – let's say – a barbarity, but it can
happen) and you can also paint a tree on canvas and accept in the same way that
that happens in the forest. Alright – but what if something really happens in the
forest? In the theatre we have lighting, which creates the effect of the moon or the
sun. Alright – but there is in fact a real moon and a real sun. Let's imagine that
there is no scenery. We are in the forest – and it's a real forest, we are on the road
– and it's a real road, there is sun – and it's a real sun, it's night – and it's really
night and not the dimming of the lighting. Someone might say that that is the most
naturalistic or realistic scenery that can exist. Only that that is not scenery at all.
Quite simply the place of action is the real place of action. Short and to the point.

Centuries ago Aristotle defined the unity of place, time and action. This was said
about tragedy, and thus about theatre. And here we have the place – it happens
where it happens, the time – it happens when it happens, and the action – what
happens, happens. There is no relating about something that happened at some
other time or could happen. It emerges from the participants or it is born from the
leading group, but it is born here and now – it is unrepeatable, once and for all,
at another time and in another place it will be different. We have that unity of
action, time and place.

First of all, then: the 'actor' can mean an individual who portrays or experiences
some character, who acts somebody. That is one concept. Another possibility: the
'actor' means an individual in action, who aims not at acting, but at acting less than
in daily life and who draws others to the simplest, the most human, the most direct
actions – something so simple that it borders on the childish. Two polar possibilities.

Secondly: 'theatre' may be associated with a building, in which there is a room.
In the room is a stage and an auditorium. On the stage is scenery, which suggests
the place of action. But equally well, what happens may happen there, where it
happens. There is no need to represent the forest, for there is a real forest, no need
to represent the street, for there is a real street, no need to represent the sun, for
there is a real sun, no need to represent the grass for there is real grass, no need

to represent a house, for there is a real house. That's the second possibility: the reality of place.

Thirdly: what happens may be erected around a certain scaffolding, such as a written drama. And it can be born from human improvisation. Like in jazz music, there is in fact a starting motif around which there are then improvisations – in the same way action can be improvised, and running, movement, song, voice, moments of contact, fooling, something which is on the border of flight. All that may be improvisation. The individual indeed may be their own improvisation. That's the other possibility. For did improvisation not exist in theatre? It did indeed exist – centuries ago the *commedia dell'arte* was based exclusively on improvisation.

Fourthly – other polar possibilities: there can be a spectator, and there can be a participant. That can also have blurred borders – to be one, and the other. One way now, and later another.

Fifthly: there may be a group which gets together solely because that is the place of work and profession, and there may be a group which gets together because there is something in life of particular interest. For that, they have come together. Does that group have to be amateur? If through profession we understand a certain competence or responsibility, then it should be professional. In this meaning – yes. But if through profession we understand simply a connection with employment, it is better if that group is united more in other ways. There may apart from that be employment, because you must have something to live on. It's better not to patch up your life. It is better to have a place in which your work and your life can intersect.

Finally, as a postscript to these extracts, and indeed to the entire book, I offer the following words of Grotowski's, with which he concluded a talk given at the Brooklyn Academy in New York on 16 December 1969:

All of the detailed matters I have expressed may function only as examples amongst others. No formula, from an intellectual point of view, is very precise, and to repeat these formulae or to find them important would be a mistake. All that can be put within a system from what I have said is of no value. That system would paralyse in the same way as all other systems. If, in what I have said, there has been something that anyone listening was able to understand as a purely personal message, only for them and not for all the others, that has been the thing I wanted to express. Anything that has been a sort of general formula for everybody has already missed the point, it is a device for creating new slogans, and to make people believe that these are new truths. There remains what exists solely on the level of an appeal for an individual, a concrete appeal in the context of their life and their experience. For another individual, it will already be something different. Only that is not falsified. And so I will end, asking your pardon for all the confusion I have created in the past and all the confusion I am at this moment recreating. Perhaps one must create an abundance of confusion in order to create also an individual understanding which surpasses the level of words. [51/28]

91 Jerzy Grotowski.

APPENDIX
Apocalypsis Cum Figuris
Translation and personal account

What follows are my own personal recollections of the events of *Apocalypsis Cum Figuris*, after attendance at performances over many years. I was helped with the dialogue by having a Polish 'script', and was able to track down most of the sources on my return to this country. I have not indicated where texts have been edited by the Laboratory Theatre or slightly altered from their original sources, so as not to inhibit the flow of the dialogue. One detail – the part of Mary Magdalene was taken on different nights by either Rena Mirecka (Polish) or Elizabeth Albahaca (South American). The resulting variation only slightly affects the text and action. I have chosen to describe the performance in which Rena Mirecka takes part.

The first spectator enters the dim, rectangular, windowless room to find it empty. There are two 'attendants', whose job becomes increasingly demanding as the audience grows. There is no seating, and the only objects are two spotlights: placed side by side on the floor their beams reflect off one wall, and this arrangement gives a tangible, spatial quality to the lighting. The spectators begin to swarm in, skilfully manipulated into position against the walls by the attendants. The sea of bodies heaves and wriggles and squirms, leaving an area empty in the middle.

Meanwhile the actors have been entering, from a separate, curtained-off doorway. They take up their positions in their own time, the same every night, maybe jostled by unaware spectators, their eyes moving around the room with the same curiosity displayed by the audience. First comes Lazarus, dressed casually. He is small, wiry and alert, with aristocratic deep-lined features, and a pair of piercing cruel eyes. Then Simon Peter, a tall slim man with a strong chest – a long black waistcoat over his clothes. He has thinning hair and a beard – a lively, curious face. Mary Magdalene enters quickly and almost shyly, clutching a loaf of bread and a knife wrapped in a white cloth. Fine black hair hangs straight to her shoulders past a pointed weary face, whispy strands getting in her eyes or mouth. She wears a brilliantly patterned long-sleeved dress, cut low, and her legs and feet are bare. Judas enters quickly and furtively to recline near her – respectably dressed in shirt and slacks, he somehow manages to look seedy. And at some point the Simpleton has slipped in unobtrusively to crouch unseen against the wall. Finally, with the room nearly full, in stalks John, barefoot and wary – very tight worn jeans, jacket and cap. Although the immediate impression is of youth, the hair beneath the cap is receding, and the face is very slightly debauched.

The last spectators are being ushered in. The actors sink down into reclining but watchful positions – all save Simon Peter who remains kneeling in one corner of the playing area,

92 Poster for *Apocalypsis Cum Figuris*.

in a commanding position. The last spectator in place, a final look around from the attendants, and the door is pulled to.

Silence settles and grows.

In the waiting, the eyes of Mary Magdalene and John meet, and a spark leaps across the space dividing them. John, shuffling on his knees to the middle of the room, addresses her intensely: *Verily, verily I say unto you, Except ye eat the flesh of the Son of Man and drink his blood, ye have no life in you.*[1] Mary Magdalene, now sitting, responds wearily: *You think so?* John continues: *Whoso eateth my flesh, and drinketh my blood, hath eternal life; and I will raise him up on the last day.*[2] Mary Magdalene, pityingly: *That's not true.* John reaches out before him and with a taut finger draws the sign of the cross on the ground between them, saying: *For my flesh is meat indeed, and my blood is drink indeed.*[3]

Mary Magdalene comes swiftly to kneel before him, and gently lays the bread and knife on the white cloth between them. John watches her, excitement on his face. Then violently shrugging the jacket off his shoulders to bare his chest, he spreads his arms wide and turns aside his face in a gesture of painful surrender. Mary Magdalene is unmoved but interested. John plunges a cupped hand into the front of his jeans, and his body jerks spasmodically. Withdrawing his hand he lifts it reverently to his lips and sups noisily. Mary Magdalene gazes on, now fascinated and a little repulsed. John repeats the action, this time offering his hand to Mary Magdalene. She takes it greedily with both hands and drains it.

Then all is violent action.

Leaping at him, Mary Magdalene repeats his movements. His body, held captive by hers, shudders helplessly. She lifts her hand to his mouth and forces the offering between his lips. As he kneels, body limp and head averted, Mary Magdalene reaches for the knife. She places it in his unresisting hand, and thrusts the hand towards his genitals. John reacts with fury, throwing Mary Magdalene aside, and drives the knife quivering into the floor. Grabbing the bread he collapses on the floor face down, and thrusts it between his legs, his body jerking. Mary Magdalene retrieves the cloth and circles around him warily, watching his actions in distress. There is silence except for John's laboured breathing.

Springing into action again Mary Magdalene tries to flay John with the cloth. There is a brief and violent struggle, their bodies slamming to the floor. Mary Magdalene fights like an animal until John throws her off and rolls onto his back, his body again arching against the bread. Mary Magdalene, determined now, retrieves the knife. She awaits her moment, and as John lies back in helpless spasms, she drags the bread from him. Crouching over it on the ground, she drives the knife into it, one, two, three times – each time John's body arches in agony as he cries out. There is a few seconds' pause, then Simon Peter takes the bread and knife gently from Mary Magdalene's hands, and replaces the bread on the cloth.

He looks calmly around the room at the spectators: *Let us rise.*

So saying, Simon Peter gets up. Cautiously circling the perimeter of the playing area he throws himself before Lazarus, and burying his face in his lap, cries: *Saviour!* Lazarus, calmly and with dignity (but looking at John with a playful expression in his eyes) puts his arms around Simon Peter and accepts the accolade: *Blessing and having been blessed, sit down beside me. Where have you come from? You're a lot of fatheads! How do you keep the fasts?*[4] Lazarus starts to giggle and collapses on his side. Simon Peter walks away from him, and, suddenly pouncing behind some spectators, drags the Simpleton, who has been curled up

93 *Apocalypsis* – Mary Magdalene (Rena Mirecka).

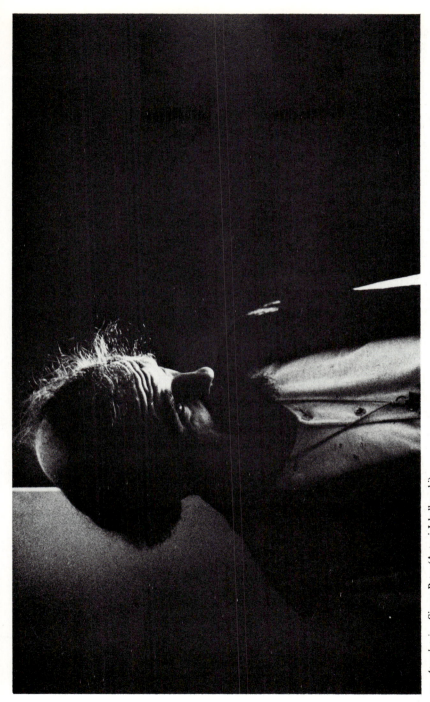

94 *Apocalypsis* – Simon Peter (Antoni Jahołkowski).

unnoticed all this time, to his feet. He hauls him to the centre of the room, where the Simpleton, dressed only in a black knee-length raincoat and carrying a wooden staff, stands obviously bewildered. Licking his lips, his eyes wildly search for reassurance.

Simon Peter: *Mary Magdalene, wash, anoint and wipe his feet.* With scarcely a glance at the Simpleton, Mary Magdalene goes directly to Lazarus. Reclining back, Lazarus elegantly lifts one foot which she wipes with spittle. As she returns to her place, he addresses Simon Peter with confidence, even insolence: *Aye, I'm thinking of giving up their bread, for I don't need it at all, and going away into the woods and living on wild berries. They can't give up their bread here and so they're still in bondage to the devil. Nowadays the infidels say there's no need to fast. Haughty and impious is this judgement of theirs ... and have you seen devils amongst those?*[5] Simon Peter ignores him and addresses Judas: *Judas, indicate him.*

Judas has been sitting to one side silently watching the proceedings. Circling the Simpleton with a disparaging backward glance, he approaches Lazarus and indicates his choice by placing his hand on Lazarus's head, playfully pushing him over as he does so. From his position on the floor Lazarus watches Simon Peter return in determination to kneel before the bread again and say to the Simpleton, with a wily smile: *You were born in Nazareth.* They all grin at the Simpleton. *You are the Saviour.* They begin to laugh. *You died on the cross for them.* The laughter becomes uproarious and the Simpleton simpers guilelessly back at them. *You are God.* Then to Judas: *You are Judas . . .* and turning to the girl who is screeching uncontrollably: *Mary Magdalene.*

As the laughter dies away, Simon Peter approaches the Simpleton, lifting his waistcoat to expose his side. With a single leap the Simpleton vaults onto him, legs tucked up together, arms tightly clutching, his face buried in Simon Peter's neck. With delicate, mincing steps, Simon Peter slowly circles the playing area. Lazarus has thrown himself face downwards on the ground before him, arms spread in supplication. John, who is kneeling upright, closes his eyes and begins to explore his own body slowly and sensually with his hands, singing an old Polish hymn:

He is hanging on the Cross
The Creator of Heaven
Men, you must weep for your sins
Ah! Ah! That man is dying
And suffering for my wilfulness.

As John reaches the final notes, Simon Peter gently lays the Simpleton, still curled up on his side, on the floor, saying vehemently: *Twenty centuries have passed since he gave the promise to come into his kingdom, twenty centuries since his prophet wrote: 'Behold I come quickly. Of that day and hour knoweth no man, but my Father only.' But mankind awaits him with the same faith and the same yearning. Oh, with greater faith even, for the pledges given to man from heaven have ceased: Trust what thy heart doth tell thee, trust no pledges from above.*[6]

Simon Peter turns and runs frantically towards the curtained exit, but is halted as Judas cuts off his escape. Judas circles furtively, and says in the tones of someone telling a particularly dirty story: *A certain man made a great supper, and bade many: And sent his servant at suppertime to say to them that were bidden, Come; for all things are now ready. And they all with one consent began to make excuse. The first said unto him, I have bought a piece of ground, and I must needs go and see it: I pray thee have me excused.* Judas leaps wildly into the air like a badly handled puppet. *And another said, I have bought five yoke of oxen and I go to prove them: I pray thee have me excused.* Judas leaps again. *And another said, I have married a wife, and therefore I cannot come. So the servant came and shewed his lord these things. Then the master of the house being angry said to his servant, Go out quickly into the streets and lanes of the city, and bring in hither the poor, and the maimed, and the halt, and the blind.*[7] On these final phrases Judas walks away, his voice trailing off.

Simon Peter returns to bend over and address the Simpleton, saying accusingly: *Man is born a rebel, and can rebels be happy? You were warned. There has been no lack of warnings and signs, but you did not heed the warnings. You rejected the only way by which men might be made happy, but, fortunately, in departing, you handed on the work to us. You have promised and you have confirmed it by your own word. You have given us the right to bind and unbind, and of course you can't possibly think of depriving us of that right now. Why, then, have you come to interfere with us?*[8] Simon Peter backs away, his voice trailing off, to come up short against John, who steadies him.

There is an expectant silence. Then the Simpleton, still lying on his side, begins to speak. The words are low and musical, but build up in intensity, until driven by some great emotion, he is writhing in anguish on the ground:

> *Because I do not hope to turn again*
> *Because I do not hope*
> *Because I do not hope to turn*
> *I no longer strive to strive towards such things*
> *(why should the agèd eagle stretch its wings?)*
> *Why should I mourn*
> *The vanished power of the usual reign?*
> *Because I do not hope to know again*
> *The infirm glory of the positive hour*
> *Because I do not think*
> *Because I know I shall not know*
> *The one veritable transitory power*
> *Because I cannot drink*
> *There, where trees flower, and springs flow, for there is nothing again.*
> *Because I know that time is always time*
> *And place is always and only place*
> *And what is actual is actual*
> *Because I do not hope to turn again*
> *Let these words answer*
> *For what is done, not to be done again*
> *May the judgement not be too heavy upon us*
> *Because these wings are no longer wings to fly*
> *But merely vans to beat the air*
> *The air which is now thoroughly small and dry*
> *Smaller and dryer than the will*
> *Teach us to care....*[9]

The last words come out brokenly and sobbingly. The others have been staring with dispassionate curiosity. Simon Peter replies grandly: one hand stretched out above his head, he crashes to his knees, and stumbles around the room: *The terrible and wise spirit, the spirit of self-destruction and non-existence, the great spirit talked with you in the wilderness, and we are told in the books that he apparently 'tempted' you. Is that so? And could anything truer have been said than what he revealed to you in his three questions and what you rejected, and what in the books are called 'temptations'? And yet if ever there has been on earth a real, prodigious miracle, it was on that day, on the day of the three temptations. Indeed, it was in the emergence of those three questions that the miracle lay. Decide yourself who was right – you or he who questioned you then? Call to your mind the first question; its meaning, though not in these words, was this: 'You want to go into the world and you are going empty-handed, with some promise of freedom, which men in their simplicity and their innate lawlessness cannot even comprehend, which they fear and dread – for nothing has ever been more unendurable to man and to human society than freedom! And do you see the stones in this parched and barren desert? Turn them into loaves, and mankind will run after you like a flock of sheep, grateful and obedient, though for ever trembling with fear that you might withdraw your hand and they would no longer have your loaves.'*[10]

The Simpleton, transfixed by Simon Peter's actions, has jumped up to follow him, and the progress around the room is jerky and frenetic. Simon Peter's words rise in a crescendo as the Simpleton leaps ahead to confront him. As Simon Peter bares his chest, the Simpleton charges to spear him in the belly with his staff. Then it is the Simpleton who leads the procession, stumbling, the staff over his shoulder in a parody of the cross, his face aching with silent laughter. He confronts Simon Peter once more, on his knees, and his face is suddenly confused and vulnerable. Then the Simpleton lunges forward, and their foreheads meet with a resounding crack, as of sparring stags. Glaring into his eyes, his face suffused and devilish, Simon Peter shrieks: *I can see nothing there but cunt!*

And then the other actors, who during this tortured duet have mingled into obscurity with the rest of the spectators, spring into frenzied activity. They encircle the kneeling Simpleton,

95 *Apocalypsis* – Mary Magdalene (Elizabeth Albahaca) Lazarus (Zbigniew Cynkutis), The Simpleton (Ryszard Cieślak), and Judas (Zygmunt Molik).

who is stunned by the sudden uproar, and collapse in a circle of writhing arms and legs, shrieking hysterically. Rising above the sea of their bodies, the Simpleton stretches one hand out to Simon Peter, who now stands aloof, and raises his voice above the chaos: *Take no thought ... take no thought for your life, for the life is more than meat, and the body is more than raiment.*[11] And in the sudden quiet Simon Peter announces: *And I saw water flowing from the right side of the temple, Allelujah; and all unto whom the water came were saved.*[12]

In response, Lazarus whips up the raincoat the Simpleton is wearing, to expose his naked side: putting his mouth to it he drinks deeply. The others watch greedily, until Judas pulls him off like a leech and takes his place. Lazarus rolls in slow motion onto his back to rock there, mouth open and pouting like an infant deprived of the nipple. In between each fresh assault the Simpleton, stunned and weakened, manages to stagger a couple of steps further away from his parasites, to be caught afresh each time. Next it is Mary Magdalene's turn, and she clasps him to her eagerly, her body seeming to fill up with each intake. And finally John throws Mary Magdalene off with glee, and attacks the source with animal grunts. He collapses back like the others, bloated, croaking: *It's liquor in his veins, not blood!*

The Simpleton has collapsed, drained, upon the floor. For several moments the other four roll around, the voices of Mary Magdalene and John blending in a drunken duet of repletion. Eventually Judas's voice brings them back to some level of sanity, as he drones out one of his parables: *Call the labourers ... call the labourers, and give them their hire, beginning from the last unto the first. And when they came that were hired about the eleventh hour, they received every man a penny. But when the first came, they supposed that they should have received more; and they likewise received every man a penny.*[13]

By now they are all on their feet, and have formed into a swaying procession. Mary Magdalene and John lead, followed by Judas in possession of the staff and hobbling like an old man. Lazarus and Simon Peter are in the rear. John begins to sing a slow, lyrical melody, his body swaying to the rhythm, his hands stroking Mary Magdalene. She clings to him, never taking her eyes from his face. All is now peaceful and calm and romantic. The room is mesmerized by the slow, interminable procession, as it makes a full circuit of the playing area.

For some time the Simpleton has remained motionless, and unnoticed. But the gentle rhythms gradually ease him back to life, and he takes a few tentative steps towards the centre of the room. His body becomes tense and his face suffused with ecstasy. Now on a second circuit of the room, the procession falters before him, and as he looks at each of them, they seem to reach out towards him, their faces full of love. Incredulous of their acceptance, he fixes his gaze on Lazarus, and seeing the same love there, stretches out his hands to touch his face. For an instant a frozen tableau forms, the Simpleton's hands a bare inch away from contact. And then Lazarus snaps backwards like a tight spring, and sidesteps around the group, leaving the Simpleton shocked and clutching at nothing.

Slowly the procession moves off again, the Simpleton scampering around, aping their movements. But eventually he returns to the centre of the room, to kneel down, eyes closed, and immerse himself in the gentle melody. A few moments later the procession and singing ceases abruptly, and the Simpleton begins to speak with passionate intensity:

Who walked between the violet and the violet
Who walked between
The various ranks of varied green

96 *Apocalypsis* – Simon Peter (Antoni Jahołkowski), Lazarus (Zbigniew Cynkutis), Judas (Zygmunt Molik), Mary Magdalene (Elizabeth Albahaca), and John (Stanisław Scierski).

97 *Apocalypsis* – Lazarus (Zbigniew Cynkutis), The Simpleton (Ryszard Cieślak) and Judas (Zygmunt Molik).

> *Going in white and blue, in Mary's colour,*
> *Talking of trivial things*
> *In ignorance and in knowledge of eternal dolour*
> *Who moved among the others as they walked,*
> *Who then made strong the fountains and made fresh the springs*
> *Redeem the time, redeem the dream*
> *The token of the word unheard, unspoken*
> *And after this our exile.*[14]

The procession begins again and completes another half-circuit of the room before breaking up, still gently singing. John and Mary Magdalene, hands outstretched, slowly approach the kneeling Simpleton. His face is streaked with tears and sweat, and his head goes back trustingly as Mary Magdalene swoops forward to clasp his face. But at that instant Simon Peter, with a wild whoop, stamps his boots on the floor and the idyllic interlude is shattered. The air is filled again with wildly whirling, shrieking bodies, who dance an orgiastic fandango around the Simpleton. They fling themselves to the ground, Lazarus and Judas in a parody of a lovers' embrace, Mary Magdalene and John supine before the Simpleton. Simon Peter crouches at their heads, an avenging angel, waistcoat swept over his shoulders like black wings. John chants in a rising crescendo: *May the angels lead you into Paradise. May the martyrs await your coming and bring you into the Holy City, the heavenly Jerusalem. May a choir of angels welcome you and with the poor man Lazarus of old, may you enjoy eternal rest.*[15] Simon Peter climaxes the final note with the frenzied clucking of a lunatic hen, which breaks the Simpleton's frozen paralysis.

98 *Apocalypsis* – The Simpleton (Ryszard Cieślak).

Bare feet rhythmically thudding on the floor, arms wildly flailing in a crazed and uncontrolled war-dance, he weaves in circuits around the tableau created by the other performers, whipping himself to ever greater frenzy, until coming to a sudden halt behind Simon Peter, he softly and breathlessly whistles his distress to the others.

But they take no notice of him, now bent on pursuit of other prey. Simon Peter has broken away, and again makes for the exit. But he is engulfed by Lazarus, Judas, John and Mary Magdalene, who taunt and assault him. Mary Magdalene, crouching on the ground, eyes raised provocatively to Simon Peter, begins to hum a sleazy, teasing tune. Gradually the others join in. And now they approach him one by one as he stands before them, helpless and shocked: first Judas, then Lazarus, leering into his face until he turns away in disgust. Then Mary Magdalene flaunts her breasts and buttocks as she kneels before him, squirming away with a shriek of laughter as he reaches for her. The singing becomes raucous, and it is the turn of the irrepressible John to insult him unrestrainedly with the lavatory gestures of a schoolboy. The singing momentarily drops to a hushed and expectant crooning, as Mary Magdalene reapproaches. Simon Peter grabs her, and it is the cue for the others to pounce. He stiffens into catalepsy as they thrust him to the floor and begin to abuse him.

It is the Simpleton who breaks them up. Having been ignored for so long, he simply wants to join in the fun. But at his impetuous arrival the others scatter swiftly, leaving him with the stiffened body of Simon Peter. He leans over the body cautiously, and then begins to slap the face vigorously. Simon Peter leaps back to life, to stand commandingly over the Simpleton crouched at his feet. He places one foot forward. Using a corner of his raincoat, the Simpleton briskly polishes his boot. Then at the parade-ground command 'Hup!', he slips his head between Simon Peter's legs, and jerks to his feet with Simon Peter sitting on his shoulders. Simon Peter whips him into action, and the Simpleton thuds around the room with his burden, eyes bulging, his lips drawn back in sheer physical effort. Simon Peter, shrieking in delight, spurs him on until finally the Simpleton throws him off his back, and careers madly around the room until he literally drops. Juddering to the ground, the impact jerks his body violently, and the impetus of his headlong flight sends him sliding across the floor to be brought to a halt against the feet of some spectators.

The jeering crowd have fallen silent, and Simon Peter returns quietly to his corner where he kneels to watch the ensuing action. The others circle and fidget around the Simpleton, rapidly shooting speeches at him that range in tone from sullen disappointment to vicious baiting, as they attempt again to raise a response in their inert victim. Judas: *He that entereth not by the door into the sheepfold, but climbeth up some other way, the same is a thief and a robber.*[16] Mary Magdalene: *Our bed is green.*[17] Lazarus: *If mine heart have been deceived by a woman, or if I have laid wait at my neighbour's door; Then let my wife grind unto another, and let others bow down upon her. For this is an heinous crime.*[18] Mary Magdalene: *There will I give thee my loves.*[19] Lazarus: *I have said to corruption, Thou art my father: to the worm, Thou art my mother, and my sister. And though after my skin worms destroy this body, yet in my flesh shall I see God.*[20] Mary Magdalene: *My beloved is mine and I am his.*[21] John: *And there went out another horse that was red: and the power was given to him that sat thereon to take....*[22]

The constant rainfall of words breaks through the Simpleton's stupor, as he lies on the floor. He shakes his head from side to side at his tormentors, like a chained and baited bear. Judas: *When I went out to the gate through the city the young men hid themselves: and the aged arose, and stood up. And I brake the jaws of the wicked, and plucked the spoil out of his teeth.*[23] Mary Magdalene: *My beloved put in his hand by the hole.*[24] Lazarus: *Can'st thou draw leviathan out with an hook? or his tongue with a cord which thou lettest down? Can'st thou put an hook into his nose? or bore his jaw through with a thorn? Wilt thou play with him as with a bird? or wilt thou bind him for thy maidens? Can'st thou fill his skin with barbed irons? or his head with fish spears?*[25] John: *And I saw three unclean spirits like frogs come out of the mouth of the dragon, and out of the mouth of the beast, and out of the mouth of the false prophet.*[26]

Judas has picked up the Simpleton's staff. Placing the crook under the Simpleton's chin, he draws him up from his prone position, saying tauntingly: *He that hath ears to hear, let him hear. But whereunto shall I liken this generation? It is like unto children sitting in the markets, and calling unto their fellows, And saying, We have piped unto you, and ye have not danced.*[27]

At last there is response. The Simpleton staggers to his feet, grabbing the staff back from Judas. But the jeering group now melt away from him and scatter around the room to lie curled up on their sides with their backs to him. The Simpleton begins to speak, and as he approaches each one, they cower further away from him, only to reveal laughing faces once he has passed them by:

Although I do not hope to turn again
Although I do not hope
Although I do not hope to turn
Wavering between the profit and the loss
In this brief transit where the dreams cross
The dreamcrossed twilight between birth and dying
(Bless me father) though I do not wish to wish these things
This is the time of tension
The place of solitude where three dreams cross
But when the voices shaken from the yew-tree drift away
Let the other yew be shaken and reply.
Blessed sister, holy mother, spirit of the fountain, spirit of the garden,
Suffer us not to mock ourselves with falsehood.[28]

But Lazarus has abandoned the game and is now sitting, watching the Simpleton intently. His words, addressed to the Simpleton's back, come out ominously: *I despaired . . . for now shall I sleep in the dust; and thou shalt seek me in the morning, but I shall not be.*[29]

The Simpleton stiffens in response, and turns in dread to watch Lazarus as he sinks back motionless on the ground, his face hidden by his shirt. Mary Magdalene and Judas arise slowly and ponderously and cross over to the body of Lazarus, humming a funeral tune. Judas at the head, and Mary Magdalene at the feet, they swoop down with exaggerated gestures to lift the corpse and carry it rigid between them to lay it down, feet facing the Simpleton. John scoops up the bread from where it has been lying on the white cloth, in front of Simon Peter, and carries it over to the mourning group. He breaks off small pieces and distributes them.

The Simpleton has been watching the events with a growing horror. Mary Magdalene is now squatting on the corpse's legs, Judas on his chest, and John stands at his head. When the funeral dirge shows indications of abating, it is Simon Peter, from his position on the other side of the room, who leans forward evilly to prompt them. They pick up the rhythm and carry on enthusiastically, until all discipline breaks down into a cacophony of hysterical wails and grief-torn shrieks.

Three sharp raps of the Simpleton's rod on the floor, and the row ceases abruptly. The Simpleton: *Lazarus, I say unto thee, Arise.*[30]

The words are spoken softly, but with confidence. The room is transfixed by the awful, vulnerable waiting on the Simpleton's face. And the corpse, in slow motion, lifts itself up until kneeling, faceless, before the miracle worker. The hands slowly lift to drag the material, inch by inch, back over the head. Above the cloth the eyes stare into the Simpleton's own, slightly maddened by the return to reality. A movement of hope creeps across the Simpleton's face, broken off by a high-pitched whinny of mockery from Lazarus.

The Simpleton falls back a few paces, as the laughter freezes into a mask of pure hatred on Lazarus's face. Lazarus reaches out a careless hand, into which Judas thrusts the loaf of bread. He rises to his feet to stalk his cowering victim, breaking the loaf in two and throwing one half at the Simpleton's feet. Lazarus: *Who can bring a clean thing out of an unclean? not one. Seeing his days are determined, the number of his months are with thee, thou hast appointed his bounds that he cannot pass.*[31] Thrusting a hand into the soft dough, he has been scattering crumbs at the Simpleton's feet and through his reaching fingers, mesmerizing his prey with trusting tones. Lazarus: *For there is hope of a tree, if it be cut down, that it will sprout again, and that the tender branch thereof will not cease.*[32]

The couple inch slowly backwards, as if in a grotesque dance, until they have almost penetrated the ranks of the spectators. As his fingers dig deeper into the dough, Lazarus's voice has dropped to a deceptive plea. *But man dieth, and wasteth away: yea, man giveth up the ghost, and where is he?*[33] Swiftly he brings back his arm, and with all his strength hurls a heavy pellet of bread into the Simpleton's face. It explodes full in his stricken eyes, sending a shower of crumbs over the spectators. Lazarus's voice rises grief-stricken and tragic: *Let the day perish wherein I was born, and the night in which it was said, There is a man-child conceived. Let that day be darkness; let not God regard it from above, neither let the light shine upon it. Let darkness and the shadow of death stain it.*[34]

He grabs the Simpleton by the front of his coat and hurls him towards the centre of the room: *Let the stars of the twilight thereof be dark; let it look for light, but have none; neither let it see the dawning of the day.*[35] Following, he kneels at the Simpleton's feet: *Because it shut not up the doors of my mother's womb, nor hid sorrow from my eyes. Why died I not from the womb? why did I not give up the ghost when I came out of the belly? Why did the knees prevent me? or why the breasts that I should suck?*[36] Reaching out his hands, he slides them under the Simpleton's coat and up his thighs. His voice softens into lulling tones: *For my sighing cometh before I eat, and my roarings are poured out like the waters. I was not in safety, neither had I rest, neither was I quiet....*[37]

The Simpleton gives one start, and then his head relaxes back with a sigh, and his eyes close. His hands reach caressingly for Lazarus's face. The Simpleton:

My nerves are bad tonight. Yes, bad. Stay with me.
Speak to me
I have heard the key
Turn in the door ... each in his prison
Thinking of the key, each confirms a prison.[38]

Then the caress turns to violence as the hands seize Lazarus's head and throw him violently across the room. On Lazarus's face there is a look of cruel satisfaction. Reaching for his abandoned staff, the Simpleton makes for the exit door. But even as he reaches it, he is stopped by Lazarus's words: *As a servant earnestly desireth the shadow, and as an hireling looketh for the reward of his work: So I am made to possess months of vanity, and wearisome nights are appointed to me. When I lie down, I say, When shall I arise and the night be gone? My flesh is clothed with worms and clods of dust. My days are swifter than a weaver's shuttle. O remember that my life is wind.*[39]

Now Simon Peter steps forward, and taking away again the Simpleton's staff, begins to pull him towards the spotlights, saying: *So when they had dined, Jesus saith to Simon Peter, Simon, son of Jonas, lovest thou me more than these? He saith unto him, Yea, Lord; thou knowest that I love thee.*[40] At first the Simpleton has gone willingly enough. But now he holds back, driving his heels into the floor, and Simon Peter has to drag him forcibly, tolling his words like a death sentence: *He saith unto him, Feed my lambs. He saith to him again the second time, Simon, son of Jonas, lovest thou me? He saith unto him, Yea, Lord; thou knowest that I love thee. He saith unto him, Feed my sheep.*[41]

He has thrust the Simpleton before the spotlights, and he himself steps to the other side of them, to squat in their full glare, throwing a looming shadow up the wall. John, who has been writhing on the floor in some barely contained emotion, jumps to his feet and runs across to the passively watching girl. *Go*, he snarls. She rises swiftly and subserviently, and, a little frightened now, goes to stand facing the Simpleton, very close. John is in a demented rage, and bellows at the Simpleton, ripping off his cap and jacket to hurl them on the ground: *Come hither; I will shew unto thee the judgement of the great whore that sitteth upon many waters; With whom the kings of the earth have committed fornication, and have been made drunk with the wine of her fornication. The beast that thou sawest was, and is not; and shall ascend and go into perdition: and they shall wonder when they behold the beast that was, and is not.*[42] John is poised before the Simpleton and Mary Magdalene like a wrestler, head thrust forward belligerently. His bare chest and arms glisten in the filtered light. The Simpleton replies quietly and soothingly: *And here is the mind which hath wisdom.*[43]

The Simpleton turns to Mary Magdalene and takes her face gently in his hands. Judas moves quickly to join Simon Peter in the glare of the spotlights, and the darkened room is filled with the sound of their laboured breathing, night wind blowing through a forest. Lazarus is curled up on his side, some way away. John has not moved a muscle, but remains taut and eager and expectant.

All attention is fixed on the couple. He runs his fingers exploringly through her hair, rubbing the soft strands across his face and mouth. Arms limp at her side, eyes closed, she waits apprehensively. Grabbing her, he kisses her violently, only to stop and reach out blindly towards John in silent supplication. The muscles in John's body ripple as he slowly starts to run on the spot, his bare feet making a gentle rhythm on the floor. The Simpleton

100 *Apocalypsis* – The Simpleton (Ryszard Cieślak) and Mary Magdalene (Rena Mirecka).

turns back to his partner and covers her face wildly with kisses. The noise of John's feet on the floor builds up to an aching rhythm, and then his body lurches to a halt as the two forms before him break apart in a tense, held, bow shape. The wind ceases abruptly and in the silence a distant coyote howl echoes from the corners of the room.

John springs to a new position. The wind begins again as Mary Magdalene drops slowly to lie at the Simpleton's feet. He looks at her for a moment, then kneels between her legs. With a sobbing breath John begins again his rippling sprint. The building rhythms are again repeated, background music to the clutching bodies on the floor. Again comes the climax – John's body lurching as though shot in flight, the two outflung bodies before him, and the eerie howl. And the cycle of sensual effects begins for the third time.

101 *Apocalypsis* – The Simpleton (Ryszard Cieślak) and Mary Magdalene (Rena Mirecka).

John's body is now streaming with perspiration and his face is tortured. As the third climax is reached, the pattern is broken and John slumps to the ground on hands and knees like a mighty slain animal, head bowed. The sweat runs forward down his body to stream from his forehead and form a pool beneath him. His body shudders with painful gasps. The Simpleton breaks away from Mary Magdalene, and throwing her to the ground, thrusts himself face forward against the wall, crying:

> *Lady, three white leopards sat under a juniper tree*
> *In the cool of the day, having fed to satiety*
> *on my legs my heart my liver and that which had been contained*
> *In the hollow round of my skull. And God said*
> *Shall these bones live? shall these*
> *Bones live? And that which had been contained*
> *In the bones (which were already dry) said chirping:*
> *There is no life in them*
> *And God said*
> *Prophesy to the wind, to the wind only, for only*
> *The wind will listen*
> *Lady of silences*
> *Calm and distressed*
> *Torn and most whole*
> *Rose of Memory*
> *Rose of forgetfulness*
>
> *Terminate torment*
> *Of love unsatisfied.*
> *Speech without word and*
> *Word of no speech*
> *Grace to the Mother*
> *For the Garden.*[44]

In the desultory aftermath of these events, Judas and Lazarus get up and wander matter-of-factly around the room. They conspicuously avoid looking at one another until Lazarus stops abruptly in front of Judas to address: *Behold, thou art fair, my love.* Judas responds: *Behold thou art fair, my love; my sister, my spouse, they neck is as a dove's.*[45] But they skitter backwards and forwards, half shyly, half eagerly, like two rustic pubescents. Lazarus: *Behold thou art fair.* Judas: *Behold thou art fair.*

They turn aside from each other and enact a comic mime of collecting fruit and flowers. It is Judas who next takes the initiative, halting Lazarus in his game with the falsetto chant: *Make haste my beloved, and be thou like to a roe or to a young hart upon the mountain of spices.*[46] He begins to hum a slow waltz rhythm, which Lazarus takes up, and they eagerly lurch towards each other in a parody of dance steps. Then the flippancy is shattered as Judas grabs Lazarus and forces him to the ground. Legs entwined, they stiffen in brief and sordid climax.

John now jumps to his feet and dances over to fatuously address the Simpleton – he is still leaning weakly against the wall, and gazes back wearily: *Notwithstanding I have a few things against thee, because thou sufferest that woman Jezebel to teach and to seduce my servants to commit fornication, and to eat things sacrificed unto idols.*[47] Receiving no response from the Simpleton, John prances into the middle of the room to continue his tirade, becoming progressively more elated and unrestrained: *Behold I will cast her into a bed, and them that*

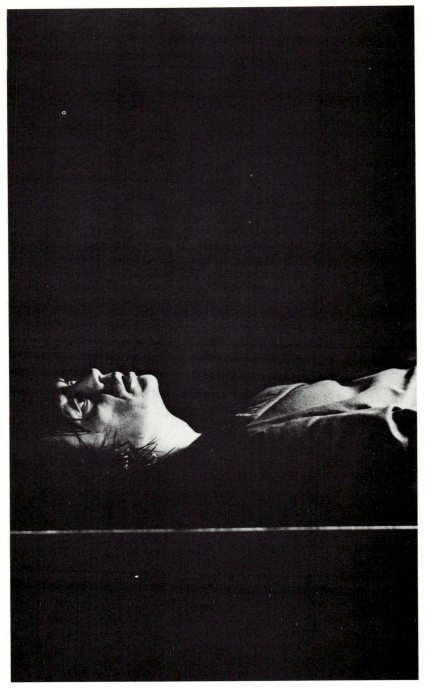

102 *Apocalypsis* – The Simpleton (Ryszard Cieślak).

commit adultery with her into great tribulation. And I will kill her children with death; and all the churches shall know that I am he which searcheth the reins and hearts.[48]

Mary Magdalene breaks into a contemporary pop song, and the others mill around the centre of the room, singing and dancing. There is a renewed surge of energy through the group, but it is chaotic and highly disorganized. Each individual seems to be pursuing private associations and the speeches tumble out haphazardly. Simon Peter is lying on his back, his legs tucked up in a strange position, grimacing with feigned pains. Lazarus, crouched at his feet, is playing an obscure nursery-level game of his own. Simon Peter: *... there thy mother brought thee forth: there she brought thee forth that bare thee.*[49] Judas: *Man is like unto a certain king, which made a marriage for his son. But when the king heard thereof, he was wroth: and he destroyed those murderers and burned up their city. Take him away, and cast him into outer darkness.*[50] Mary Magdalene: *My beloved is white and ruddy.*[51] Lazarus: *They have gaped upon me with their mouth; they have smitten me upon the cheek reproachfully; they have gathered themselves together against me. He cleaveth my reins asunder, and doth not spare; he poureth out my gall upon the ground.*[52]

The group is in a state of extreme excitement, and the tableau in the centre of the room is never still for a moment as they dance and leap around, turning from one to another. Mary Magdalene is alternately seductive and repelling: *His left hand is under my head, and his right hand doth embrace me.*[53] Judas: *And at midnight there was a cry made, Behold the bridegroom cometh; go ye out to meet him. Then all the virgins arose, and trimmed their lamps. And the foolish said unto the wise, Give us of your oil; for our lamps are gone out. But the wise answered, saying, Not so.*[54] John: *I saw the horses and them that sat on them, having breast-plates of fire, and of jacinth and the heads of the horses were as the heads of lions; and out of their mouths issued fire and smoke and brimstone. For their power is in their mouth, and in their tails.*[55]

With all the frenetic activity, the Simpleton is drawn irresistibly back into their orbit. But they form a closed group in the centre of the room and he pads softly around them, whistling pleadingly, both attracted and repulsed by their orgiastic fervour. Lazarus: *It is the gall of asps within him. He hath swallowed down riches, and he shall vomit them up again: God shall cast them out of his belly.*[56] Judas: *Then appeared the tares also. Sir, did'st thou not sow good seed in thy field? from whence then hath it tares? He said unto them, An enemy hath done this. The servants said unto him, Wilt thou then that we go and gather them up? But he said, Nay.*[57]

The Simpleton tries to mimic their dancing, and Lazarus encourages him, displaying a wild war-dance. But it is John who fascinates most, with his animal exuberance and obscene gestures. It is this obscenity that finally drives the Simpleton back again, after his brief contact with the group, and he runs in helpless, confused circles around them, raincoat pulled over his head. John: *And another came crying with a loud voice to him that sat on the cloud, Thrust in thy sickle, and reap. And he that sat on the cloud thrust in his sickle. And another cried with a loud cry to him that hath the sharp sickle, saying, Thrust in thy sharp sickle, and gather the clusters of the vine of the earth; for her grapes are fully ripe. And he thrust in his sickle into the earth. And the winepress was trodden without the city, and blood came out of the winepress.*[58]

Still in the centre of the room, they stand watching the Simpleton as he circles them continuously. Lazarus: *For vain man would be wise, though man be born like a wild ass's colt.*[59] Mary Magdalene: *I have put off my coat. I have washed my feet.*[60] Lazarus: *Your remembrances are like unto ashes, your bodies to bodies of clay.*[61] Mary Magdalene: *By night on my bed I sought him whom my soul loveth: I sought him, but I found him not.*[62] Lazarus: *Because he covereth his face with his fatness, and maketh collops of fat on his flanks.*[63]

The group breaks up during John's final apocalyptic speech, and dispersing around the

103 *Apocalypsis* – The Simpleton (Ryszard Cieślak), John (Stanisław Scierski), Mary Magdalene (Elizabeth Albahaca), Lazarus (Zbigniew Cynkutis), Simon Peter (Antoni Jahołkowski) and Judas (Zygmunt Molik).

room begins to buffet the still-blinded Simpleton violently from one to another. Completely disorientated, he spins helplessly around, whistling his distress again, arms reaching out for guidance. John: *And I beheld another beast coming up out of the earth; and he had two horns like a lamb, and he spake as a dragon. And deceiveth them that dwell on the earth by means of those miracles which he had power to do in the sight of the beast; saying to them that dwell on the earth, that they should make an image to the beast that the image of the beast should both speak, and cause that as many as would not worship the image of the beast should be killed.*[64]

Simon Peter has been standing behind the spotlights. On the final word from John, he spreads wide his waistcoat and swoops down to completely cover the two beams of light, and plunge the room abruptly into blackness.

The blackness and near-silence are oppressive. The abrupt cessation of vision and action have robbed those present of a sense of orientation, and there is a feeling of threat and of vulnerability. Occasionally, soft whistlings can still be heard from the Simpleton, and pacing footsteps echo from wall to wall. And then a passage of welcome fresh air is felt and the room is filled with crazily lurching shadows as Simon Peter enters, carrying candles. He halts by the doorway and wax flows freely to the floor.

As he slowly circles the room, to where the Simpleton is kneeling before the white cloth, the positions of the others are dimly made out. Lazarus is alone, crouched over in a corner – his fingers, which have been involved in some unknown business with the discarded bread, suddenly stilled. Judas is lying astride Mary Magdalene on the floor, one hand on her breast. John is lying seemingly unconscious in a pool of his own sweat.

From now on, the actions unfold consumed by their own impetus, and the events move swiftly and unavoidably to inbuilt, unforeseen conclusions.

Judas says ironically: *Behold the bridegroom cometh; go ye out to meet him.*[65] And from the inert figure of John is wrung, reluctantly and painfully: *Give us of your oil; for our lamps have gone out.*[66] Simon Peter stands over the Simpleton, the candles a bright glare in the surrounding dimness. The Simpleton wets the palm of his hand with his tongue, and reaches down to wipe Simon Peter's shoe. Simon Peter says, sincerely astonished: *Lord, dost thou wash my feet?*[67] And the Simpleton, now dignified and resolute, replies calmly: *What I do thou knowest not now; but thou shalt know hereafter. Ye are not all clean. Now I tell you before it come, that, when it is come to pass, ye may believe that one of you shall betray me.*[68]

Simon Peter bends over to place the mass of candles before the white cloth, and squats down beside them. Looking across the room, he prompts: *John, ask him, who it is he means.*[69] John writhes on the floor, tormented out of his exhaustion, and the words are torn from his body: *Jesus, who is it?*[70]. The Simpleton reaches over swiftly to the candles before him. Lifting up high one candle, he douses the flame with two damp fingers and smears the sign of the cross with ash on Simon Peter's forehead. There is an interjection from Judas: *And I, Lord?* Simon Peter, getting up and walking away, says softly: *Judas, Son of Iscariot....* And the Simpleton replies: *Yet a little while I am with you. Ye shall seek me: and as I said unto the Jews, Whither I go, ye cannot come; so now I say to you.*[71] Simon Peter asks him: *Lord, whither goest thou?*[72] And he replies with an indulgent laugh: *Whither I go, thou can'st not follow me now; but thou shalt follow me afterwards.*[72] And turning to the entire room he says in ringing and exultant tones: *Before I am delivered unto them, sing we a hymn to the Father.*

To this, Judas replies, with anticipation of pleasure: *The Suffering of the Lamb?* There comes a long, drawn-out, affirmatory *Amen* from Mary Magdalene beneath him, and the others join in fervently. All confidence gone, the Simpleton is once again the bewildered victim, as Lazarus places the white cloth around his neck, and, together with Simon Peter, drags the Simpleton to the centre of the room. The candles are distributed amongst the participants, and Simon Peter places one carefully on the floor before the Simpleton, about four feet away. Holding the candles out before them, all five kneel, facing the Simpleton. Simon Peter gives them the lead. Bending slightly forward in an attitude of humility and adoration, he softly begins to sing: *Glory to the Great and Just, Glory to the Great and Just, Glory to....*

One by one, the others join in, swaying backwards and forwards, their candles weaving mesmerizing patterns of light. The Simpleton gazes from one to another, seeking enlightenment but finding only blind and frightening adoration. He crouches, a fascinated prey, eyes held by the candle inches away from Lazarus's hypnotic eyes. Simon Peter rises, and shuffles forward, head and shoulders bent over like an ancient monk. Crossing behind the kneeling Simpleton, he leans over to place a kiss on his shoulder. The tempo and volume of the liturgical chant rises sharply, as they begin to shuffle around the Simpleton on their knees, candles still weaving to and fro. Faster and faster they move, their voices mingling discordantly and feverishly in prayer-meeting abandon. The noise and hysteria reaches an unbearable level, until they gather in unison behind the Simpleton, candles held aloft, and their voices slide imperceptibly into derisive bleating.

In a single, slow, controlled movement, the Simpleton rotates around, still on his knees, to face them and crumples backwards, his head cracking to the floor an inch from the flickering candle. They listen in respectful silence to his incoherent, crucified words:

If the lost word is lost, if the spent word is spent
If the unheard, unspoken
Word is unspoken, unheard;
Still is the unspoken word, the Word unheard,
The Word without a word ...
O my people, what ...
Where shall the word be found, where will the word
Resound? Not here ...
The right time and the right place are not here
No place of grace
For those who walk among noise and deny the voice
Will the sister pray for
Those who walk in darkness, who chose and oppose
Those who are torn on the horn between season and season between
Power and power, those who wait
... between
The desert in the garden ... the desert
of drouth, spitting from the mouth the withered apple-seed.[73]

The watching group disperse respectfully to scatter around the room, repositioning the candles. Simon Peter returns once more to kneel at his own corner of the room, placing two candles before him about two feet apart. He is framed in their glow. He is murmuring: *In nomine Patris et Filii et Spiritus Sancti, amen. Kyrie Eleison, Kyrie Eleison, Kyrie Eleison.*[74] Lazarus replies: *Christe Eleison.* Simon Peter: *Sursum Corda. Habemus ad dominum gratias agamus domino deo nostro dignum et iustum est. Sequentia sancti evangelii secundum ...* And he returns now to his earlier accusation, directed at the slumped figure of the Simpleton in the centre of the room: *I repeat again ... if for the sake of bread from heaven thousands and tens of thousand will follow you, what is to become of the millions and scores of thousands of millions of creatures who will not have the strength to give up the earthly bread for the bread of heaven?*[76]

The reverence of the other participants has not lasted. The room is now filled with an obscene hissing and bartering, as they offer their wares. John: *I sell myself.* Judas: *Hag!* Mary Magdalene: *His legs are as pillars of marble.*[77] Simon Peter continues through it all: *Or are only the scores of thousands of the great and strong dear to you, and are the remaining millions, numerous as the sand of the sea, who are weak but who love you, to serve only as the material for the great and the strong?*[78] The Simpleton has come back to life, and he whips around from his crouching position to glare angrily from one to another of his tormentors. Simon Peter: *No, to us the weak, too, are dear. They are vicious and rebellious, but in the end they will become obedient too. They will marvel at us and they will regard us as gods because, having become their masters, we consented to endure freedom and rule over them – so dreadful will freedom become to them in the end! But we shall tell them that we do your bidding and rule in your name. We shall deceive them again, for we shall not let you come near us again.*[79]

Lazarus scuttles forward to kneel behind the Simpleton, and arches his body concavely

104 *Apocalypsis* – The Simpleton (Ryszard Cieślak), Mary Magdalene (Rena Mirecka), Judas (Zygmunt Molik), Lazarus (Zbigniew Cynkutis), Simon Peter (Antoni Jahołkowski) and John (Stanisław Scierski).

over him in a graceful, protective gesture. Lazarus: *Naked came I out of my mother's womb, and naked shall I return thither.*[80] ... His voice soars pleadingly: *Behold, happy is the man whom God correcteth: For he maketh sore, and bindeth up: he woundeth.*[81] ... The Simpleton leaps to his feet, and with the white cloth begins to flay Lazarus, who proffers his back. The others rush eagerly forward to claim their punishment, turning their backs to him. The Simpleton beats them in an orgy of cathartic scourging and purification, until he collapses in their midst. Hands raised in ecstasy above their heads, they turn in silence and rush one by one from the room. Judas delays only to consolingly pat the Simpleton's back, saying: *I sell fresh meat.*

Apart from Simon Peter and the Simpleton, only John remains. He has faltered by the doorway and now hesitatingly returns. Standing to one side, not facing the Simpleton, he begins to speak rapidly and accusingly: *You came into my room and said: 'You poor wretch who understands nothing and knows nothing. Come with me and I will teach you things you never dreamed of.' You told me to leave and go with you to the attic, where from the open window one could see the entire city, a sort of wooden scaffolding and a river on which boats were being unloaded. We were alone. From a cupboard you took bread, which we shared. That bread truly had the taste of bread. Never again did I find such a taste. You promised to teach me but you taught me nothing. One day you told me: 'And now go.' I never tried to find you again. I understood you came to me by mistake.*[82]

The Simpleton has come up behind him to listen, unbearably moved. At these last words he raises again the white cloth and brings it down in fury, three times, on John's bare and glistening back. The sound cracks shockingly around the room, and John arches in agony. He turns and drops to his knees before the Simpleton. He is now near weeping. As he speaks, he reaches out to caress the Simpleton's feet, and the Simpleton kneels to join him. Their faces and bodies reach forward to meet, perspiration mingling. John: *My place is not in that attic. Anywhere else: in the prison cell, a railroad waiting room, anywhere, but not in that attic. Sometimes I can't keep from repeating, in fear and contrition, a little of what you told me. But how can I convince myself that I remember? You won't tell me, you are not here. I well know that you don't love me. How could you love me? And yet, there is within me something, a small part of myself which, in the depths of my soul, trembling with fear, cannot defend itself against the thought that maybe, in spite of everything, you....*[82]

The final word is no more than a sob. The Simpleton wrenches himself upright from the embrace. Again the blows, twice. A shudder passes in one movement through John's body, and like an arrow from the bow he springs from the room.

Only Simon Peter and the Simpleton remain.

The Simpleton turns to throw the cloth wearily to the centre of the room, and slumps between two clusters of candles in the corner diagonally opposite to Simon Peter. Simon Peter's words come insidiously again: *And instead of firm foundations for appeasing man's conscience once and for all, you chose everything that was beyond the strength of men, acting, consequently, as though you did not love them at all – you who came to give your life for them! Instead of taking possession of men's freedom you multiplied it and burdened the spiritual kingdom of man with its sufferings for ever. You wanted man's free love so that he should follow you freely, fascinated and captivated by you. Instead of the strict ancient law, man in future had to decide for himself with a free heart what is good and what is evil, having only your image before him for guidance. But did it never occur to you that he would at last reject and call in question even your image and your truth, if he were weighed down by so fearful a burden as freedom of choice? They will at last cry aloud that the truth is not in you, for it was impossible to leave them in*

105 *Apocalypsis* – John (Stanisław Scierski) and The Simpleton (Ryszard Cieślak).

greater confusion and suffering than you have done, by leaving them with so many cares and insoluble problems.[83]

A strange duo erupts into the room. It is Mary Magdalene, hair now swept purposefully back, and Judas with his trouser legs rolled up. They bring with them an assortment of objects: a pail of water, black garment, glass phials, old shoes and white starched cloths. Before the bemused gaze of the Simpleton they enact a comic ritual of washing and dressing themselves, then form into a procession to stomp up and down the room in a long pilgrimage – Mary Magdalene leading and Judas stumbling along behind, like an old woman. Arriving at their destination, they slow down abruptly and assume pious attitudes, quietly and waveringly singing a mournful chant: *He knows the anguish: he knows the tears of sorrow.* Mary Magdalene clasps the white cloth to her face, and Judas slumps heavily to his knees. They remain in these attitudes.

The Simpleton, now ignoring them, is looking across the room at Simon Peter, who asks: *And why are you looking at me silently and so penetratingly with your gentle eyes? Get angry. I do not want your love because I do not love you myself.*[84]

(Mary Magdalene and Judas, their roles performed, lunge forward, and scooping up their props exit hastily).

As Simon Peter continues speaking, the Simpleton swings around on his knees to face the spectators nearest him. With blind, unseeing, distant eyes he searches their faces, one by one. Simon Peter: *And what have I to hide from you? Or don't I know to whom I am speaking? All I have to tell you is already known to you. I can read it in your eyes. And would I conceal our secret from you? Perhaps it is just what you want to hear from my lips. Well, then, listen. We are not with you but with* him*: that is our secret! It's a long time – many centuries – since we left you and went over to* him.[85]

The Simpleton is now standing before his candles, facing Simon Peter across the room. Placing his feet solidly apart, he begins to speak softly, but his voice gradually rises in volume towards uncontrolled delirium:

I was neither at the hot gates
Nor fought in the warm rain
Nor knee-deep in the salt marsh, heaving a cutlass,
Bitten by flies, fought.
My house is a decayed house
The goat coughs at night in the field overhead;
Rocks, moss, stone-crop, iron, merds.
The woman keeps the kitchen, makes tea,
sneezes at evening, poking the peevish gutter.
After such knowledge, what forgiveness? Think now
History has many cunning passages, contrived corridors
And issues, deceives with whispering ambitions,
Guides us by vanities. Think now
She gives when our attention is distracted
And what she gives, gives with such supple confusions
That the giving famishes the craving. Gives too late
What's not believed in, or if still believed,
In memory only, reconsidered passion. Gives too soon
Into weak hands, what's thought can be dispensed with
Till the refusal propagates a fear. Think

Neither fear nor courage saves us. Unnatural vices
Are fathered by our heroism. Virtues
Are forced upon us by our impudent crimes.
These tears are shaken from the wrath-bearing tree.
The tiger springs in the new year. Us he devours, Think at last
We have not reached conclusion, when I
Stiffen in a rented house. Think at last
I have not made this show purposelessly
And it is not by any concitation
Of the backward devils.
I would meet you upon this honestly.
I that was near your heart was removed therefrom
To lose beauty in terror, terror in inquisition.
I have lost my passion: Why should I need to keep it
Since what is kept must be adulterated?
I have lost my sight, smell, hearing, taste and touch:
How should I use them for your closer contact?[86]

Simon Peter: *Know that I, too, was in the wilderness, that I, too, fed upon locusts and roots, that I, too, blessed freedom, with which you have blessed men, and that I, too, was preparing to stand among your chosen ones, among the strong and mighty, thirsting 'to make myself of the number'. But I woke up and refused to serve madness.*[87]

With deep breaths, the Simpleton has brought himself back to a level of control. Exhaustion shows in his face, and utter despair. He begins to sing. The voice is low, vibrant, sobbing. As he drops to his knees it deepens to envelop the room:

Cogitavit Dominus dissipare
Murum Filiae Syon
Tetendit funiculum suum, et
Non avertit manum suam a
Perditione luxitque antemurale
Et murus pariter dissipatus est.

Simon Peter crawls stealthily around towards him, extinguishing the candles one by one as he goes, viciously stabbing them on the floor. The darkness and the soaring voice grow together:

Sederunt in terra conticuerent
Senes Filiae Syon
Consperserunt cinere capita
Sua accincti sunt ciliciis
Abiecerunt in terram capita
Sua virgines Jerusale.

Simon Peter has reached the final two candles near the exit. Lying out flat beside them, he holds the two dying flames to mingle in a blue aura. The Simpleton flounders near him — a dying moth craving the last rays of light:

Defecerunt prae lacrimis
Oculi mei, conturbata
Sunt viscera mea, effusum est

106 *Apocalypsis* – The Simpleton (Ryszard Cieślak).

In terra iecur meum super
Contritione filiae populi mei
Cum deficeret parvulus et
Lactens in plateis oppidi.
Jerusale, Jerusale
Convertere ad Dominum
Deum tuum.[88]

There is darkness. Then Simon Peter's words: *Go, and come no more.* Mercilessly the lights are flicked on and the room is empty.

Literary Sources
Apocalypsis Cum Figuris

1. The Gospel according to St John, Ch 6:53
2. The Gospel according to St John, Ch 6:54
3. The Gospel according to St John, Ch 6:55
4. Fyodor Dostoyevsky: *The Brothers Karamazov I*: trans. David Magarshack: Penguin 1974: pp 194–195
5. *The Brothers Karamazov I*: p 196
6. *The Brothers Karamazov I*: pp 289–290
7. The Gospel according to St Luke, Ch 14:16–21
8. *The Brothers Karamazov I*: p 295
9. T.S. Eliot: Collected Poems 1909–1962: Faber 1974: from 'Ash Wednesday I': pp 95–96
10. *The Brothers Karamazov I*: pp 295–296
11. The Gospel according to St Luke, Ch 12:22–23
12. Anthem used between Easter and Whitsuntide during the *Asperges* preceding High Mass. See also Ezekiel, Ch 47:2,9
13. The Gospel according to St Matthew, Ch 20:8–10
14. T.S. Eliot: from 'Ash Wednesday IV': pp 100–101
15. *Rituale Romanum*: Pauli V. Pontificis Maximi Iussu Editum: Editio Novissima Paris Peter Aegidius Le Mercier 1758: Exsequiarum Ordo pp 198–199
16. The Gospel according to St John, Ch 10:1
17. Solomon's Song, Ch 1:16
18. Job, Ch 31:9–11
19. Solomon's Song: Ch 7:12
20. Job, Ch 17:14, Ch 19:26
21. Solomon's Song, Ch 2:16
22. Revelation, Ch 6:4
23. Job, Ch 29: 7,8,17
24. Solomon's Song, Ch 5:4
25. Job, Ch 41:1,2,5,7
26. Revelation, Ch 16:13
27. The Gospel according to St Matthew, Ch 11:15–17
28. T.S. Eliot: from 'Ash Wednesday VI': pp 104–105
29. Job, Ch 7:21

30. The Gospel according to St Luke, Ch 7:14
31. Job, Ch 14:4–5
32. Job, Ch 14:7
33. Job, Ch 14:10
34. Job, Ch 3:3–5
35. Job, Ch 3:9
36. Job, Ch 3:10–12
37. Job, Ch 3:24,26
38. T.S. Eliot: from 'The Wasteland' – 'II. A Game of Chess' and 'V. What the Thunder said': pp 67, 79
39. Job, Ch 7:2–7
40. The Gospel according to St John, Ch 21:15
41. The Gospel according to St John, Ch 21:15–16
42. Revelation, Ch 17:1,2,8
43. Revelation, Ch 17:9
44. T.S. Eliot: from 'Ash Wednesday II': pp 97–98
45. Solomon's Song, Ch 4:1,10
46. Solomon's Song, Ch 8:14
47. Revelation, Ch 2:20
48. Revelation, Ch 2:22,23
49. Solomon's Song, Ch 8:5
50. The Gospel according to St Matthew, Ch 22:2,7,13
51. Solomon's Song, Ch 5:10
52. Job, Ch 16:10,13
53. Solomon's Song, Ch 2:6
54. The Gospel according to St Matthew, Ch 25:6–9
55. Revelation, Ch 9:17,19
56. Job, Ch 20:14–15
57. The Gospel according to St Matthew, Ch 13:26–29
58. Revelation, Ch 14:15–16, 18–20
59. Job, Ch 11:12
60. Solomon's Song, Ch 5:3
61. Job, Ch 13:12
62. Solomon's Song, Ch 3:1
63. Job, Ch 15:27
64. Revelation, Ch 13:11, 14–15
65. The Gospel according to St Matthew, Ch 25:6
66. The Gospel according to St Matthew, Ch 25:8
67. The Gospel according to St John, Ch 13:6
68. The Gospel according to St John, Ch 13:7,11,12,21
69. The Gospel according to St John, Ch 13:24
70. The Gospel according to St John, Ch 13:25
71. The Gospel according to St John, Ch 13:33
72. The Gospel according to St John, Ch 13:36
73. T.S. Eliot: from 'Ash Wednesday V': pp 102–103
74. The *Kyrie*, which follows the *Introit* in the Ordinary of the Mass
75. From the Preface, preceding the *Sanctus* in the Ordinary of the Mass
76. *The Brothers Karamazov I*: p 297

77. Solomon's Song, Ch 5:15
78. *The Brothers Karamazov I*: p 297
79. *The Brothers Karamazov I*: p 297
80. Job, Ch 1:21
81. Job, Ch 5:17, 18
82. Simone Weil: *La Connaissance Surnaturelle*: Editions Gallimard 1950: pp 9–10
83. *The Brothers Karamazov I*: p 299
84. *The Brothers Karamazov I*: p 301
85. *The Brothers Karamazov I*: pp 301–302
86. T.S. Eliot: from 'Gerontion': pp 39–41
87. *The Brothers Karamazov I*: p 305
88. Lamentationes Jeremiae II verses 8, 10, 11: *Breviarum Romanum* ex decreto ss Concilii Tridentini restitutum, S. Pii V Pontificis Maximi iussu editum, Clementis VIII et Urbani VIII auctoritate recognitum: 1854 Mechliniae: Pars Verna: Feria Sexta In Parasceve Ad Matutinum In Primo Nocturno: p 259

BIBLIOGRAPHY

This Bibliography is not exhaustive of every single literary or journalistic reference concerning the work of Grotowski and the Laboratory Theatre that I have come across in my research on the subject. It is, however, fairly extensive, and has two main aims. Firstly, as explained in the introductory chapter, it serves as a system of reference for quotations used in the main text. Secondly, it is a bibliographical record of practically all the published work I have read by Grotowski and members of his company, and particularly relevant works from many other sources, and as such it may be useful for other researchers.

The Bibliography is divided into three sections, of which the first two – comprising material by Grotowski and by other members of his company – are in chronological order of publication. The third section – material by other writers about the Laboratory Theatre – is in alphabetical order. As far as possible I have cross-referenced to indicate where one source is a translation of, an alternative version of, or is contained within another work.

I. GROTOWSKI

1. JG: 'Marzenie o teatrze': *Dziennik Polski* 1955 nr 46
2. JG: 'Szkoła Szczerości': *Echo Tygodnia* (Supplement to *Gazeta Krakowska*) 1955 nr 9
3. JG: 'Jakie dostrzegłem zmiany w życiu kulturalnym ZSRR': *Dziennik Polski* 1956 nr 216
4. JG: 'Między Iranem i Chinami: Prorok odchodzi z trzech pustyń': *Dziennik Polski* 1956 nr 216
5. JG: 'Między Iranem i Chinami: Wieża Babel': *Dziennik Polski* 1956 nr 227
6. JG and Ógorzałek, A: 'Lewica Akademicka': *Gazeta Krakowska* 1957 nr 87: p 3
7. JG: 'Cywilizacja i wolność – nie ma innego socjalizmu': *Walka Młodych* 1957 nr 6: p 4
8. JG: 'Twórcze ambicje teatru': *Współczesność* 1958 nr 29/19
9. JG: 'Z Jerzym Grotowskim o teatrze' (interviewer J. Falkowski): *Współczesność* 1958 nr 30/20
10. JG: 'Śmierć i reinkarnacja teatru': *Współczesność* 1959 nr 13
11. JG: 'Wokól teatru przyszłości': *Ekran* 1959 nr 21
12. JG: 'Co to jest teatr': *Dziennik Polski* 1959 nr 200
13. JG: '11 pytań o 13 Rzędow' (interviewer B. Zagórska): *Echo Krakowa* 1959 nr 248
14. JG: 'Inwokacja do przedstawienia Orfeusz': *Materiały-Dyskusje* October 1959 nr 1

15. JG: 'Dziady jako model teatru nowoczesnego' (interviewer J. Falkowski): *Współczesność* 1961 nr 21: p 8

16. JG: *Możliwość Teatru – Materiały Warsztatowe Teatru 13 Rzędow:* Opole February 1962

17. JG: 'Ankieta o krytyce – żeby za słowem kryło się pojęcie' (statement by Grotowski inter alia): *Współczesność* 1962 nr 3: pp 2–3

18. JG: 'Doktor Faustus in Poland': *Tulane Drama Review* T24 1964: pp 120–133

19. JG: 'Teatr – Godzina Niepokoju' (interviewer J. Falkowski): *Odra* 1964 nr 6: pp 55–58

20. JG: 'Ku teatrowi ubogiemu': *Odra* 1965 nr 9: pp 21–27 (28) (35) (73) (121)

21. JG: 'Perspektywy wrocławskich teatrów' (statement by Grotowski inter alia): *Odra* 1965 nr 11: pp 29–36

22. JG: 'Aktor Ogołocony': *Teatr* 1965 nr 17: pp 8–10

23. JG: 'Czy portret?': *Teatr* 1965 nr 21

24. JG: 'Pour une interprétation totale – For a total interpretation': *World Theatre* 1966 Vol 15 nr 1: pp 18–22

25. JG: '10 Minut z Jerzym Grotowskim' (interviewer K. Zbijewska): *Dziennik Polski* 13.4.66 nr 86

26. JG: 'Po skandynawskim tournée 13 Rzędów' (interviewer T. Buski): *Gazeta Robotnicza* 1966 nr 105

27. JG: 'Rencontres avec Grotowski' (interviewer E. Barba): *Théâtre et Université* February 1965 nr 5: pp 6–26 (73) (121)

28. JG: 'Vers un Théâtre Pauvre': *Cahiers Renauld-Barrault* May 1966: pp 52–65 (20) (35) (73) (121)

29 JG: 'Poszukiwaniu Perspektywy': *Współczesność* 1966 nr 23: pp 2–3

30. JG: 'Studium nie dla gwiazd' (interviewer J. Bajdor): *Słowo Polskie* 1966 nr 31

31. JG and Flaszen, L: 'Na Rynku czeka na nas ofiarowanie' (interviewer K. Krzyżagórski): *Słowo Polskie* 1966 nr 288

32. JG: 'Nie Był Cały Sobą': *Odra* 1967 nr 1: pp 31–34 (37) (73)

33. JG: 'Contemporary Perspectives': *The Theatre in Poland/Le Théâtre en Pologne* 1967 nrs 2–3: pp 42–49

34. JG: 'Faire de l'acteur part entiere' (interviewer R. Desné): *L'Humanité* 15.3.67

35. JG: 'Towards the Poor Theatre': *The Drama Review* T35 Spring 1967: pp 60–65 (20) (28) (73) (121)

36. JG: 'Laboratorium w teatrze' (interviewer B. Czarmiński): *Tygodnik Kulturalny* 1967 nr 17: pp 1, 6 (73) (121)

37. JG: 'He wasn't entirely himself': *Flourish* Summer 1967 nr 9: p 14 (32) (73)

38. JG: 'Le théâtre est une rencontre' (interviewer Naim Kattan): *Arts et Lettres* (Supplement to *Le Devoir*) July 1967 (73)

39. JG: 'Przepraszamy, tylko 3 pytania. Odpowiada Jerzy Grotowski po powrocie z USA i Francji' (interviewer M.K. Osińska): *Życie Warszawy* 19.12.67 nr 300

40. JG: 'Techniki Aktorskie' (interviewer Denis Bablet): *Odra* 1968 nr 4: pp 34–39 (73) (121)

41. JG: 'Institute for the Study of Acting Methods': *The Theatre in Poland/Le Théâtre en Pologne* 1968 nrs 7–8: pp 3–9

42. JG: 'An interview with Grotowski' (interviewers R. Schechner and T. Hoffman): *The Drama Review* T41 Fall 1968: pp 29–45 (73)

43. JG: 'Au delà de l'art dramatique': *Les Nouvelles Littéraires* 10.10.68: p 13

44. JG: 'Rozmowa z Grotowskim' (interviewer Witold Filler): *Kultura* 1968 nr 11: p 10

45.   JG: 'Grotowski et ses Épigones' (interviewer Claude Sarrauté): *Le Monde* 16.5.69 (Supplement)

46.   JG: 'Teatr a Rytuał' (Statement during a Paris Conference 15.10.68): *Dialog* 1969 nr 8: pp 64–74

47.   JG: 'External Order, Internal Intimacy' (interviewer Marc Fumaroli): The Drama Review T45 Fall 1969: pp 172–177

48.   JG: 'Propozycja Współpracy': *Słowo Polskie* 1970 nr 215
        'Teatr Laboratorium – Propozycja Współpracy': *Sztandar Młodych* 1970 nr 217
        'Propozycja Współpracy Teatru Laboratorium': *Przekrój* 1970 nr 1327

49.   JG: 'Jerzy Grotowski o swoim teatrze – spotkanie z krytykami we Wrocławiu': *Teatr* 1970 nr 8: pp 23–24

50.   JG: 'W poszukiwaniu szczerości' (unauthorized interview by Z. Raducka): *Tygodnik Demokratyczny* 1970 nr 13

51.   JG: 'Un inédit de Jerzy Grotowski – L'obscenité au théâtre' (Statement at the Brooklyn Academy of Music in New York December 1969): *La Quinzaine Littéraire* 1–15.9.70 nr 101: pp 26–28

52.   JG: 'Po sukcesach w Iranie i Libanie Teatr Laboratorium powrócił do Wrocławia': *Gazeta Robotnicza* 1970 nr 244

53.   JG: 'La Voix': *Le Théâtre* (*Cahiers dirigés par Arrabal*) 1971 nr 1: pp 87–131 (90)

54.   JG: 'Les Exercises': *Action Culturelle du Sud-Est*, Supplement to nr 6 Marseille 1971 (89)

55.   JG: 'Statement of Principles': *Poland* 1971 nr 7: pp 34, 36 (73)

56.   JG: 'Wypowiedź Grotowskiego dla Życia Warszawy. W Niedzielę, o godzinie 12 otwarła konferencja prasowa' (interviewer M.K.): *Życie Warszawy* 1971 nr 241

57.   JG: 'Jak żyć by można' (Statement at press conference organized by Polish ITI in Warsaw 10.10.71): *Odra* 1972 nr 4: pp 33–38 (74)

58.   JG: 'Takim, jakim się jest cały' (Statement at a meeting in the New York Town Hall 12.12.70): *Odra* 1972 nr 5: pp 51–56 (64)

59.   JG: 'Święto' (transcript of a meeting with students and professors at New York University 13.12.70): *Odra* 1972 nr 6: pp 47–51 (64) (65) (139)

60.   JG: 'Meeting with Grotowski' (at the 3rd International Student Festival in Wrocław): *The Theatre in Poland/Le Théâtre en Pologne* 1972 nr 7: pp 8–10 (64)

61.   JG: 'To święto stanie się możliwe' (Statement at a Polish-French Conference in Royaumont, France 11.10.72): *Kultura* 1972 nr 52 (64) (67)

62.   JG: 'Osterwa po ćwierćwieczu': *Dialog* 1972 nr 9: pp 115–117

63.   JG: 'Co było – Kolumbia – Lato 1970 – Festival Ameryki Łacińskiej': *Dialog* 1972 nr 10: pp 111–118

64.   JG: 'Holiday – the day that is holy' (trans. B. Taborski): *The Drama Review* T58 June 1973: pp 113–135 (58) (59) (60) (61) (65) (67) (139)

65.   JG: 'Jour Saint' in *Jour Saint et Autres Textes* (trans. G. Lisowski and Grotowski): Gallimard 1973: pp 3–24 (64) (59) (139)

66.   JG: 'Obok Teatru' (conversation between Grotowski and Konstanty Puzyna 19.12.72): *Dialog* 1973 nr 7: pp 95–107

67.   JG: 'This holiday will become possible' (abridged version of Grotowski's statement at Royaumont 11.10.72): *The Theatre in Poland/Le Théâtre en Pologne* 1973 nr 12: pp 5–6 (61) (64)

68   JG: 'Theatre as unarmed confrontation' (interviewer Katharine Brisbane): *The Australian* 18.8.73: p 24

69. J G: 'Grotowski w mowie pozornie zależnej' (report by J. Kelera of Grotowski's meeting with participants and guests at the 4th International Student Festival in Wrocław 27.10.73): *Odra* 1974 nr 5: pp 35–44 (72)

70 J G: 'Grotowski w Recamier': *Odra* 1974 nr 5: pp 45–50

71. J G: 'Self-discovery in the Laboratory' (interviewer Katharine Brisbane): *The Australian* 19.6.74

72 J G: 'Grotowski in free indirect speech' (reported by J. Kelera): *The Theatre in Poland/Le Théâtre en Pologne* 1974 nr 10: pp 9–13 (69)

73. J G: *Towards a Poor Theatre*: Eyre Methuen Ltd., London 1975 (First published Denmark 1968 by Odin Teatrets Forlag; Simon and Schuster New York 1968; French translation by C.B. Levenson, La Cité, Lausanne 1971) (20) (28) (35) (27) (36) (38) (40) (42) (55) (117) (121) (179) (299)

74. J G: 'How one could live': *The Theatre in Poland/Le Théâtre en Pologne* 1975 nrs 4–5: pp 33–34 (57)

75. J G: 'Przedsięwzięcie Góra': *Odra* 1975 nr 6: pp 23–27

76. J G: 'Rozmowa z Grotowskim' (interviewer Andrzej Bonarski): *Kultura* 1975 nr 13 (139) (169)

77. J G: 'Instytut Laboratorium: Program 1975–1976': *Teatr* 1975 nr 7

78. J G: 'We simply look for those close to us' (statement at an international conference in Paris 15–18.7.74): *International Theatre Information*, Paris, Winter 1975: pp 6–8

79. J G: 'Le double stage de Jerzy Grotowski. Ce n'est pas la santé des gens qui nous préoccupe, mais celle de leur métier' (interviewer C. Godard): *Le Monde* 18.3.76: p 17

80. J G: 'The healthy state of their work': *International Theatre Information*, Paris, Winter-Spring 1976

81. J G: 'Poszukiwania Teatru Laboratorium' (interviewer T. Burzyński): *Trybuna Ludu* 1976 nr 252

82. J G: 'The art of the beginner' (statement at I T I conference in Warsaw June 1978): *International Theatre Information* Paris, Spring/Summer 1978: pp 7–11 (87) (96)

83. J G: 'Grotowskiego Teatr Źródeł – Rozmowa z twórcą Teatru Laboratorium' (interviewer T. Burzyński): *Trybuna Ludu* 21.6.79 nr 143 (86) (88)

84. J G: 'Działanie jest dosłowne' (statement at a conference in New York at the Kościuszko Foundation 19.4.78): *Dialog* 1979 nr 9: pp 95–101 (88)

85. J G: 'Świat powinien być miejscem prawdy' (statement at a Polish-Russian conference in Moscow November 1976): *Dialog* 1979 nr 10: pp 138–141

86. J G: 'Jerzy Grotowski on the Theatre of Sources' (interviewer T. Burzyński): *The Theatre in Poland/Le Théâtre en Pologne* 1979 nr 11: p 24 (83) (88)

87. J G: 'Wędrowanie za Tearem, Źródeł' (statement at I T I conference in Warsaw June 1978 plus other material): *Dialog* 1979 nr 11: pp 94–103 (82) (96) (88)

88. J G: *La Frontiera del Teatro* (documentary material for a conference held by Il Centro di Ricerca per il Teatro in Milan): Milan, November/December 1979 (84) (83) (86) (87) (82) (96) (92)

89. J G: 'Ćwiczenia': *Dialog* 1979 nr 12: pp 127–137 (54)

90. J G: 'Głos': *Dialog* 1980 nr 1: pp 109–123 (53)

91. J G: 'Pogadanka o teatrze dla młodzieży szkolnej' (school programme broadcast by Polish Radio October 1979): *Dialog* 1980 nr 2: pp 132–137

92. J G: 'O praktykowaniu Romantyzmu' (statement by Grotowski at C R T Congress in Milan January 1979): *Dialog* 1980 nr 3: pp 112–120 (88)

93. JG: 'Jerzy Grotowski, Oggi' (interviewer Ugo Volli): *Alfabeta*, Milan, April 1980: pp 3–5

94. JG: 'Odpowiedź Stanisławskiemu' (statement at a meeting with actors and directors at the Brooklyn Academy in New York 22.2.69): *Dialog* 1980 nr 5: pp 111–119

95. JG: 'The Laboratory Theatre: 20 years after: a working hypothesis' (statement at 20th anniversary celebrations of Laboratory Theatre held in Wrocław 15.11.79): *Polish Perspectives*, Warsaw, May 1980: pp 31–40

96. JG: 'Wandering towards a Theatre of Sources' (trans. J. Kumiega): *Dialectics and Humanism*, The Polish Academy of Sciences, Warsaw, Spring 1980: pp 11–23 (82) (87)

II. LUDWIK FLASZEN AND MEMBERS OF THE LABORATORY THEATRE COMPANY

97. Flaszen, L: '*Kain*-Informacja': *Materiały-Dyskusje*, Opole, January 1960 nr 2

98. Teatre 13 Rzędów: 'Kabaret Błażeja Sartra': Materiały-Dyskusje, Opole, May 1960 nr 3

99. Flaszen, L: '*Kain* – czyli jak zabić autora?': *Dialog* 1960 nr 6: pp 138–145

100. Flaszen, L: '*Misterium Buffo* – Informacja': *Materiały-Dyskusje*, Opole, July 1960 nr 4

101. Flaszen, L: '*Siakuntala* – Regulamin patrzenia dla widzów a szczególnie dla recenzentow': *Materiały-Dyskusje*, Opole December 1960 nr 5

102. Flaszen, L: '*Dziady* – Komentarz do inscenizacji J Grotowskiego': *Materiały-Dyskusje*, Opole, June 1961 nr 6

103. Flaszen, L: 'Teatr 13 Rzędów': *Materiały*, Opole 1961 (104) (105)

104. Flaszen, L: 'The Theatre with Thirteen Rows': *The Theatre in Poland/Le Théâtre en Pologne*: 1961 nr 12: pp 16–19 (103) (105)

105. Flaszen, L: '13 Rzędów Teatr bez sceny': *Współczesność* 1962 nr 5 (103) (104)

106. Flaszen, L: '*Kordian* – Komentarz do inscenizacji J. Grotowskiego': *Materiały-Dyskusje*, Opole, February 1962 nr 7

107. Mirecka, R: 'Przejazdem w Krakowie: Mówi Siakuntala' (interviewer A.M.): *Dziennik Polski* 1962 nr 77

108. Flaszen, L: '*Akropolis* – Komentarz do przedstawienia': *Materiały-Dyskusje*, Opole, October 1962

109. Flaszen, L: 'Teatr Laboratorium 13 Rzędów': *Materiały*, Opole 1962

110. Flaszen, L: '*Tragiczne Dzieje Doktora Fausta* – Komentarz do przedstawienia': *Materiały-Dyskusje*, Opole, April 1963

111. Teatr Laboratorium: 'Wprowadzenie w Metodę': Opole 1964 (a printed pamphlet containing Polish translation of foreign press articles from 1963)

112. Flaszen, L: '*Dziady, Kordian, Akropolis* w Teatrze 13 Rzędów': *Pamiętnik Teatralny* 1964 nr 3: pp 220–234

113. Flaszen, L: '*Studium o Hamlecie*': Opole, March 1964

114. Barba, E: *Alla Ricerca del Teatro Perduto – una proposta dell' avanguardia Polacca*: Marsilio Editori, Padova 1965

115. Barba, E: 'Theatre Laboratory 13 Rzędów': *The Drama Review* T27 Spring 1965: pp 153–165

116. Flaszen, L: and Barba, E: 'A Theatre of Magic and Sacrilege': *The Drama Review* T27 Spring 1965: pp 172–189

117. Flaszen, L: '*Książe Niezłomny* – przypisy do przedstawienia': *Materiały–Dyskusje*, Wrocław 1965 (73)

118. Flaszen, L: '*Książe Niezłomny* – przebieg seen': Wrocław 1965

119. Mirecka, R: 'Wierzę w teatr' (interviewer H. Garlińska): *Gazeta Robotnicza – Magazyn Tygodniowy* 1965 nr 252

120. Flaszen, L: 'Filolog w teatrze i inni': *Odra* 1965 nr 11: pp 79–81

121. *Institute de Recherche sur le jeu de l'acteur – Théâtre Laboratoire* Wrocław 1967 (pamphlet published by Laboratory Theatre – pp 40 (20) (27) (28) (35) (36) (40) (73) (124) (125)

122. Barba, E: 'The Kathakali Theatre': *The Drama Review* T36 Summer 1967: pp 37–50

123. Flaszen, L: 'Z Ludwikiem Flaszenem a Teatrze Laboratorium: Sukcesy – Zadania – Zamiary': *Wieczór Wrocławia* 31.7.67

124. Flaszen, L: 'Po Awangardzie': *Odra* 1967 nr 4: p 41 (121) (125) (135)

125. Flaszen, L: 'After the Avant-Garde': *The Theatre in Poland/Le Théâtre en Pologne* 1968 nrs 7–8: pp 11–17 (121) (124) (135)

126. Cieślak, R: 'Wrocławscy twórcy kultury. Ryszard Cieślak' (interviewer Z. Frąckiewicz): *Słowo Polskie* 1969 nr 225

127. Cieślak, R: 'Spotkanie nie przypadkowe z Ryszardem Cieślakiem. Maksymalna szczerość i prostota – oto tajemnica sukcesów aktorskich' (interviewer S. Jabłonski): *Wieczór Wrocławia* 1970 nr 280

128. Cieślak, R: 'Aktor – Marzenia, Myśli, Rozterki. Ryszard Cieślak' (interviewer L. Jabłonkowna): *Teatr* 1971 nr 14

129. Flaszen, L: 'An unusual actor': *Poland* 1971 nr 7: pp 37–39

130. Flaszen, L: 'Eklektycy czy doktrzynerzy?': *Dialog* 1971 nr 11: pp 117–127

131. Flaszen, L: 'Dać znak: to jestem ja' (interviewer H. Wolniak): *Literacki Głos Nauczycielski* 1972 nr 3

132. Flaszen, L: 'Spotkanie z Grotowskim. Uczestników i Gości III Międzynarodowego Festiwalu Studenckiego': *Teatr* 1972 nr 5: pp 17–20

133. Flaszen, L: 'Księga': *Odra* 1973 nr 9: pp 59–61 (139) (135)

134. Cynkutis, Z: 'Ku Znalezieniu': *Dialog* 1973 nr 12: pp 132-135

135. Flaszen, L: *Cyrograf*: Krakow 1974 (133) (124) (125)

136. Scierski, S: '*Apocalypsis Cum Figuris*' (interviewer K. Starczak): *Odra* 1974 nr 6: pp 85–95 (139)

137. Flaszen, L: 'Grotowski na V kontynencie – Korespondencja z Australii' (interviewer B. Majorek): *Słowo Polskie* 1974 nr 177

138. Cieślak, R: 'Bez Gry' (interviewer B. Gieraczyński): *Kultura* 16.3.75 (139) (140)

139. Teatr Laboratorium: *Teksty*: Wrocław 1975 (printed on the occasion of the Theatre of Nations Festival, 88 pp): (56) (64) (65) (76) (133) (136) (138) (140)

140. Cieślak, R: 'No Play-Acting' (interviewer B. Gieraczyński): *The Theatre in Poland/Le Théâtre en Pologne* 1975 nr 8: pp 5–6 (138) (139)

141. Zmysłowski, J: 'Na przeciwległym biegunie potoczności' (interviewer T. Burzyński): *Scena*, Warsaw, November 1978

142. Cynkutis, Z: '*Drzewo Ludzie i Teatr Źródeł*': *Odra* 1978 nr 11: pp 83–86

143. Flaszen, L: 'Conversations with Ludwik Flaszen' (reported by Eric Forsythe): *Educational Theatre Journal* 1978 Vol 30/3: pp 301–328

144. Teatr Laboratorium: '*Polish Thanatos*': May 1981 (printed pamphlet 8 pp trans. J. Kumiega)

145. Flaszen, L et al: 'Trwało 25 lat....': *Gazeta Robotnicza* 28.1.84

III. OTHER WRITERS

146. Abirached, Robert: 'Théâtre pour l'avenir': *Le Nouvel Observateur* 29.6.66: p 33
147. *ACT*: 'Grotowski in retrospect – three views': Wellington, New Zealand, December 1973 nr 21: pp 12–13
148. Addenbrooke, David: *The Royal Shakespeare Company*: London 1974
149. Attoun, L: 'Le Godot du théâtre': *Les Nouvelles Littéraires* 10.10.68: p 13
150. Attoun, L: 'À propos de Grotowski': *Le Théâtre (Cahiers dirigés par Arrabal)* 1969 nr 1: pp 241-264
151. Bablet, Denis: 'Techniki Aktorskie' (interview with Grotowski translated from French): *Odra* 1968 nr 4: pp 34–39
152. Bajdor, J: 'Studium nie dla gwiazd' (interview with Grotowski): *Słowo Polskie* 1966 nr 31
153. Bąk, B: Review of *Dziady*: *Słowo Polskie* 1961 nr 272: p 3
154. Bąk, B: Review of *The Constant Prince*: *Słowo Polskie* 1965 nr 106
155. Barnes, Clive: Review of *Akropolis*: *New York Times* 5.11.69: p 40
156. Barnes, Clive: Review of *Apocalypsis Cum Figuris*: *New York Times* 20.11.69
157. Bentley, Eric: 'Dear Grotowski – Open Letter from Eric Bentley': *New York Times* 30.11.69 (Sunday Arts Supplement) pp 1,7
158. Błońska, W: 'The Theatre Workshop of Wrocław. Le Theatre Laboratoire': *Young Cinema and Theatre*, Prague, 1967 nr 1: pp 4–8
159. Błoński, Jan: '13 Rzędów nie takich jak inne': *Przekrój* 1965 nr 1025: pp 5–6
160. Błoński, Jan: 'Teatr Laboratorium': *Dialog* 1969 nr 10: pp 110–118 (161)
161. Błoński, Jan: 'Grotowski and his Laboratory Theatre': *Dialog* 1970 Special Edition: pp 142–150 (160)
162. Błoński, Jan: 'Znaki, Teatr, Świętość': *Teksty*, Warsaw, 1976 nrs 4–5: pp 27–43
163. Błoński, Jan: 'Holiday or Holiness': *Gambit*, London, 1979 nrs 33–34: pp 67–76
164. Bonarski, Andrzej: 'Rozmowa z Grotowskim' (interview with Grotowski): *Kultura* 1975 nr 13 (169)
165. Bonarski, Andrzej: 'O czym warto mówic' (interview with Joseph Chaikin): *Dialog* 1975 nr 11: pp 103–110 (169)
166. Bonarski, Andrzej: 'Misterium Rozwojowe' (interview with Professor Kazimierz Dąbrowski): *Odra* 1975 nr 11: pp 38–41 (169)
167. Bonarski, Andrzej: 'Tu bije serce teatru' (interview with André Gregory): *Dialog* 1976 nr 2: pp 92–97 (169)
168. Bonarski, Andrzej: 'Staż': *Polityka* 21.2.76
169. Bonarski, Andrzej: *Ziarno*: Warsaw 1979 (76) (165) (166) (167)
170. Brach-Czaina, Jolanta: 'Proces Indywiduacji w wersji Grotowskiego' *Dialog* 1980 nr 4: pp 80–93
171. Braun, Edward: *Meyerhold on Theatre*: London 1969
172. Braun, Edward: *The Theatre of Meyerhold*: London 1979
173. Braun, Kazimierz: *Nowy Teatr na Świecie 1960–1970*: Warsaw 1975: pp 149–226 'Jerzego Grotowskiego droga do święta'
174. Brecht, Stefan: 'On Grotowski – A Series of Critiques': *The Drama Review* T46 Winter 1970: pp 178–192
175. Brisbane, Katherine: 'Land of the Living Theatre': *The Guardian*, London, 17.1.70: p 8

176. Brisbane, Katharine: 'Theatre as unarmed confrontation' (interview with Grotowski): *The Australian* 18.8.73: p 24

177. Brisbane, Katharine: 'Self-discovery in the Laboratory' (interview with Grotowski): *The Australian* 19.6.74

178. Brook, Peter: 'Oh for empty seats': *Encore* January 1959

179. Brook, Peter: 'O Jerzym Grotowskim' (translated from English by Henry Machoń): *Odra* 1967 nr 2: pp 69–70 (73)

180. Brook, Peter: *US*: Calder & Boyars Playscript 9: 1968

181. Brook, Peter: *The Empty Space*: Pelican 1972

182. Brook, Peter: 'Knowing what to celebrate': *Plays and Players* March 1976: pp 17–19

183. Bryden, R: 'A Myth in Stepney. At Grotowski's *The Constant Prince*': *The Observer Review*, London, 28.9.69: p 27

184. Buski (Burzyński) Tadeusz: 'Po Skandynawskim tournée 13 Rzędów' (interview with Grotowski): *Gazeta Robotnicza* 1966 nr 105

185. Buski (Burzyński) Tadeusz: 'Grotowskiego "wątpię więc jestem"': *Gazeta Robotnicza – Magazyn Tygodniowy* 1974 nr 4/1

186. Buski (Burzyński) Tadeusz: 'Grotowskiego wyjście z teatru': *Gazeta Robotnicza – Magazyn Tygodniowy* 1975 nr 9/2 (190)

187. Burzyński, Tadeusz: 'Wyjście z teatru': *Kultura* 16.3.75

188. Buski (Burzyński) Tadeusz: 'Pole Szukania': *Gazeta Robotnicza* 27/29.6.75

189. Buski (Burzyński) Tadeusz: 'Nawet gdyby nie spać zupelnie': *Gazeta Robotnicza* 11/13.7.75

190. Buski (Burzyński) Tadeusz: 'Grotowski's exit from theatre': *The Theatre in Poland/Le Théâtre en Pologne* 1975 nr 7: pp 15–16 (186)

191. Burzyński, Tadeusz: 'University of Research': *The Theatre in Poland/Le Théâtre en Pologne*: 1975 nrs 11–12: pp 49–54

192. Burzyński, Tadeusz: 'Anty-Anty-Grotowski': *Literatura* 11.12.75: pp 11–12

193. Burzyński, Tadeusz: 'Special Project': *Scena* 1976 nr 4: pp 12–19

194. Burzyński, Tadeusz: 'Jerzy Grotowski's Special Project': *The Theatre in Poland/Le Théâtre en Pologne*: 1976 nr 8: pp 11–17

195. Burzyński, Tadeusz: 'Poszukiwania Teatru Laboratorium' (interview with Grotowski): *Trybuna Ludu* 1976 nr 252

196. Burzyński, Tadeusz: 'Grotowski's Laboratory – 1977/78 season': *The Theatre in Poland/Le Théâtre en Pologne*: 1978 nr 5: pp 19–20

197. Burzyński, Tadeusz: 'Na przeciwległym biegunie potoczności': (interview with Jacek Zmysłowski): *Scena*, Warsaw, November 1978

198. Burzyński, Tadeusz, and Osiński, Zbigniew: *Grotowski's Laboratory*: Interpress Publishers, Warsaw, 1979

199. Burzyński, Tadeusz: 'Grotowskiego Teatr Źródeł' (interview with Grotowski): *Trybuna Ludu* 21.6.79

200. Burzyński, Tadeusz: 'Tree of People at Grotowski's Laboratory': *The Theatre in Poland/Le Théâtre en Pologne* 1979 nr 7: p 23

201. Burzyński, Tadeusz: 'Premiera w Laboratorium': *Gazeta Robotnicza Magazyn Tygodniowy* 3/5.4.81: p 13

202. Byrski, M.K.: 'Grotowski a tradycja Indyjska': *Dialog* 1969 nr 8: pp 86–91

203. Bzowska, Agnieszka: 'Nieco inna relacja z Uli': *Dialog* 1976 nr 3: pp 120–122

204. Carney, Kay: 'Wrocław, the Paratheatrical Experiment: Two Experiences': *Alternative Theatre*, Baltimore, March/April 1976

205. Cashman, Daniel E.: 'Grotowski: His Twentieth Anniversary': *Theatre Journal* December 1979: pp 460–466
206. Chaikin, Joseph: *The Presence of the Actor*: New York 1972
207. Chodunowa, J: 'Po Apocalypsis': *Dialog* 1976 nr 3: pp 113–116
208. *Christchurch Press*: 'Famous Director to hold New Zealand Seminar': 31.7.73
209. *Christchurch Press*: 'Jerzy Grotowski's Theatre Seminar': 6.8.73
210. Clurman, H: *The Divine Pastime*: New York 1974: pp 221–226 'Jerzy Grotowski'
211. Collins, William B.: 'Polish Theatre is overwhelming': *Philadelphia Inquirer*: 17.9.73: p 46
212. Croyden, Margaret: 'Notes from the temple: A Grotowski seminar': *The Drama Review* T45 Fall 1969: pp 178–183
213. Croyden, Margaret: *The Contemporary Experimental Theatre: Lunatics, Lovers and Poets*: New York 1974: pp 135–168 'The Phenomenon of Jerzy Grotowski'
214. Croyden, Margaret: 'New Theatre Rule: No Watching Allowed': *Vogue*, New York, December 1975: pp 196–197 (215)
215. Croyden, Margaret: 'Nowe Przykazanie Teatru: Nie Oglądać': *Odra* 1976 nr 5: pp 55–58 (214)
216. Cushman, R: 'Polish Apocalypse': *The Observer*, London, 18.11.73: p 36
217. Ćwirko-Godycka, Ewa: 'Polemiki': *Kultura* 1975 nr 49: p 12
218. Czarmiński, Bogusław: 'Laboratorium w teatrze' (interview with Grotowski): *Tygodnik Kulturalny* 1967 nr 17: pp 1, 6
219. Czarmiński, Bogusław: 'Wrocławska szansa': *Kultura* 1968 nr 26
220. Czarmiński, Bogusław: 'Najnowsze imię boga teatru': *Współczesność* 1970 nr 25: p 9
221. Dąbrowski, Andrzej: 'Polemiki': *Kultura* 1975 nr 49: p 12
222. Dalby, A: 'Grotowski et le Living: deux conceptions opposées': *Le Théâtre (Cahiers dirigés par Arrabal)*: 1968 nr 1: pp 102–105
223. Danowicz, Bogdan: '*Orfeusz* Cocteau i problemy egzystencjalne': *Od Nowa* 1960 nr 6: p 6
224. Danowicz, Bogdan: 'Grotowski': *Argumenty* 1970 nr 13: pp 9, 12
225. Davidson, J.P.: 'Grotowski in Poland': *Plays and Players*, London, 1976 nr 6
226. Demonticelli, Roberto: 'Grotowski e Brook spiegano il nonteatro': *Corriere della Sera* 26.11.75: p 15
227. Desné, R: 'Faire de l'acteur part entiere. Entretien avec Jerzy Grotowski': *L'Humanité* 15.3.67
228. De Zuvillaga, Javier Navarro: 'The Disintegration of Theatrical Space – Mobile Theatre: *Architectural Association Quarterly* 1976 Vol 8 nr 4: pp 24–31
229. Dowlasz, Janina: 'Psycholog u Grotowskiego': *Życie Literackie* 18.9.77
230. Dumur, Guy: 'Les Exercises de Grotowski': *Le Nouvel Observateur* 29.6.66: p 33
231. Dzieduszycka, Małgorzata: *Apocalypsis Cum Figuris*: Kraków 1974
232. Dzieduszycka, Małgorzata: 'Łatać?' *Kultura* 10.8.75: p 13
233. Dziewanowski, Kazimierz: 'Wielki Dzień. Tablicza myślenia': *Literatura* 1972 nr 16: p 3
234. Dziewulska, Małgorzata: 'Uniwersytet Poszukiwań Teatru Narodów': *Dialog* 1975 nr 10: pp 161–163
235. Dziewulska, Małgorzata: 'Brook, Ronconi i Inni – we Wrocławiu': *Dialog* 1975 nr 12: pp 111–118
236. Esslin, Martin: *An Anatomy of Drama*: London 1976

237. Falkowski, Jerzy: 'Z Jerzym Grotowskim o teatrze' (interview with Grotowski): *Współczesność* 1958 nr 30/20

238. Falkowski, Jerzy: 'Biblijny Kabaret z udziałem Byrona': *Współczesność* 1960 nr 5: p 9

239. Falkowski, Jerzy: 'Majakowski na glowie i w cynowej balii': *Współczesność* 1960 nr 17: p 6

240. Falkowski, Jerzy: 'Dziady jako model teatru nowoczesnego' (interview with Grotowski): *Współczesność* 1961 nr 21: p 8

241. Falkowski, Jerzy: 'Teatr – godzina niepokoju' (interview with Grotowski): *Odra* 1964 nr 6: pp 55–58

242. Feldenkrais, M: *Body and Mature Behaviour: A Study of Anxiety Sex, Gravitation and Learning*: New York 1975

243. Feldman, Peter L.: 'On Grotowski – A series of critiques': *The Drama Review* T46 Winter 1970: pp 192–197

244. Feldshuh, David: 'Zen and the Actor': *The Drama Review* T69 March 1976: pp 79–89

245. Filler, Witold: 'Rozmowa z Grotowskim' (interview with Grotowski): *Kultura* 1968 nr 11: p 10

246. Filler, Witold: 'Z Wrocławia w swiat': *Kultura* 1969 nr 8: p 10

247. Filler, Witold: 'Grotowski: początek tematu': *Kultura* 1971 nr 41: p 10

248. Findlay, Robert: 'Grotowski's "Cultural explorations, bordering on art, especially theatre"': *Theatre Journal* October 1980: pp 349–356

249. Forsythe, Eric: 'Conversations with Ludwik Flaszen': *Educational Theatre Journal* 1978 Vol 30/3: pp 301–328

250. Frąckiewicz, Z: 'Wrocławscy twórcy kultury. Ryszard Cieślak' (interview with R. Cieślak): *Słowo Polskie* 1969 nr 225

251. Fumaroli, Marc: 'External Order, Internal Discipline' (interview with Grotowski): *The Drama Review* T45 Fall 1969: pp 172–177

252. Gaillard, Roger: 'Un Chercheur Polonais parmi nous – Presentation de Grotowski': *Le Nouveau Monde*, Haiti, 7.12.77

253. Gaillard, Roger: 'Un Chercheur Polonais parmi nous – Grotowski et l'absolu du théâtre': *Le Nouveau Monde*, Haiti, 8.12.77

254. Gaillard, Roger: 'Un Chercheur Polonais parmi nous – Grotowski et le phénomene créatif humain': *Le Nouveau Monde*, Haiti, 9.12.77

255. Garlińska, H: 'Wierzę w teatr' (interview with Rena Mirecka): *Gazeta Robotnicza – Magazyn Tygodniowy* 1965 nr 252

256. Gawlik, Jan Pawel: 'Uniwersalizacja mitu czy mit uniwersalizacji?' *Życie Literackie* 1960 nr 13: p 9

257. Gawlik, Jan Pawel: 'Grotowski and the Poor Theatre': *The Theatre in Poland/Le Théâtre en Pologne* 1968 nr 12: p 17

258. *Gazeta Robotnicza*: 'Uniwersytet Poszukiwań Teatru Narodów rozpoczął działalność. Międzynarodowa konferencja. Pojutrze spotkanie z Brookiem': 16.6.75: pp 1,2

259. *Gazeta Robotnicza*: 'Teatr Laboratorium podróżuje szlakiem Reduty': 2.1.81: p 1

260: *Gazeta Robotnicza*: 'Ulysses we Wrocławiu prosto z Anglii': 12.1.81: p 5

261. Gieraczyński, Bogdan: 'Bez Gry' (interview with R. Cieślak): *Kultura* 1975 nr 11 (262)

262. Gieraczyński, Bogdan: 'No Play-Acting': *The Theatre in Poland/Le Théâtre en Pologne* 1975 nr 8: pp 5–6 (261)

263. Grimes, Ronald, L.: 'Route to the Mountain: a prose meditation on Grotowski as pilgrim': *New Directions in Performing Arts*, Hamilton, December 1976

264. Godard, C: 'Grotowski à Paris. Après l'expérience Américaine': *Le Monde* 18.10.73: p 29

265. Godard, C.: 'Le double stage de Jerzy Grotowski. Ce n'est pas la santé des gens qui nous préoccupe mais celle de leur métier' (interview with Grotowski): *Le Monde* 18.3.76: p 17

266. Gordon, Mel: 'Meyerhold's Biomechanics': *The Drama Review* T63 September 74: pp 73–88

267. Grodzicki, August (ed): *Théâtre des Nations Varsovie 1975*: Warsaw 1976

268. Grodzicki, August (ed): *Polish Theatre Today*: Warsaw 1978: pp 31–32 'News from Grotowski's Institute and The Theatre of Sources'

269. Grześczak, Marian: 'O teatrze Grotowskiego': *Scena*, Warsaw, 1970 nr 3: pp 2–3

270. Grześczak, Marian: 'O teatrze Grotowskiego': *Scena*, Warsaw, 1970 nr 4: pp 8–11

271. Gussow, Mel: 'Grotowski, 88 lbs lighter, explains his "method"': *The New York Times* 14.12.70: p 76

272. Guszpit, Ireneusz: 'Polemiki': *Kultura* 1975 nr 49: p 12

273. Guszpit, Ireneusz: 'Ewolucja *Apocalypsis Cum Figuris*': *Dialog* 1976 nr 3: pp 106–112

274. Guszpit, Ireneusz: 'Partytura słowna *Apocalypsis Cum Figuris* Jerzego Grotowskiego': *Litteraria 8*, Wrocław 1976: pp 115–154

275. Hardwick, Elizabeth: 'The theatre of Grotowski': *The New York Review of Books*: 12.2.70: pp 3–5

276. Harris, H: 'PBL offers US premiere of Polish Director's *Akropolis*': *Philadelphia Inquirer* 13.1.69

277. Hausbrandt, Andrzej: 'Czy pan wierzy w Grotowskiego?': *Kultura i Ty* 1972 nr 4: pp 31–34

278. Hayman, R: 'Meyerhold and Grotowski': *London Magazine* June 1970: pp 62–66

279. Ikanowicz, Andrzej: 'On the Jerzy Grotowski Laboratory Theatre': *The Theatre in Poland/Le Théâtre en Pologne*: 1971 nr 5: pp 23–40

280. Jabłonkówna, Leonia: 'Książę Niezłomny w Teatrze 13 Rzędów': *Teatr* 1966 nr 2: pp 8–9

281. Jabłonkówna, Leonia: 'Klucz od przepaści': *Teatr* 1969 nr 18: pp 4–5

282. Jabłonkówna, Leonia: 'Grotowski w Stanach Zjednoczonych': *Teatr* 1970 nr 4: pp 23–24

283. Jabłonkówna, Leonia: 'Aktor – Marzenia, Myśli, Rozterki' (interview with R. Cieślak): *Teatr* 1971 nr 14

284. Jabłonski, S: 'Spotkanie nieprzypadkowe z Ryszardem Cieślakiem' (interview with R. Cieślak): *Wieczór Wrocławia* 1970 nr 280

285. Jacquot, Jean (ed): *Les Voies de la Création Théâtrale*: Paris 1970

286. Janion, M: *Gorączka Romantyczna*: Warsaw 1975: pp 7–13

287. Janov, Arthur: *The Primal Scream*: Abacus Books 1973

288. Jotterand, F: 'Grotowski à New York. Le Théâtre est à l'agonie': *Le Monde* 28.1.71: p 17

289. Jourdheuil, J-M: 'Grotowski et Calderon – tracé d'un rivage': *Théâtre et Université*, Nancy, 1967 nr 9: p 17

290. Kajzar, Helmut: 'O cudach teatru Grotowskiego': *Teatr* 1968 nr 19: pp 9–11

291. Kaplan, Donald M: 'On Grotowski – A series of critiques': *The Drama Review* T46 Winter 1970: pp 197–199

292. Karpiński, M: 'W stronę widza ubogiego': *Teatr* 1972 nr 1

293. Karpiński, M: 'Anty-Grotowski': *Kultura* 1975 nr 44: pp 11–12

294. Karpiński, M: 'Polemiki': *Kultura* 1975 nr 49: p 12

295. Karwat, Krzysztof: 'Koniec pewnej epoki?': *Tak i Nie*, Katowice, 3.8.84: p 6

296. Kattan, Naim: 'Le théâtre est une rencontre' (interview with Grotowski): *Arts et Lettres* July 1967

297. Kaufman, Wolfe: 'Unhappy week for drama critics': *New York Herald Tribune*, Paris, 25–26.6.66: p 5

298. Kelera, Józef: 'Hamlet i Inni': *Odra* 1964 nr 5: pp 77–79

299. Kelera, Józef: 'Teatr w stanie łaski': *Odra* 1965 nr 11: pp 71–74 (73)

300. Kelera, Józef: '*Apocalypsis*': *Odra* 1969 nrs 7–8: pp 93–95

301. Kelera, Józef: 'Grotowski w mowie pozornie zależnej': *Odra* 1974 nr 5: pp 35–44

302. Kelera, Józef: 'Antyfelieton o szkodliwości sypania piaskiem w oczy': *Kultura* 1975 nr 49: pp 11–12

303. Kerr, Walter: 'Is Grotowski right – did the word come last?': *New York Times* 30.11.69: pp 1, 8

304. Kijowski, Andrzej: 'Grotowski jest geniuszem': *Tygodnik Powszechny* 1971 nr 41: p 8

305. Klem, Katarzyna: 'Uniwersytet Poszukiwań Teatru Narodów – ważne spotkanie': *Wieczór Wrocławia* 24.6.75

306. Klem, Katarzyna: 'Pozostawić ślad': *Wieczór Wrocławia* 26.6.75: p 9

307. Klem, Katarzyna: 'Po co tu przyszedłeś?': *Wieczór Wrocławia* 1.7.75: p 9

308. Klimczyk, J: 'Opolski teatr awangardowy? O Teatrze 13 Rzędów – nieteatralnie': *Kwartalnik Opolski* 1963 nr 1: pp 103–114

309. Kłossowicz, Jan: 'Grotowski in Poland': *The Theatre in Poland/Le Théâtre en Pologne* 1971 nr 5: pp 3–10

310. Kłossowicz, Jan: 'Dlaczego nie jesteś szczery?': *Współczesność* 1971 nr 21: p 9

311. Kłossowicz, Jan: 'The theatre reform in Poland': *The Theatre in Poland/Le Théâtre en Pologne* 1975 nr 3: pp 24–25

312. Kolankiewicz, Leszek: 'Człowiecza całość i ludzka rodzina': *Odra* 1976 nr 5: pp 64–67

313. Kolankiewicz, Leszek: 'Grotowski – Co będzie': *Kultura* 1976 nr 50

314. Kolankiewicz, Leszek: 'Nocne Czuwanie w Teatrze Laboratorium' *Kultura* 1977 nr 17

315. Kolankiewicz, Leszek: 'What's up at Grotowski's': *The Theatre in Poland/Le Théâtre en Pologne* 1977 nrs 5–6: pp 24–25

316. Kolankiewicz, Leszek: *On the Road to Active Culture* (trans. B. Taborski): Wrocław 1979

317. Kolankiewicz, Leszek: 'Doświadczenie Nieoswojone': *Dialog* 1980 nr 4: pp 94–99

318. Kołodziejczyk, Leszek: 'Zagraniczne Wawrzyny dla Grotowskiego': *Życie Warszawy* 1973 nr 268

319. Kołodziejczyk, Leszek: 'Teatr ekspresji człowieczej': *Polityka* 26.1.74

320. Kopiec, Aleksander: '*Thanatos Polski*': *Radar* 1981 nr 5: p 29

321. Korewa, Aleksandra: 'Polemika z Jean Cocteau': *Współczesność* 16–30.11.59

322. Kott, Jan: 'On Grotowski – A series of critiques': *The Drama Review* T46, Winter 1970: pp 199–203

323. Kott, Jan: 'After Grotowski: The End of the Impossible Theatre': *Theatre Quarterly* Summer 1980: pp 27–32

324. Kreczmar, Jan: 'O Grotowski – nieuczenie': *Teatr* 1968 nr 23: pp 8–9

325. Kroll, Jack: 'A legend arrives': *Newsweek* 27.10.69: p 73

326. Krzyżagórski, K: 'Na rynku czeka na nas ofiarowanie' (interview with Grotowski and Flaszen): *Słowo Polskie* 1966 nr 288

327. Kudliński, T: 'Świat się tańczuje': *Dziennik Polski* 1960 nr 61

328. Kudliński, T: '*Siakuntala* – Biomechaniczna': *Dziennik Polski* 1961 nr 15: p 4

329. Kudliński, T: 'Raczej – Łaźnia': *Dziennik Polski* 1961 nr 18: p 3

330. Kudliński, T: '*Dziady* w 13 Rzędach, czyli Krakowiacy w Opolu': *Dziennik Polski* 1961 nr 159

331. Kumiega, J: 'Laboratory Theatre/Grotowski/The Mountain Project': *Theatre Papers The Second Series* nr 9: Dartington Hall 1978

332. Kustow, Michael: 'Ludens Mysterium Tremendum et Fascinoscum': *Encore* October 1963: pp 9–14

333. Kuszewski, Marian: 'Jerzy Grotowski – nasze sylwetki': *Trybuna Ludu* 1971 nr 296: p 4

334. Lau, Jerzy: 'Poszukiwacze teatru środka': *Argumenty* 1961 nr 4: p 8

335. Lipszyc, H: 'Japończyk o Grotowskim': *Dialog* 1974 nr 11: pp 167–173

336. Łubieński, Tomasz: 'A crisis – not a demise': *Poland*, Warsaw, 1975 nr 10: p 7

337. Ludlam, Charles: 'On Grotowski – A series of critiques': *The Drama Review* T46 Winter 1970: pp 203–205

338. Łukasiewicz, Jacek: 'Rekolekcje z Flaszenem': *Odra* 1975 nr 5: pp 55–59

339. Majorek, Barbara: 'Grotowski na V kontynencie' (interview with Ludwik Flaszen): *Słowo Polskie* 1974 nr 177

340. Mamoń, B: 'Podróż do Wrocławia. Bohater jest zmęczony': *Tygodnik Powszechny* 1970 nr 12

341. Marowitz, Charles: 'Experiment': *The Encore Reader*, London 1965: pp 241–245

342. Maśliński, Józef: 'Kustosz – Jerzy Grotowski': *Życie Literackie* 1963 nr 23: p 9

343. Mayakovsky, Vladimir: *The Complete Plays* (trans. Guy Daniels): Clarion Books 1971: pp 39–139 'Mystery-Bouffe'

344. Mcnamara, Brooks: 'Performance Space: The Environmental Tradition': *Architectural Association Quarterly* April/June 1975

345. Mencwel, Andrzej: 'Grotowski – Czyli technika i metafyzika': *Argumenty* 1967 nr 21: p 9

346. Mennen, Richard: 'Grotowski's Paratheatrical Projects': *The Drama Review* T58, December 1975: pp 58–69 (347)

347. Mennen, Richard: 'Parateatralne Wprowadzenia Jerzego Grotowskiego': *Odra* 1976 nr 5: pp 58–64 (346)

348. Mickiewicz, Adam: *Polish Romantic Drama*: New York 1977: pp 72–176 'Forefathers' Eve'

349. *Le Monde*: 'Faites Holiday avec Grotowski': 29–30.4.73: p 9

350. Morawiec, E: 'Na granicy prawdy': *Życie Literackie* 1973 nr 23

351. Moscati, I: 'Il tempo secondo del mistico Grotowski': *Rinascita* 9.1.76: pp 26–27

352. Mykita-Glensk, Czesława: *Materiały do Historii Teatru 13 Rzędów w Sezonach 1958–1959 – 1961–1962*: Opole 1963

353. Mykita-Glensk, Czesława: *Życie Teatralny Opola*: Opole 1976: pp 196–216 'Teatr 13 Rzędów'

354. Natanson, W: 'Książę o Grotowskim': *Teatr* 1969 nr 11: p 23

355. Needham, Joseph: *Science and Civilization in China – Vol II*: Cambridge 1956

356. Osiński, Zbigniew: '*Książę Niezłomny* Grotowskiego': *Miesięcznik Literacki* 1966 nr 4: pp 48–53

357. Osiński, Zbigniew: 'Człowiek i jego kondycja': *Odra* 1970 nr 10: pp 44–53

358. Osiński, Zbigniew: *Teatr Dionizosa. Romantyzm w Polskim Teatrze Współczesnym*: Kraków 1972: pp 131–257, 303–336, 347–351

359. Osiński, Zbigniew: 'Symposium: The Art of the Beginner' and 'Theatre of Sources': *The Theatre in Poland/Le Théâtre en Pologne* 1978 nrs 9–10: pp 19–20

360. Osiński, Zbigniew and Burzyński, Tadeusz: *Grotowski's Laboratory*: Warsaw 1979

361. Osiński, Zbigniew: *Grotowski i jego Laboratorium*: Warsaw 1980

362. Osiński, Zbigniew: 'Twenty years of Jerzy Grotowski's Laboratory Theatre': *The Theatre in Poland/Le Théâtre en Pologne*: 1980 nr 5: pp 7–9

363. Ouaknine, Serge: 'Techniques et Esthétiques d'une Création chez Grotowski': *Théâtre et Université*, Nancy, 1968 nr 12: pp 3–40

364. Pałłasz, Alojzy: 'Frenchmen about Grotowski, Axer & Łomnicki': *The Theatre in Poland/Le Théâtre en Pologne* 1972 nr 2: pp 14–15

365. Peryt, R: 'Przeciw famie – o książce *Towards a Poor Theatre*': *Dialog* 1969 nr 8: pp 75–85

366. Planchon, R: 'Conversation avec Roger Planchon. Propos receuillis par E. Copfermann': *Les Lettres Françaises* 12–18.1.67: pp 16–17

367. *Poirot-Delpech, B: 'Akropolis': Le Monde* 27.9.68: p 12

368. Puzyna, K: 'Powrót Chrystusa': *Teatr* 1969 nr 19: pp 11–13 (369) (370)

369. Puzyna, K: '*Apocalypsis Cum Figuris*': *The Theatre in Poland/Le Théâtre en Pologne* 1971 nr 5: pp 13–21 (368) (370)

370. Puzyna, K: 'A myth vivisected – Grotowski's Apocalypse': *The Drama Review* T52 Fall 1971: pp 36–46 (368) (369)

371. Regnault, François: 'Le Prince inflexible a vous deplié': *Théâtre et Université*, Nancy, 1967 nr 9: pp 19–28

372. Richie, Donald: 'On Grotowski – a series of critiques': *The Drama Review* T46 Winter 1970: pp 205–211

373. Ronen, Dan: 'A Workshop with Ryszard Cieślak': *The Drama Review* T80 December 1978: pp 67–76

374. Rożewicz, T: 'Margines, ale ... *Apocalypsis cum Figuris* w Laboratorium Jerzego Grotowskiego': *Odra* 1969 nrs 7–8: pp 107–108

375. Rymuza, Zygmunt: 'Grotowski – między teatrem a rzeczywistością': *Literatura* 29.1.76: pp 1, 3–4

376. Ryszard: 'List z Opola – *Misterium Buffo*': *Tygodnik Powszechny* 1960 nr 40: p 6

377. Ryszard: '*Siakuntala* czyli cyrk z regulaminem': *Tygodnik Powszechny* 1961 nr: p 6

378. Ryszard: 'I co dalej?': *Tygodnik Powszechny* 1961 nr 28: p 6

379. Ryszard: 'Dostojewski współcześnie widziany': *Tygodnik Powszechny* 1961 nr 47: p 6

380. Sainer, Arthur: 'The metamorphosis of Grotowski': *The Village Voice* 31.12.70

381. Sainer, Arthur: 'Are we in the presence of great theatre?': *The Village Voice* 20.9.73: p 60

382. Salvetti, Marie-George Gervasoni (ed): *La Biennale – Annuario 1976, Eventi del 1975*: Venice 1976

383. Sarrauté, Claude: 'Grotowski et ses épigones' (interview with Grotowski): *Le Monde* 16.5.69

384. Saurel, R: 'A la Recherche du Théâtre Perdu': *Les Temps Modernes* 1965 nr 10: pp 754–763

385. Schechner, R and Hoffman, T: 'An interview with Grotowski': *The Drama Review* T41 Fall 1968: pp 29–45

386. Schevill, J: *Break Out: In Search of New Theatrical Environments*: Chicago 1973: pp 293–301 'Grotowski in New York'

387. Seymour, Alan: 'Revelations in Poland': *Plays and Players* October 1963: pp 33–34

388. Sielicki, Krzysztof: Dlaczego Grotowski nadał jest artystą': *Dialog* 1976 nr 3: pp 117–119

389. Sito, JS: 'Dialektyka Przemian': *Polityka* 1960 nr 42: p 7

390. *Słowo Polskie*: 'Nocne Czuwanie w Teatrze Laboratorium': 4.10.76: p 3

391. *Słowo Polskie*: '20 Lat Teatru Laboratorium': 19.11.79: p 1

392. *Słowo Polskie*: 'Teatr Grotowskiego we Włoszech': 7.12.79: p 1

393. *Słowo Polskie*: 'Pracowity początek roku w Teatrze Laboratorium': 5.1.81: p 3

394. *Słowo Polskie*: 'Brytyjscy Gości Teatru Laboratorium': 12.1.81: p 3

395. *Słowo Polskie*: 'Sycylijski Warsztat Twórczy Wrocławskich Aktorów': 17–20.4.81: p 1

396. Small, Christopher: 'Polish Theatre's fearful mockery of patriotism': *The Glasgow Herald* 23.8.68

397. Smektala, Zdzisław: '*Thanatos Polski* w Teatrze Laboratorium': *Walka Młodych* 17.5.81: p 18

398. Smith, A.C.H.: *Orghast at Persepolis*: London 1972

399. Srokowski, Stanisław: 'Duch teatru krąży nad nami': *Wiadomości* Wrocław, 3.7.75

400. Stanislavsky, Constantin: *My Life in Art* (trans. J. J. Robbins): New York 1924

401. Stanislavsky, Constantin: *Building a Character* (trans. Elizabeth Reynolds Hapgood): London 1968

402. Starczak, K: '*Apocalypsis Cum Figuris*' (interview with Stanisław Scierski): *Odra* 1974 nr 6: pp 85–86

403. Steiner, George: *The Death of Tragedy*: London 1968

404. Szczepanski, Jan: 'Co z tym Teatrem-Laboratorium?': *Trybuna Ludu* 1970 nr 24: pp 4, 7

405. *Sztandar Młodych*: 'Co jest na tej górze?': 12.6.75

406. Szydłowski, Roman: 'Spotkanie z Teatrem Grotowskiego': *Trybuna Ludu* 1970 nr 93

407. Szydłowski, Roman: 'Problemy Teatru Grotowskiego': *Trybuna Ludu* 1971 nr 274: p 6

408. Szydłowski, Roman: *The Theatre in Poland*: Warsaw 1972

409. Taborski, Bolesław: *Byron and the Theatre*: Salzburg 1972: pp 350–365

410. *Teatr*: 'Szkice i Projekty': 1961 nr 17: p 23

411. *Teatr*: 'Grotowski i chochoły': 1971 nr 17: p 13, nr 18: pp 4–5

412. Temkine, Raymonde: 'Fils Naturel d'Artaud': *Les Lettres Nouvelles* May/June 1966

413. Temkine, Raymonde: 'Un stage de formation de l'acteur s'est deroulé à Nancy': *Combat* 24.3.67

414. Temkine, Raymonde: *Grotowski*: Lausanne 1968 (415)

415. Temkine, Raymonde: *Grotowski*: (trans. Alex Szogyi): Avon Books 1972 (414)

416. Temkine, Raymonde: 'The Polish-French seminar on theatre at Royaumont': *The Theatre in Poland/Le Théâtre en Pologne* 1973 nr 6: pp 5–6

417. Temkine, Raymonde: 'Le Théâtre des Nations à Varsovie et Wrocław': *Europe* 1975 nr 10: pp 2–11

418. Terrier, René: 'Les impressions Polonaises d'un jeune comédien génèvois qui a passé trois mois au Théâtre Laboratoire d'Opole': *Le Dauphiné Libéré*, Grenoble, 15.2.68

419. *The Theatre in Poland/Le Théâtre en Pologne*: 'Studium o Hamlecie': 1973 nr 12

420. *The Times*: 'A Polish conception of Marlowe's *Faust*': 22.7.63: p 14

421. Trewin, JC: 'Acting with a Flourish': *Flourish* 1969 Vol 2 nr 3: p 6

422. Tyszkowska, K: 'Funkcja Teatru Laboratorium': *Gazeta Robotnicza* 26.8.65

423. Valentini, Chiara: 'Spettatori, in ginocchio' *Panorama* 9.10.75: pp 89–91

424. Volli, Ugo: 'Jerzy Grotowski, Oggi' (interview with Grotowski): *Alfabeta*, Milan, April 1980: pp 3–5

425. Waldeman, Max: The Constant Prince – A Portfolio: *The Drama Review* T46 Winter 1970: pp 164–177

426. Wardle, Irving: 'Big catch from Poland': *The Times* 24.8.68: p 18

427. Wardle, Irving: 'Grotowski the Evangelist': *The Times* 4.10.69: pIIIc

428. Weinstein, Steven: 'Wrocław, the Paratheatrical Experiment: Two Experiences': *Alternative Theatre*, Baltimore, March/April 1976

429. Wickstrom, Gordon M: '*Akropolis* at Washington Square Church': *Educational Theatre Journal* March 1970: pp 107–108

430. *Wieczór Wrocławia*: 'Nocne Czuwanie u Grotowskiego': 27.9.76: p 4

431. *Wieczór Wrocławia*: '20-lecie Teatru Laboratorium. Odznaczenia dla Zespołu Jerzego Grotowskiego': 19.11.79: pp 1, 8

432. Wojtczak, Iwona: 'Po co Uniwersytet Poszukiwań?': *Dialog* 1975 nr 11: pp 98–102

433. Wolniak, H: 'Dać znak: to jestem ja' (interview with Flaszen): *Literacki Głos Nauczycielski* 1972 nr 3

434. Wysłouch, Seweryna: 'Grotowski – Niszczyciel Znaków': *Dialog* 1971 nr 8: pp 126–131

435. Zagórska, B: '11 pytań o 13 Rzędów' (interview with Grotowski): *Echo Krakowa* 1959 nr 248

436. Zbijewska, K: '10 minut z Jerzym Grotowskim' (interview with Grotowski): *Dziennik Polski* 13.4.66 nr 86

Index

Compiled by Lesley Kelly

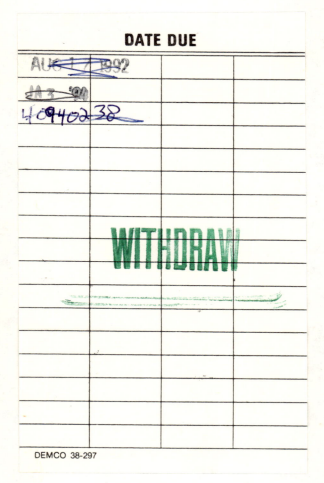